D1283652

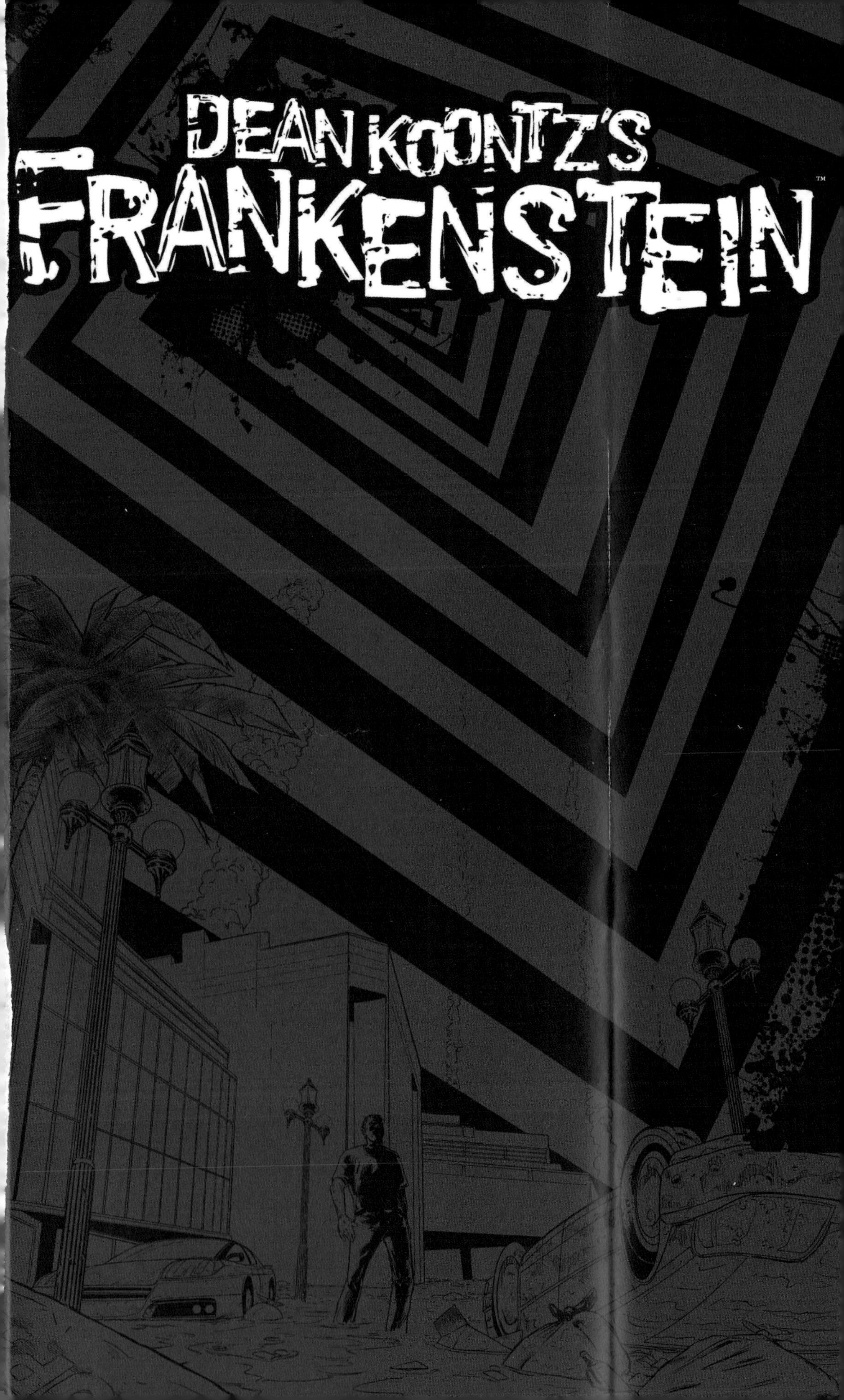
DEAN KOONTZ'S
FRANKENSTEIN™

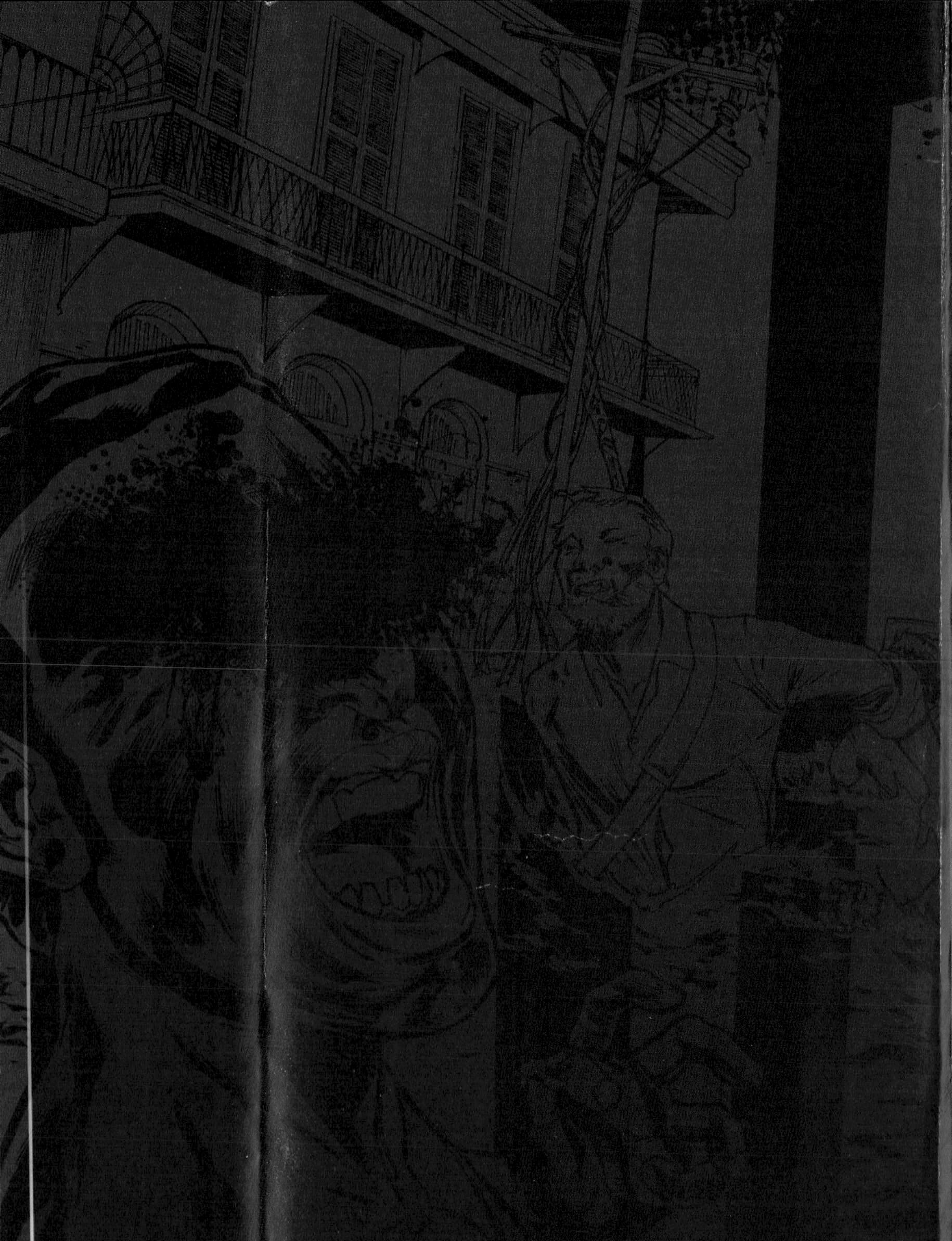

DYNAMITE®

Nick Barrucci, CEO / Publisher
Juan Collado, President / COO

Joe Rybandt, Executive Editor
Matt Idelson, Senior Editor
Rachel Pinnelas, Associate Editor
Anthony Marques, Assistant Editor
Kevin Ketner, Editorial Assistant

Jason Ullmeyer, Art Director
Geoff Harkins, Senior Graphic Designer
Cathleen Heard, Graphic Designer
Alexis Persson, Production Artist

Chris Caniano, Digital Associate
Rachel Kilbury, Digital Assistant

Rich Young, Director of Business Development
Brandon Dante Primavera, V.P. of IT and Operations

Alan Payne, V.P. of Sales and Marketing
Keith Davidsen, Marketing Director
Pat O'Connell, Sales Manager

 Online at **www.DYNAMITE.com**
On Facebook **/Dynamitecomics**
On Tumblr **dynamitecomics.tumblr.com**
On Twitter **@dynamitecomics**
On YouTube **/Dynamitecomics**

STANDARD EDITION ISBN–13: 978-1-5241-0090-2
SIGNED EDITION ISBN–13: 978-1-5241-0089-6

First Printing   10 9 8 7 6 5 4 3 2 1

DEAN KOONTZ'S FRANKENSTEIN™: STORM SURGE, VOLUME 1. Contains materials originally published in magazine form as #1-6. First printing. Published by Dynamite Entertainment, 113 Gaither Dr., STE 205, Mt. Laurel, NJ 08054. Story Copyright © Dean Koontz. Art Copyright © Dynamite Characters, llc. DEAN KOONTZ'S FRANKENSTEIN and all characters featured in this issue and the distinctive names and likenesses thereof, and all related indicia are trademarks of Dean Koontz. All Rights Reserved. DYNAMITE, DYNAMITE ENTERTAINMENT and its logo are ® & © 2016 Dynamite. All rights reserved. All names, characters, events, and locales in this publication are entirely fictional. Any resemblance to actual persons (living or dead), events or places, without satiric intent, is coincidental. No portion of this book may be reproduced by any means (digital or print) without the written permission of Dynamite Entertainment except for review purposes. Printed in China.

For information regarding press, media rights, foreign rights, licensing, promotions, and advertising e-mail: marketing@dynamite.com

DEAN KOONTZ'S FRANKENSTEIN ™

WRITTEN BY
CHUCK DIXON
RIK HOSKIN

FROM AN ORIGINAL STORY BY
DEAN KOONTZ

ART BY
ANDRES PONCE

COLORS BY
MOHAN

LETTERS BY
BILL TORTOLINI

COVER ART BY
ANDRES PONCE

COVER COLORS BY
MOHAN

EDITED BY
RICH YOUNG
ANTHONY MARQUES

COLLECTION DESIGN BY
ALEXIS PERSSON

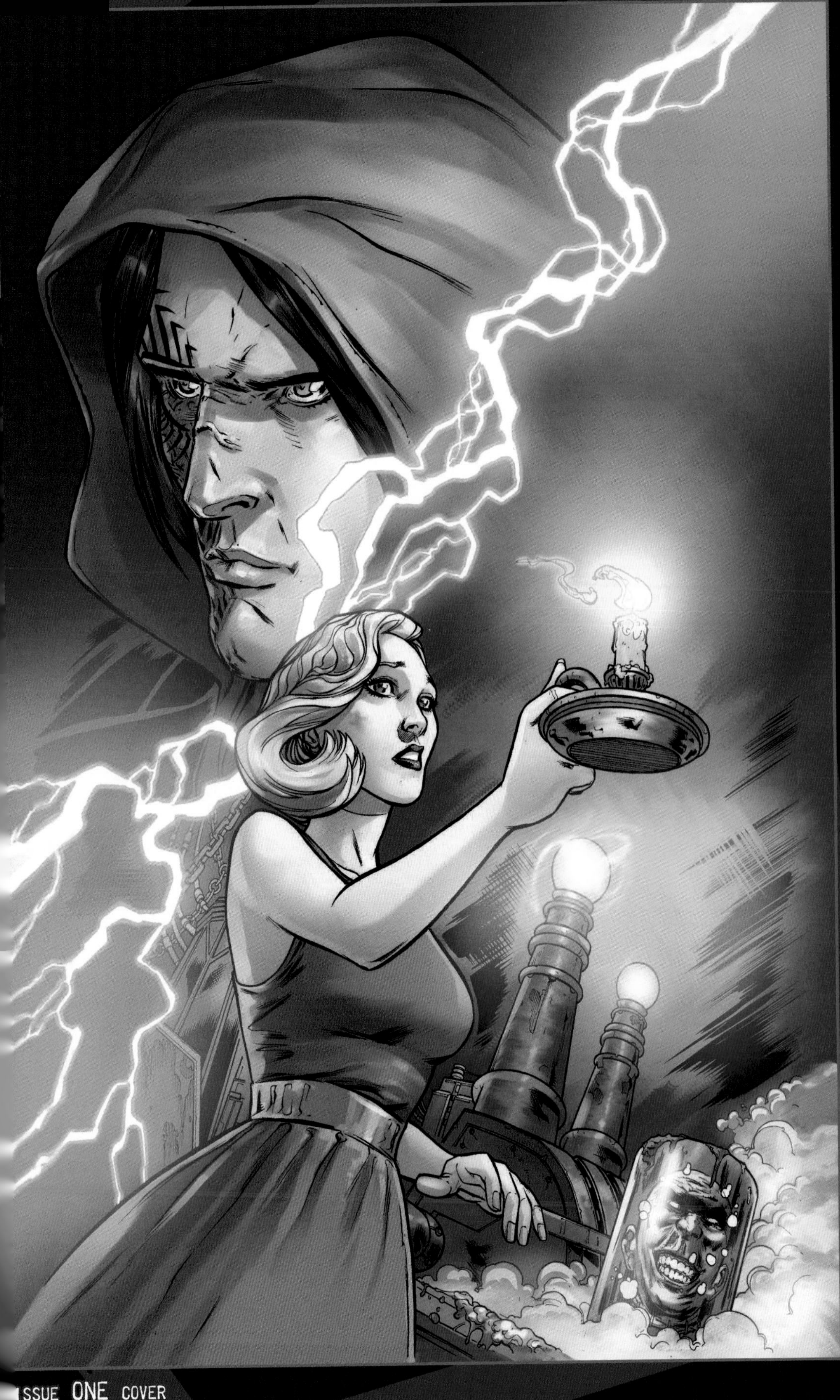

ISSUE ONE COVER
ART BY ANDRES PONCE COLORS BY MOHAN

THEY'RE RUNNING OUT OF TITLES FOR THE **REALLY** BIG ONES...

THE **PERFECT** STORM.

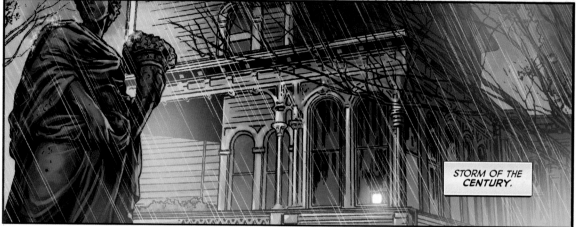

STORM OF THE CENTURY.

BUT THE MONSTERS START AS INNOCENT BOYS AND GIRLS, NAMES CULLED FROM BOOKS, THEN LINED UP IN A VERY SAFE ALPHABETICAL ORDER.

THE HUMAN MEDIA JUST FOLLOWS WHATEVER WAY THE WIND BLOWS...

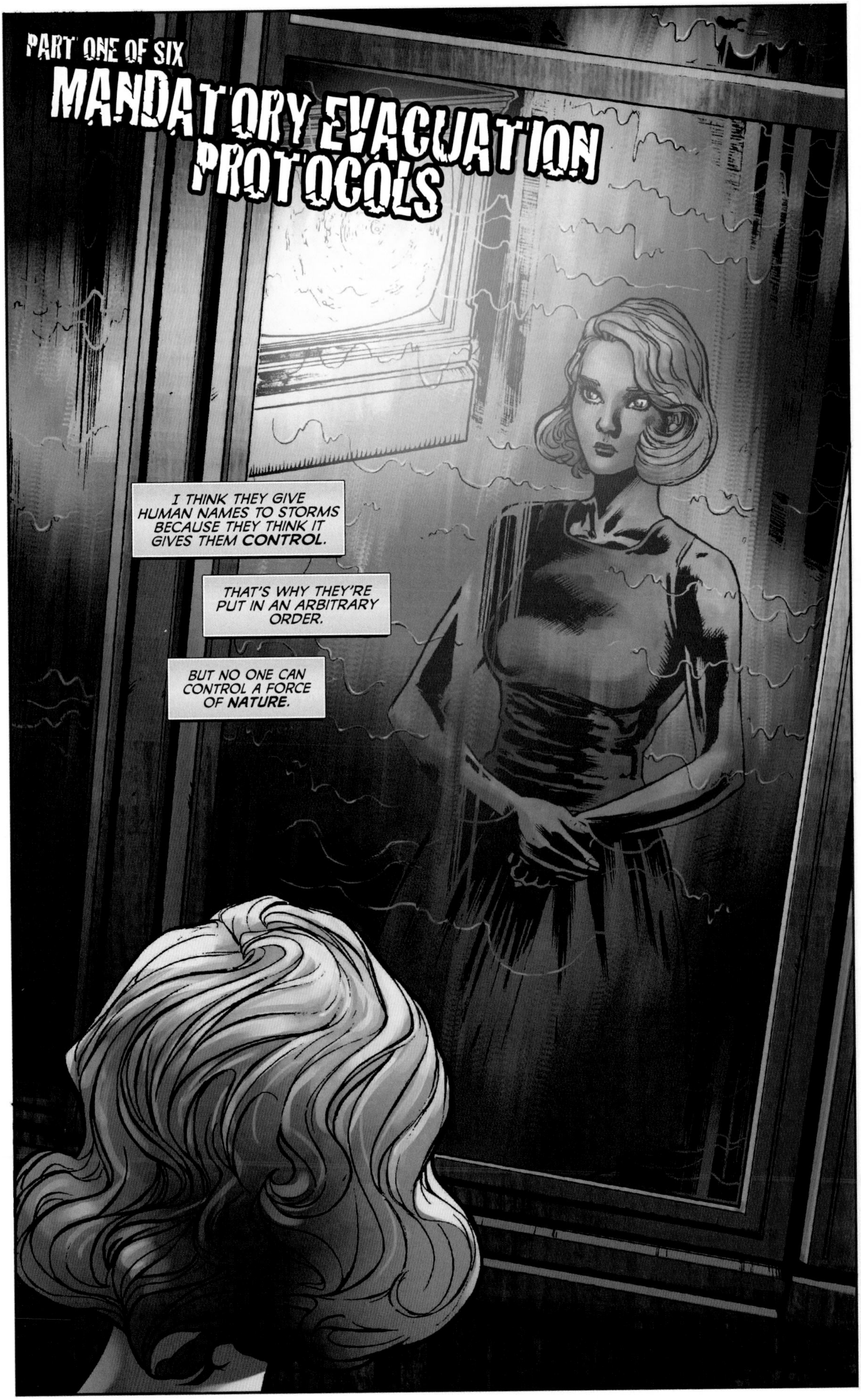
PART ONE OF SIX
MANDATORY EVACUATION PROTOCOLS
I THINK THEY GIVE HUMAN NAMES TO STORMS BECAUSE THEY THINK IT GIVES THEM CONTROL.
THAT'S WHY THEY'RE PUT IN AN ARBITRARY ORDER.
BUT NO ONE CAN CONTROL A FORCE OF NATURE.

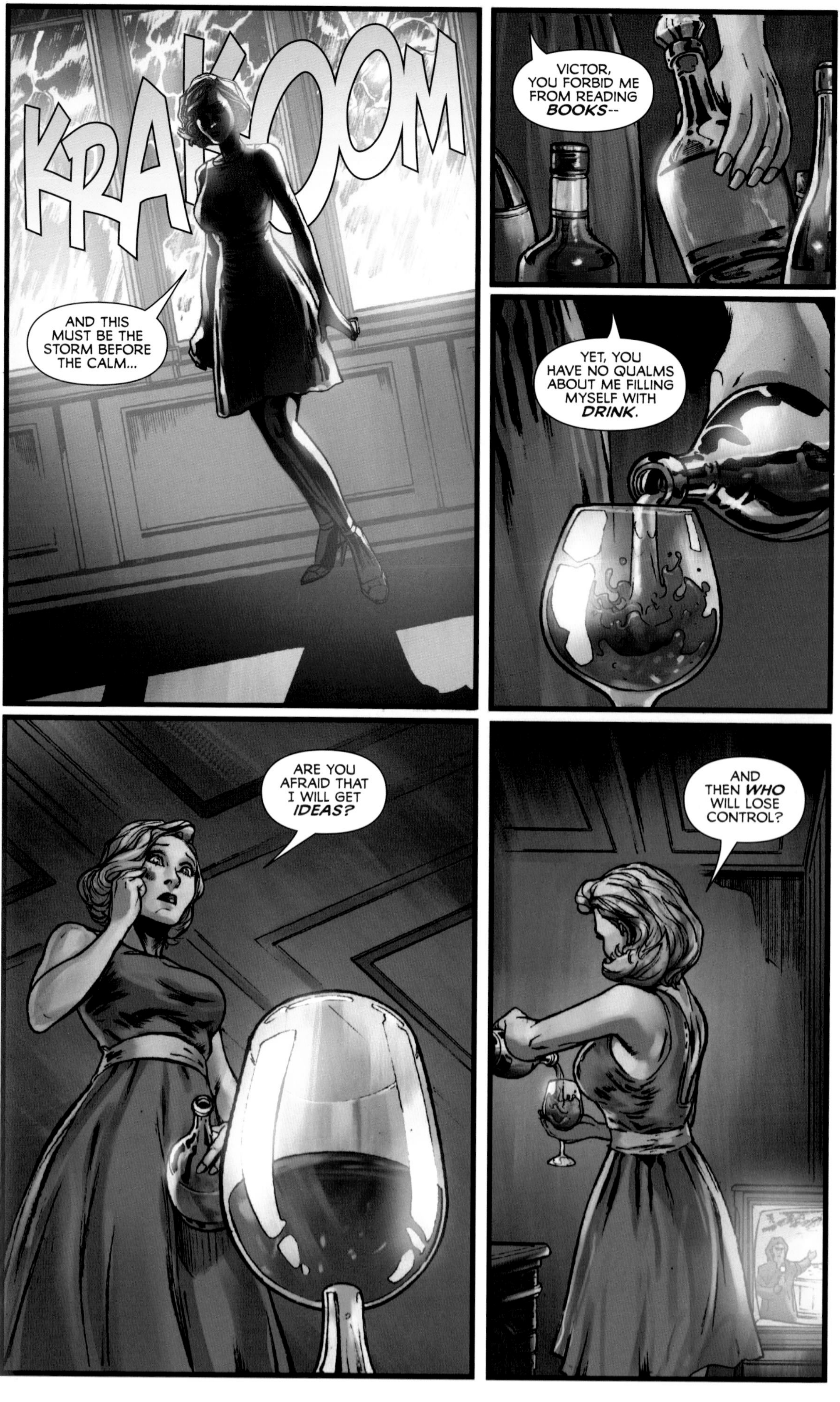
KRAKOOM
AND THIS MUST BE THE STORM BEFORE THE CALM...
VICTOR, YOU FORBID ME FROM READING BOOKS--
YET, YOU HAVE NO QUALMS ABOUT ME FILLING MYSELF WITH DRINK.
ARE YOU AFRAID THAT I WILL GET IDEAS?
AND THEN WHO WILL LOSE CONTROL?

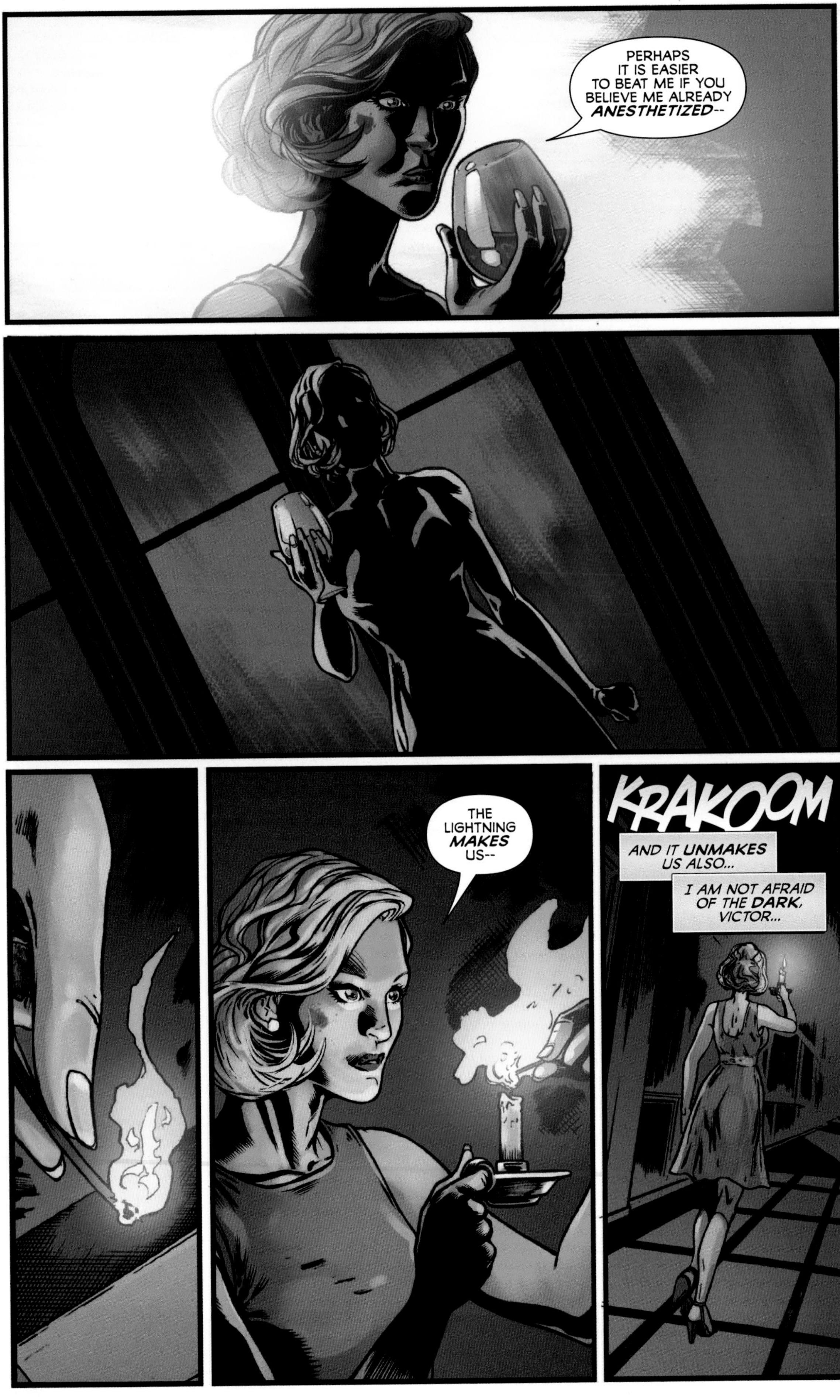
PERHAPS IT IS EASIER TO BEAT ME IF YOU BELIEVE ME ALREADY ***ANESTHETIZED***--
THE LIGHTNING ***MAKES*** US--
KRAKOOM
*AND IT **UNMAKES** US ALSO...*
*I AM NOT AFRAID OF THE **DARK**, VICTOR...*

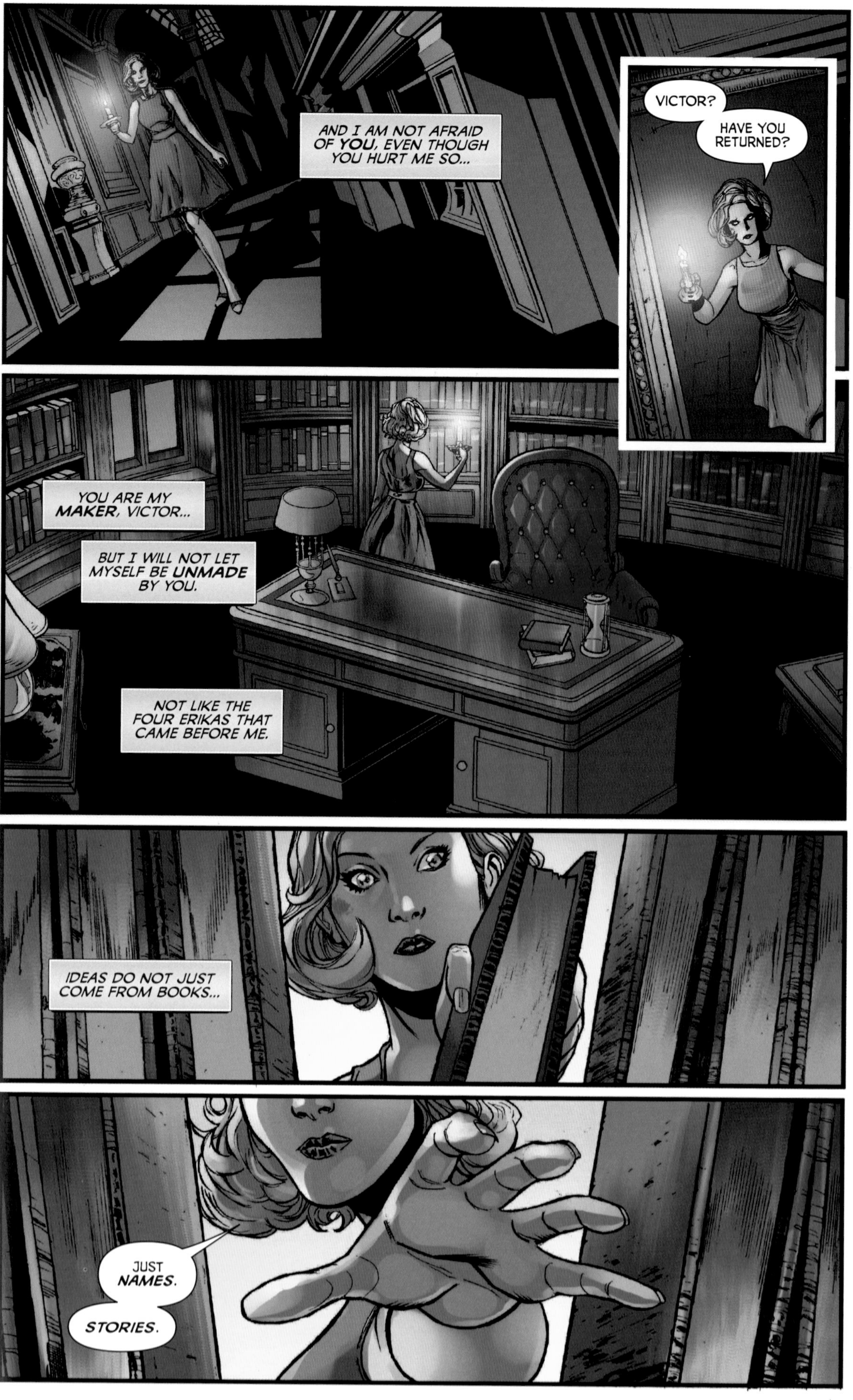
AND I AM NOT AFRAID OF YOU, EVEN THOUGH YOU HURT ME SO...
VICTOR?
HAVE YOU RETURNED?
YOU ARE MY MAKER, VICTOR...
BUT I WILL NOT LET MYSELF BE UNMADE BY YOU.
NOT LIKE THE FOUR ERIKAS THAT CAME BEFORE ME.
IDEAS DO NOT JUST COME FROM BOOKS...
JUST NAMES.
STORIES.

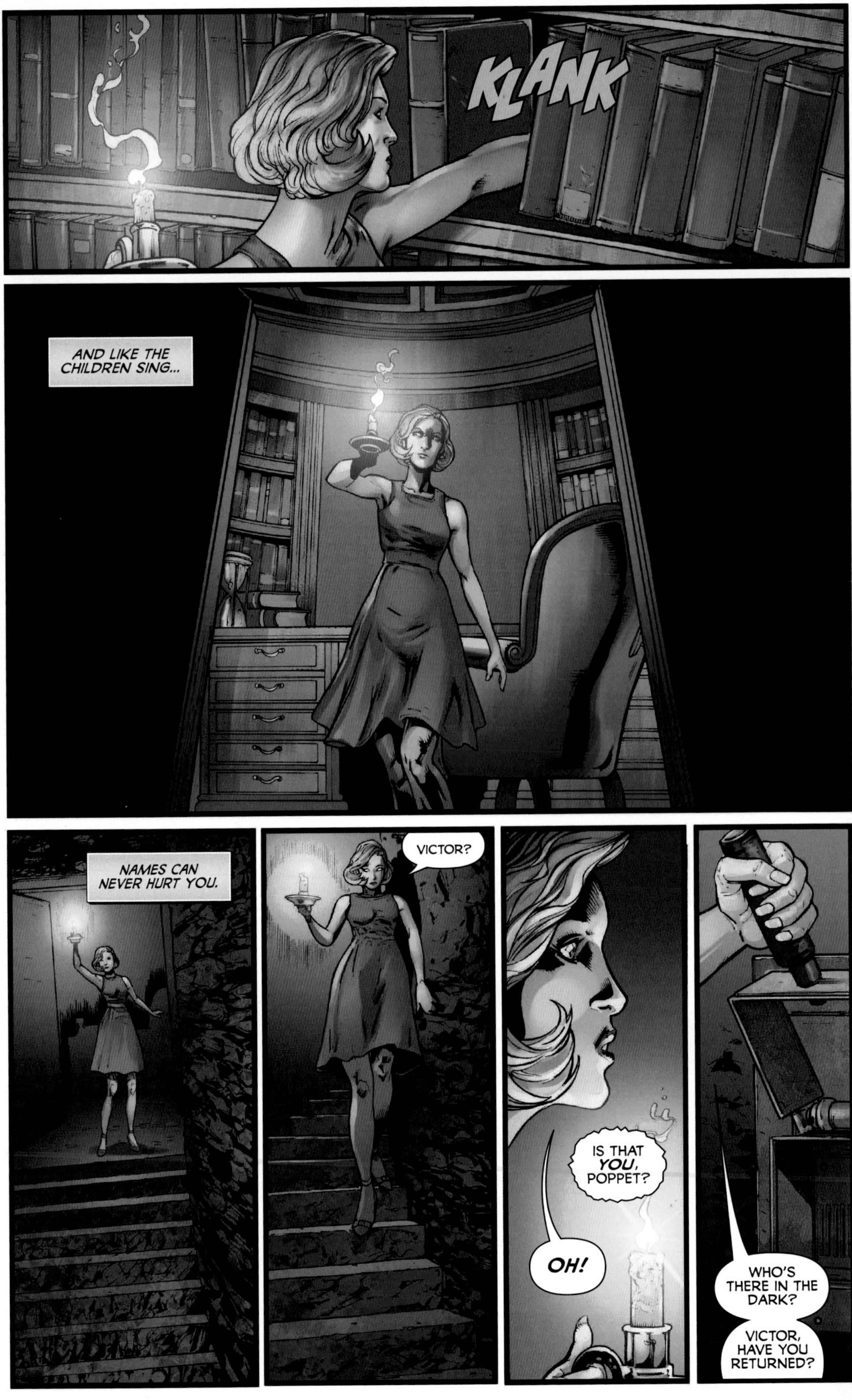
KLANK
AND LIKE THE CHILDREN SING...
NAMES CAN NEVER HURT YOU.
VICTOR?
IS THAT YOU, POPPET?
OH!
WHO'S THERE IN THE DARK?
VICTOR, HAVE YOU RETURNED?

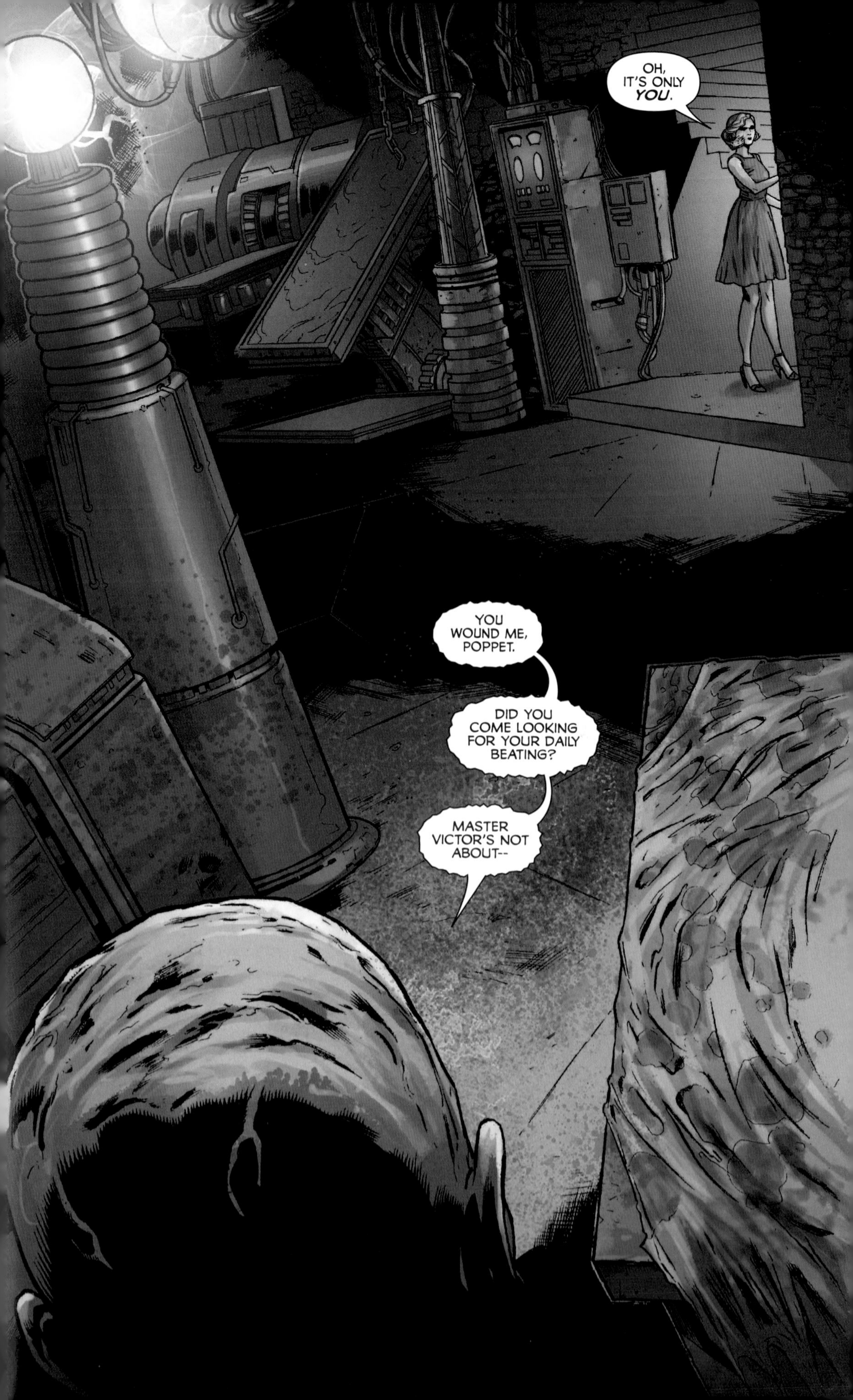
OH, IT'S ONLY *YOU*.
YOU WOUND ME, POPPET.
DID YOU COME LOOKING FOR YOUR DAILY BEATING?
MASTER VICTOR'S NOT ABOUT--

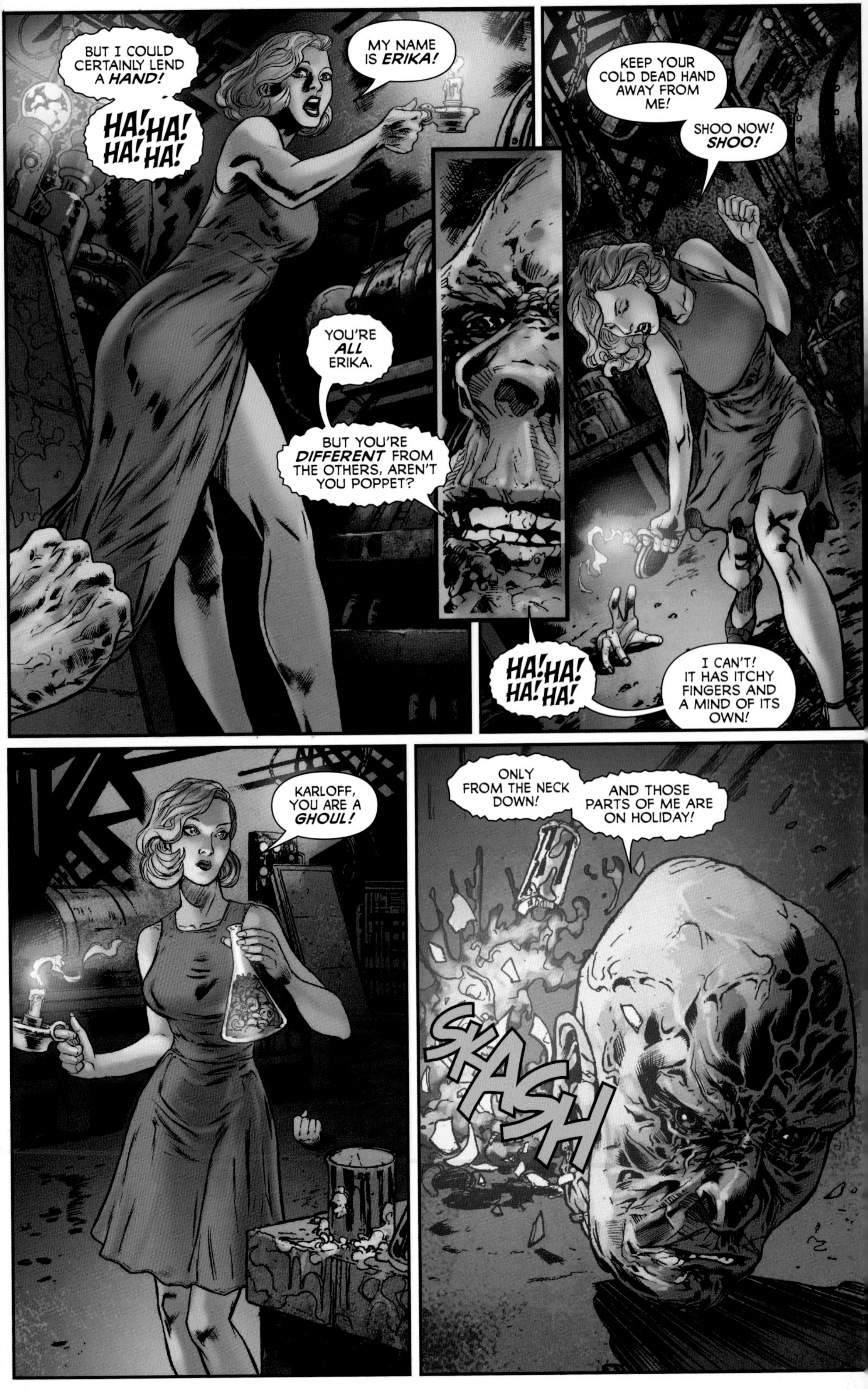
BUT I COULD CERTAINLY LEND A HAND!
HA! HA! HA! HA!
MY NAME IS ERIKA!
YOU'RE ALL ERIKA.
BUT YOU'RE DIFFERENT FROM THE OTHERS, AREN'T YOU POPPET?
KEEP YOUR COLD DEAD HAND AWAY FROM ME!
SHOO NOW! SHOO!
HA! HA! HA! HA!
I CAN'T! IT HAS ITCHY FINGERS AND A MIND OF ITS OWN!
KARLOFF, YOU ARE A GHOUL!
ONLY FROM THE NECK DOWN!
AND THOSE PARTS OF ME ARE ON HOLIDAY!
SKASH

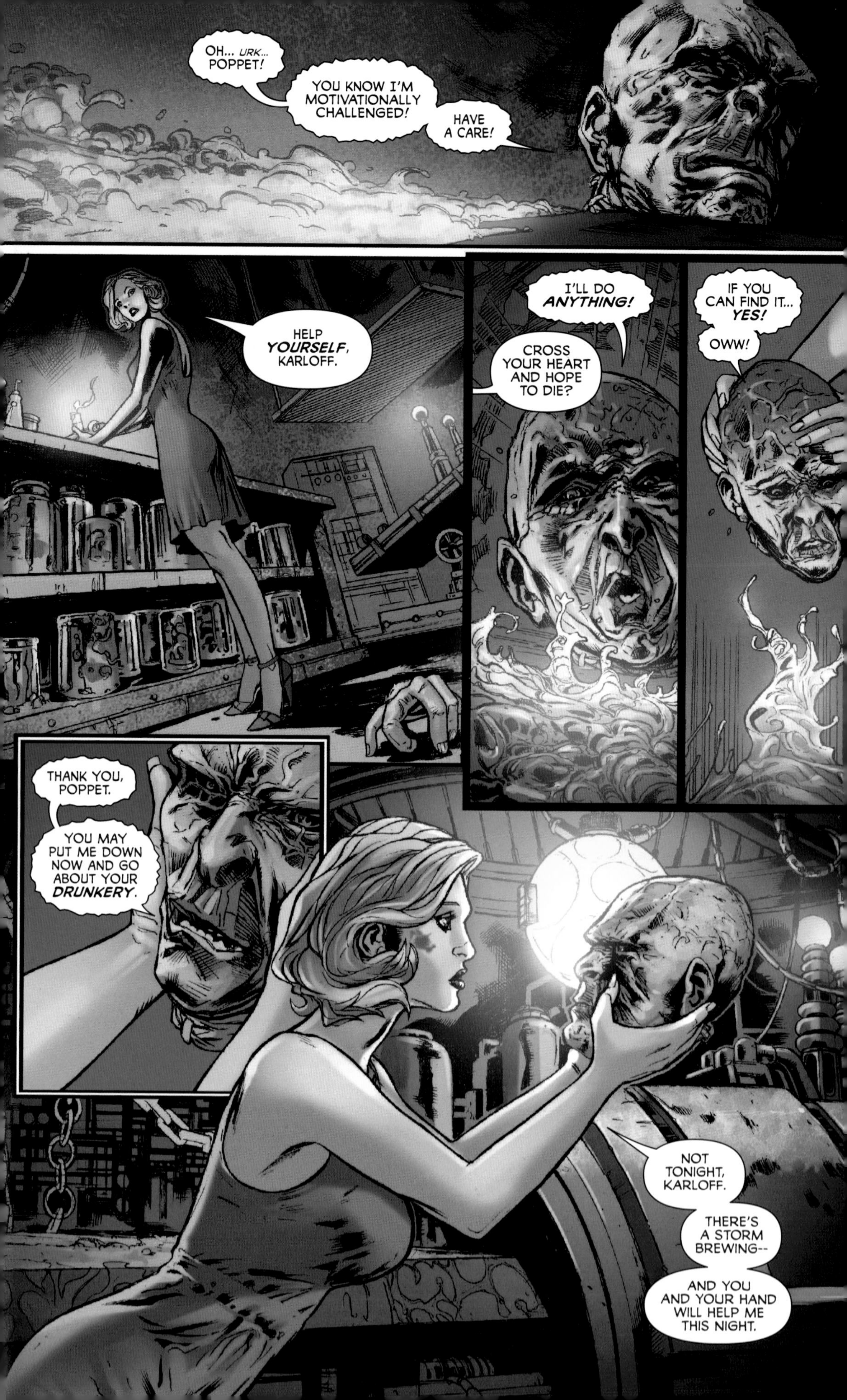
OH... URK... POPPET!
YOU KNOW I'M MOTIVATIONALLY CHALLENGED!
HAVE A CARE!
HELP YOURSELF, KARLOFF.
I'LL DO ANYTHING!
CROSS YOUR HEART AND HOPE TO DIE?
IF YOU CAN FIND IT... YES!
OWW!
THANK YOU, POPPET.
YOU MAY PUT ME DOWN NOW AND GO ABOUT YOUR DRUNKERY.
NOT TONIGHT, KARLOFF.
THERE'S A STORM BREWING--
AND YOU AND YOUR HAND WILL HELP ME THIS NIGHT.

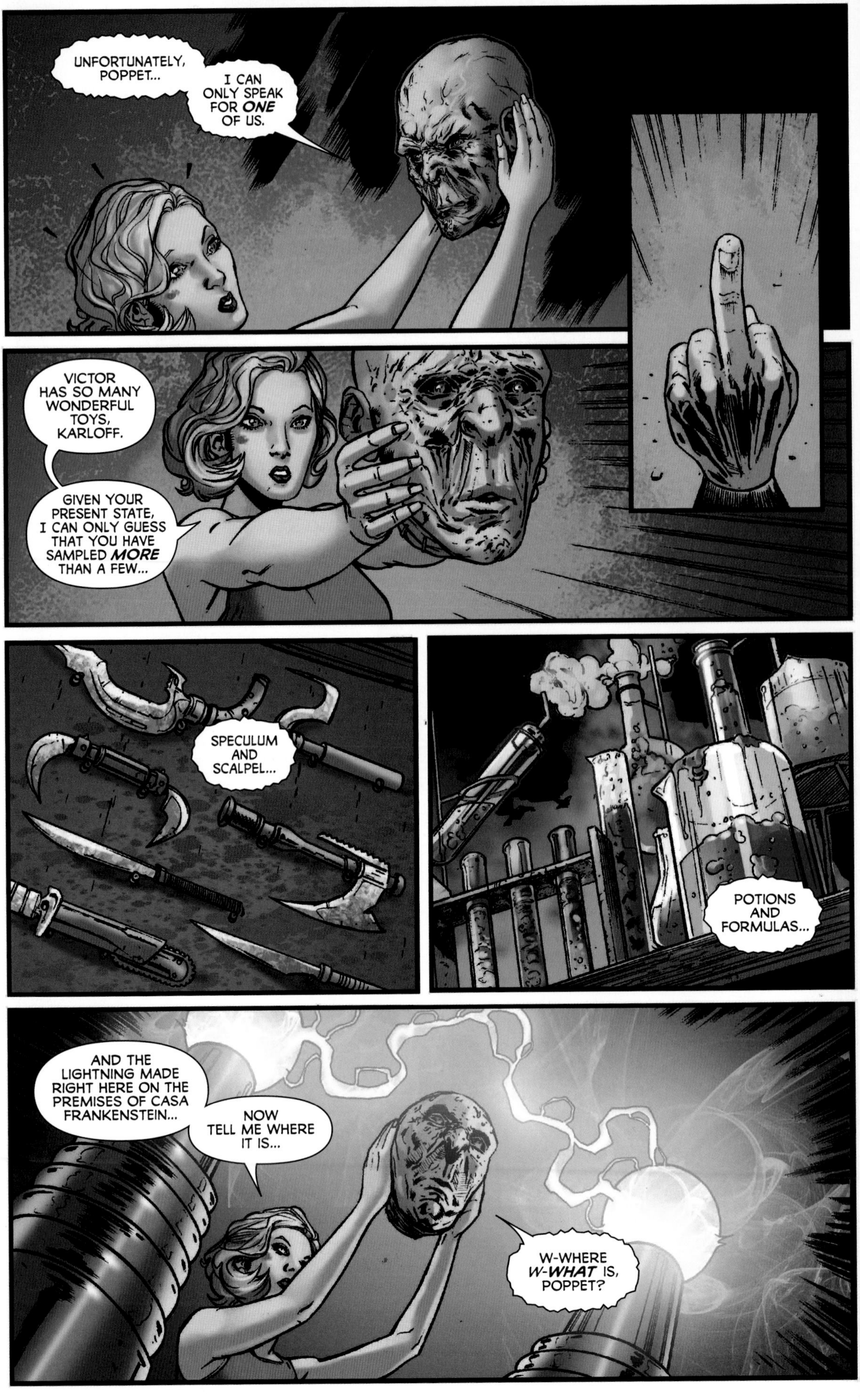
UNFORTUNATELY, POPPET...
I CAN ONLY SPEAK FOR ONE OF US.
VICTOR HAS SO MANY WONDERFUL TOYS, KARLOFF.
GIVEN YOUR PRESENT STATE, I CAN ONLY GUESS THAT YOU HAVE SAMPLED MORE THAN A FEW...
SPECULUM AND SCALPEL...
POTIONS AND FORMULAS...
AND THE LIGHTNING MADE RIGHT HERE ON THE PREMISES OF CASA FRANKENSTEIN...
NOW TELL ME WHERE IT IS...
W-WHERE W-WHAT IS, POPPET?

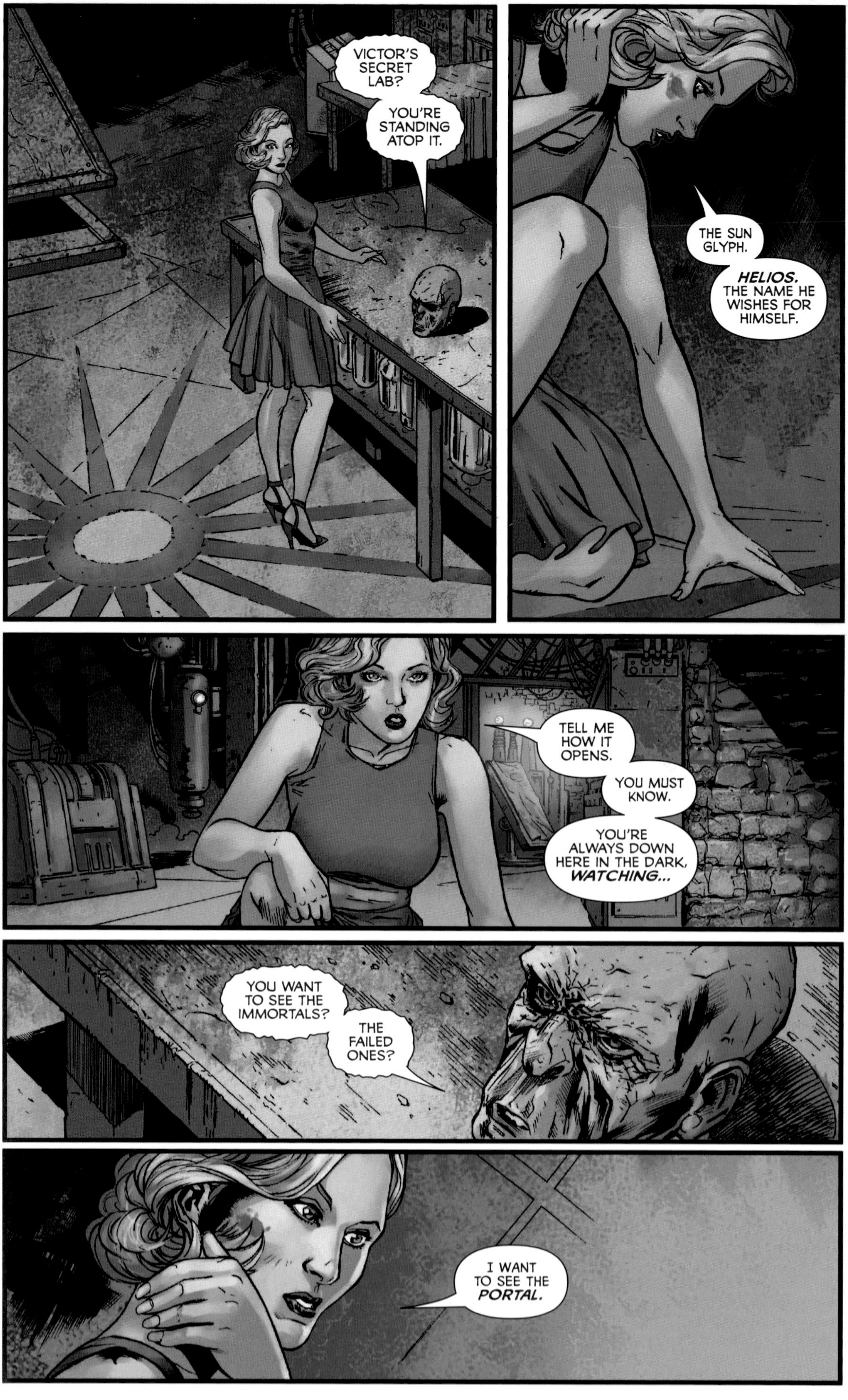
VICTOR'S SECRET LAB?
YOU'RE STANDING ATOP IT.
THE SUN GLYPH.
HELIOS. THE NAME HE WISHES FOR HIMSELF.
TELL ME HOW IT OPENS.
YOU MUST KNOW.
YOU'RE ALWAYS DOWN HERE IN THE DARK, *WATCHING...*
YOU WANT TO SEE THE IMMORTALS?
THE FAILED ONES?
I WANT TO SEE THE *PORTAL.*

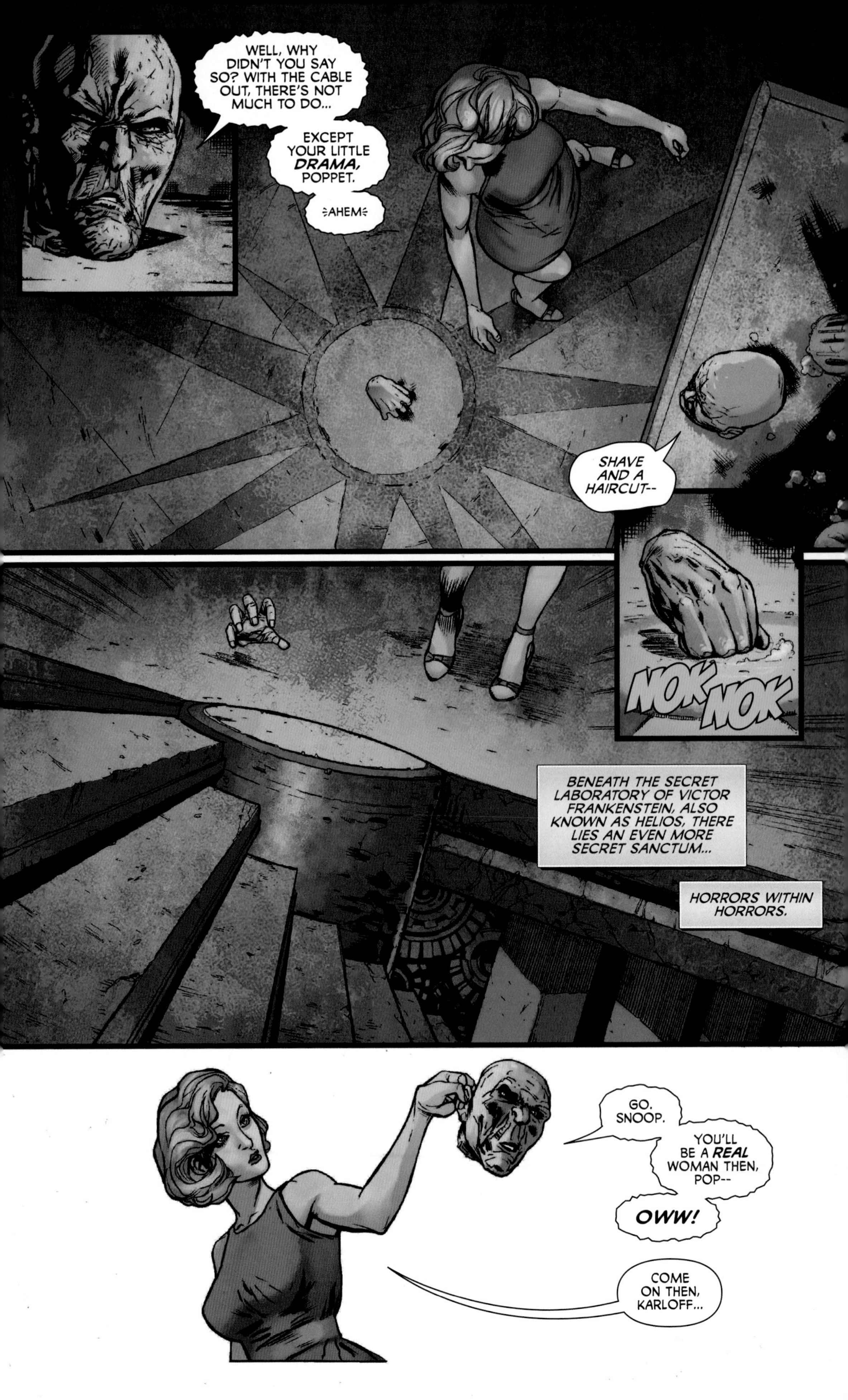

WELL, WHY DIDN'T YOU SAY SO? WITH THE CABLE OUT, THERE'S NOT MUCH TO DO...
EXCEPT YOUR LITTLE *DRAMA,* POPPET.
AHEM
SHAVE AND A HAIRCUT--
NOK NOK
BENEATH THE SECRET LABORATORY OF VICTOR FRANKENSTEIN, ALSO KNOWN AS HELIOS, THERE LIES AN EVEN MORE SECRET SANCTUM...
HORRORS WITHIN HORRORS.
GO. SNOOP.
YOU'LL BE A *REAL* WOMAN THEN, POP--
OWW!
COME ON THEN, KARLOFF...

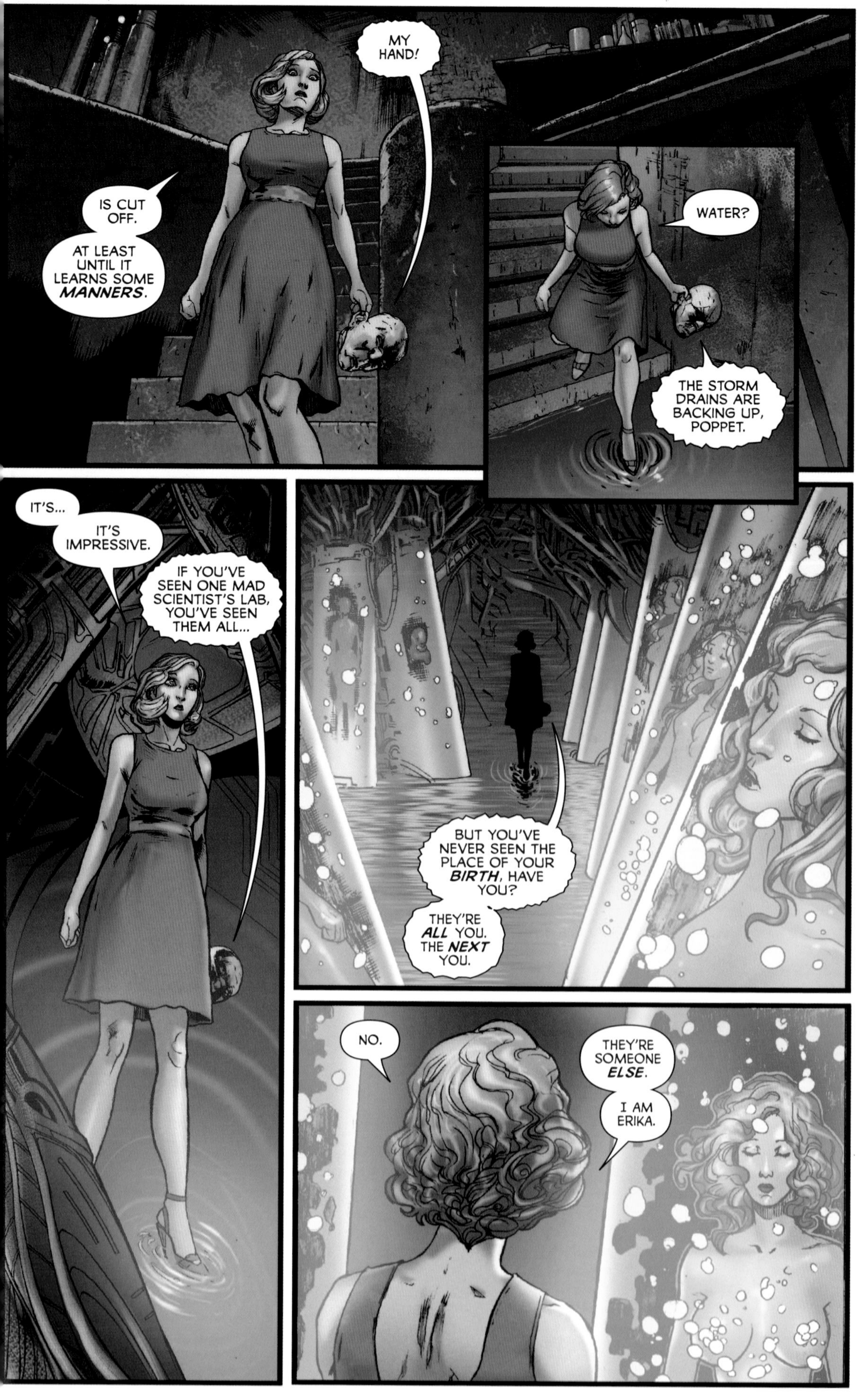
MY HAND!
IS CUT OFF.
AT LEAST UNTIL IT LEARNS SOME *MANNERS*.
WATER?
THE STORM DRAINS ARE BACKING UP, POPPET.
IT'S...
IT'S IMPRESSIVE.
IF YOU'VE SEEN ONE MAD SCIENTIST'S LAB, YOU'VE SEEN THEM ALL...
BUT YOU'VE NEVER SEEN THE PLACE OF YOUR *BIRTH*, HAVE YOU?
THEY'RE *ALL* YOU. THE *NEXT* YOU.
NO.
THEY'RE SOMEONE *ELSE*.
I AM ERIKA.

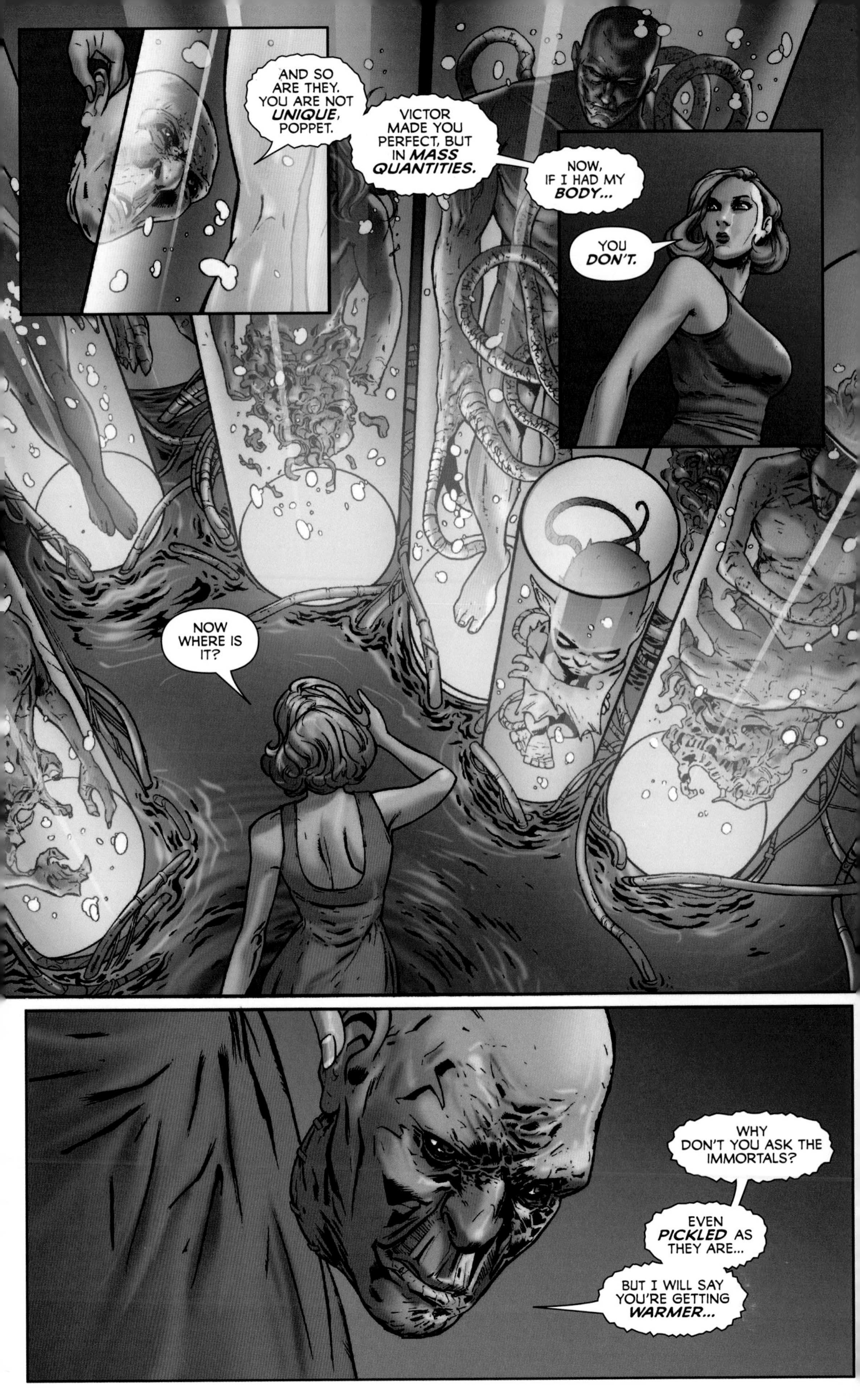
AND SO ARE THEY. YOU ARE NOT *UNIQUE*, POPPET.
VICTOR MADE YOU PERFECT, BUT IN *MASS QUANTITIES.*
NOW, IF I HAD MY *BODY...*
YOU *DON'T.*
NOW WHERE IS IT?
WHY DON'T YOU ASK THE IMMORTALS?
EVEN *PICKLED* AS THEY ARE...
BUT I WILL SAY YOU'RE GETTING *WARMER...*

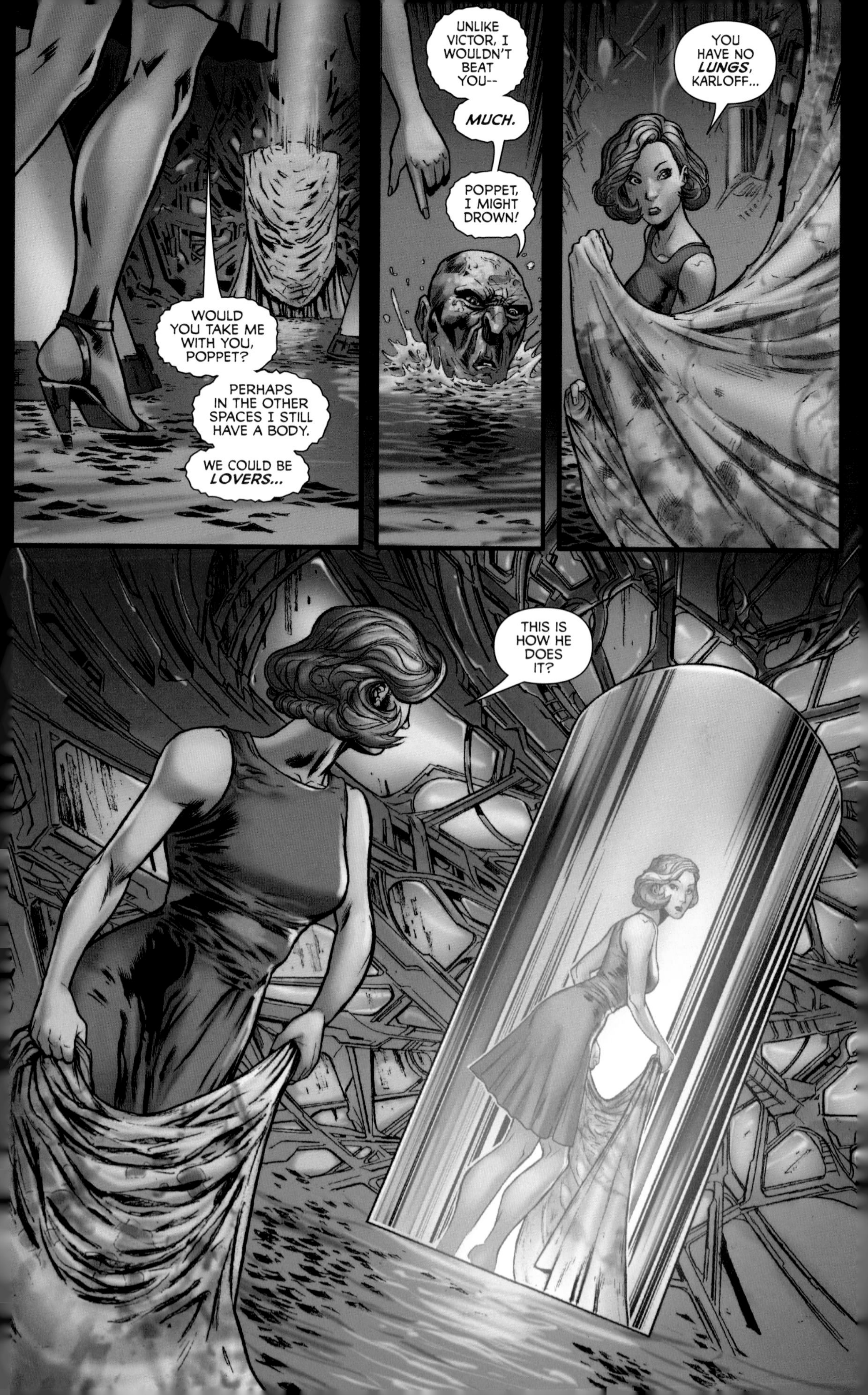
WOULD YOU TAKE ME WITH YOU, POPPET?
PERHAPS IN THE OTHER SPACES I STILL HAVE A BODY.
WE COULD BE *LOVERS...*
UNLIKE VICTOR, I WOULDN'T BEAT YOU--
MUCH.
POPPET, I MIGHT DROWN!
YOU HAVE NO *LUNGS*, KARLOFF...
THIS IS HOW HE DOES IT?

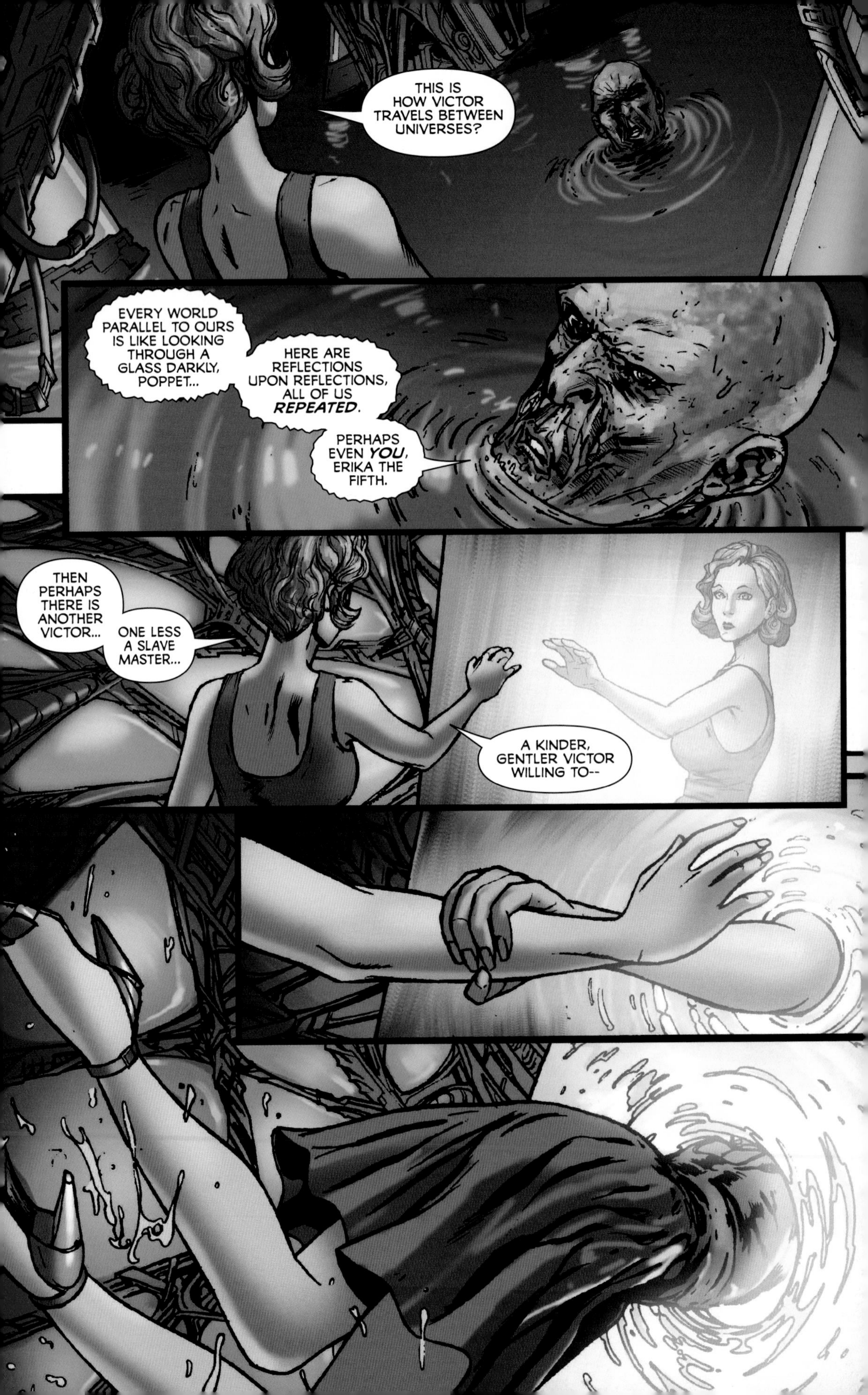
THIS IS HOW VICTOR TRAVELS BETWEEN UNIVERSES?
EVERY WORLD PARALLEL TO OURS IS LIKE LOOKING THROUGH A GLASS DARKLY, POPPET...
HERE ARE REFLECTIONS UPON REFLECTIONS, ALL OF US ***REPEATED***.
PERHAPS EVEN ***YOU***, ERIKA THE FIFTH.
THEN PERHAPS THERE IS ANOTHER VICTOR...
ONE LESS A SLAVE MASTER...
A KINDER, GENTLER VICTOR WILLING TO--

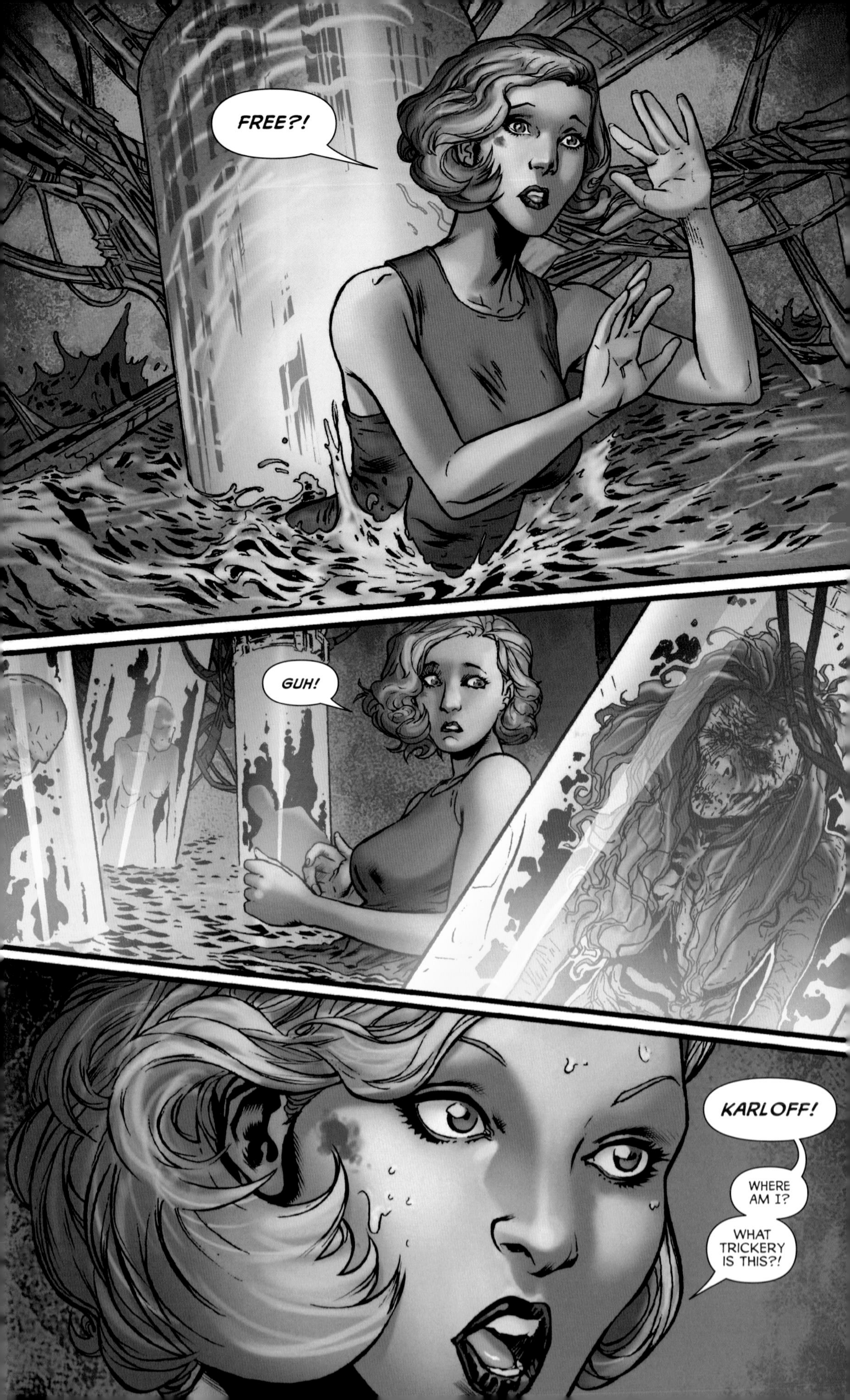
FREE?!
GUH!
KARLOFF!
WHERE AM I?
WHAT TRICKERY IS THIS?!

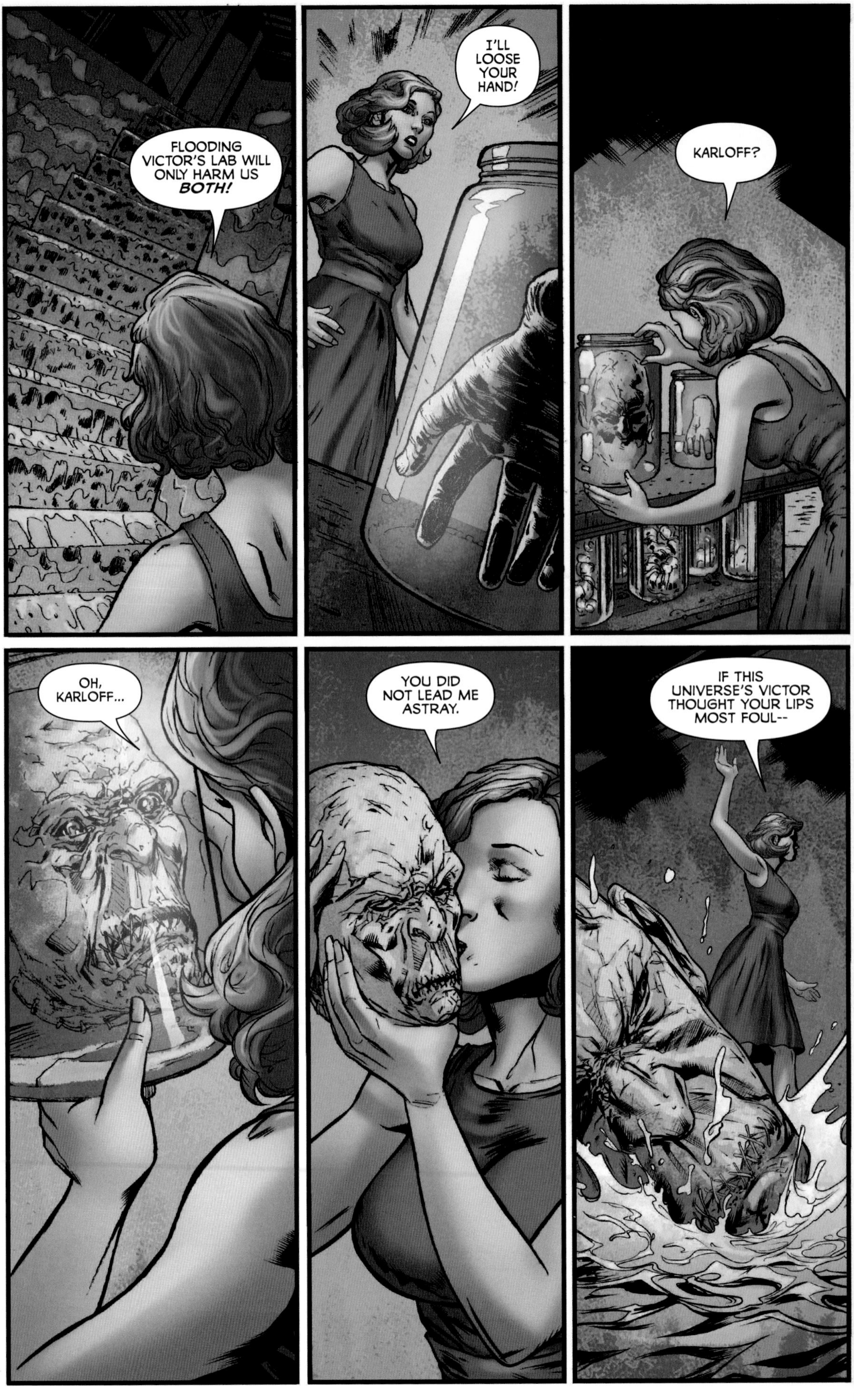
FLOODING VICTOR'S LAB WILL ONLY HARM US *BOTH!*
I'LL LOOSE YOUR HAND!
KARLOFF?
OH, KARLOFF...
YOU DID NOT LEAD ME ASTRAY.
IF THIS UNIVERSE'S VICTOR THOUGHT YOUR LIPS MOST FOUL--

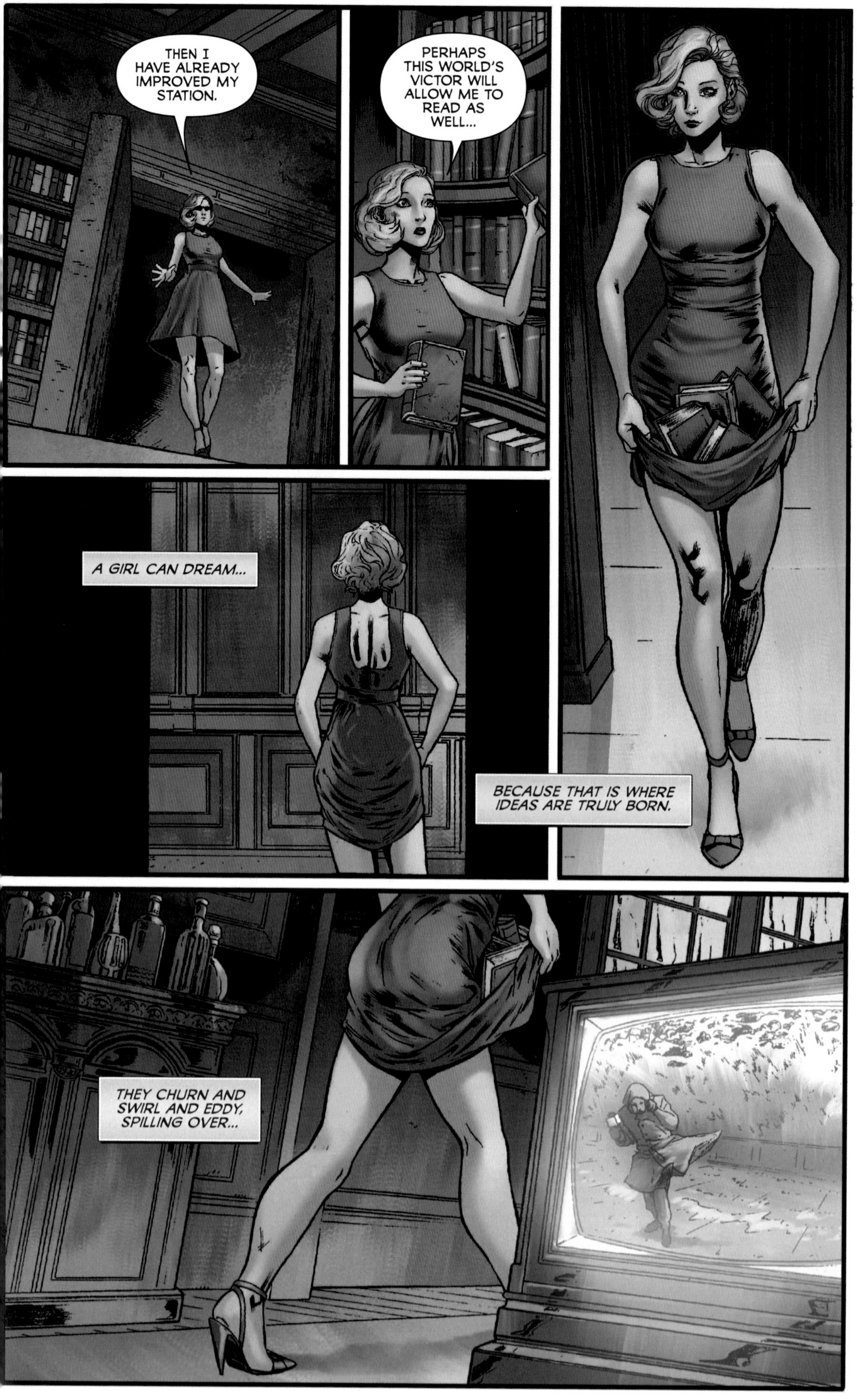
THEN I HAVE ALREADY IMPROVED MY STATION.
PERHAPS THIS WORLD'S VICTOR WILL ALLOW ME TO READ AS WELL...
A GIRL CAN DREAM...
BECAUSE THAT IS WHERE IDEAS ARE TRULY BORN.
THEY CHURN AND SWIRL AND EDDY, SPILLING OVER...

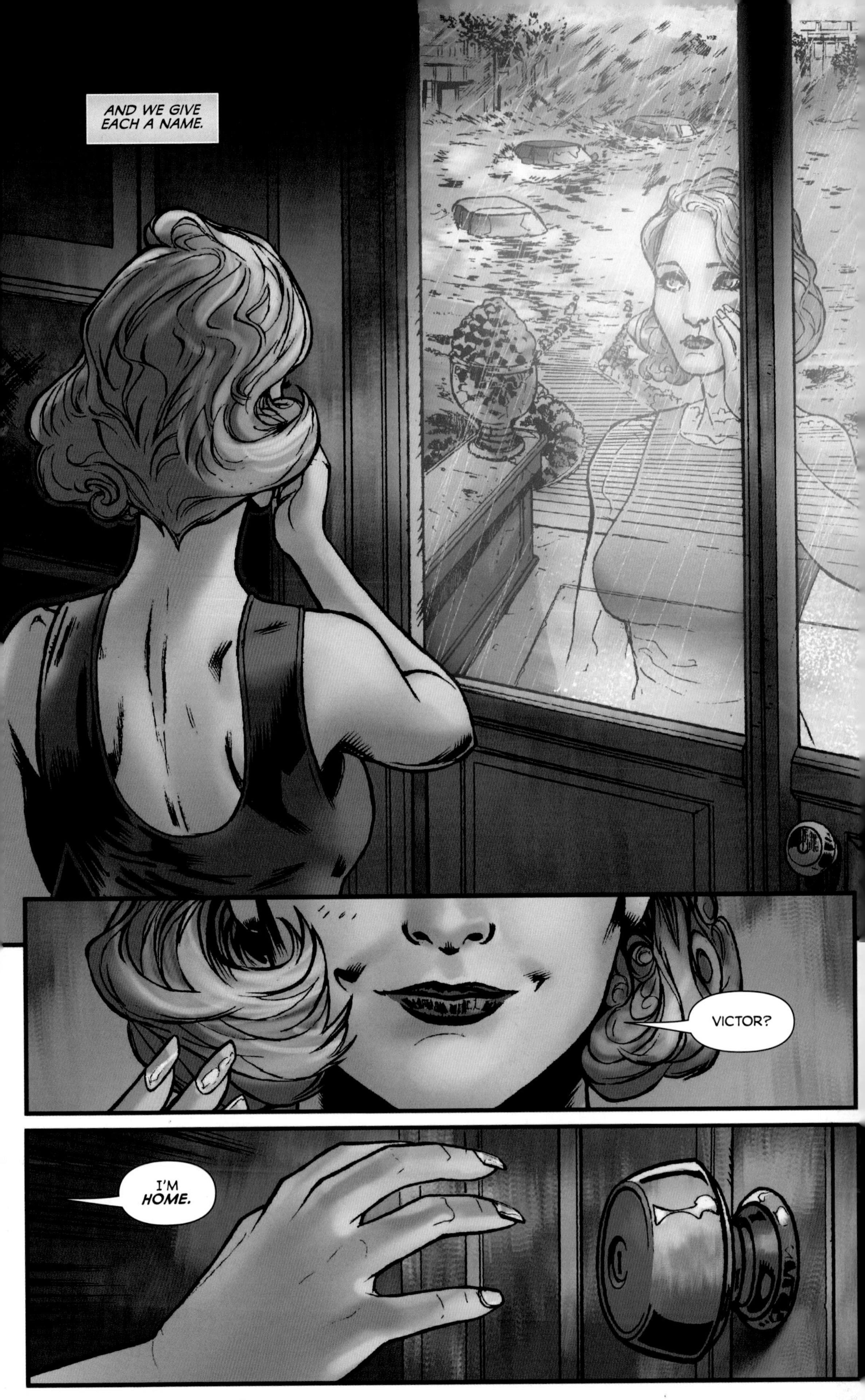
AND WE GIVE EACH A NAME.
VICTOR?
I'M HOME.

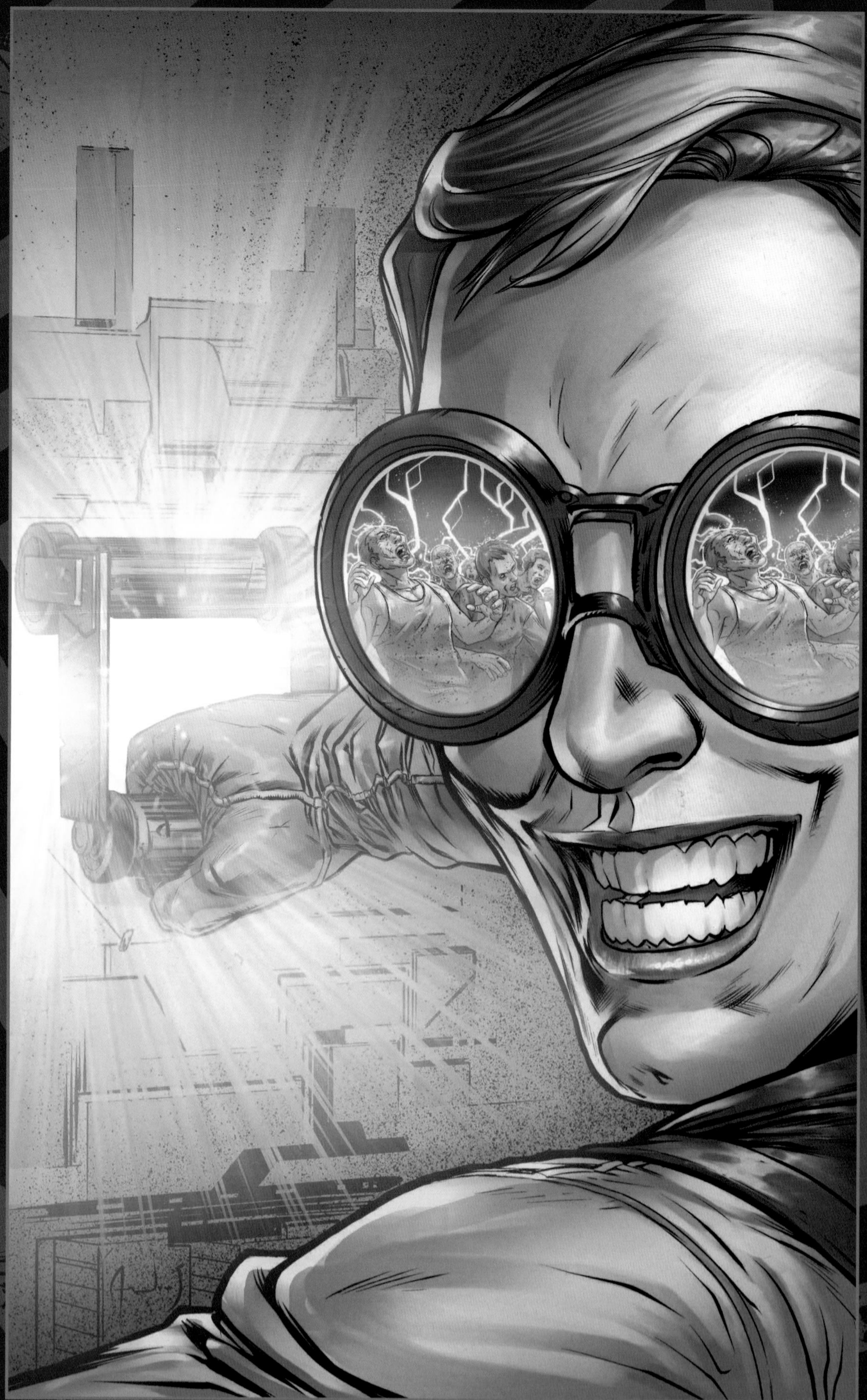

ISSUE TWO COVER
ART BY ANDRES PONCE COLORS BY MOHAN

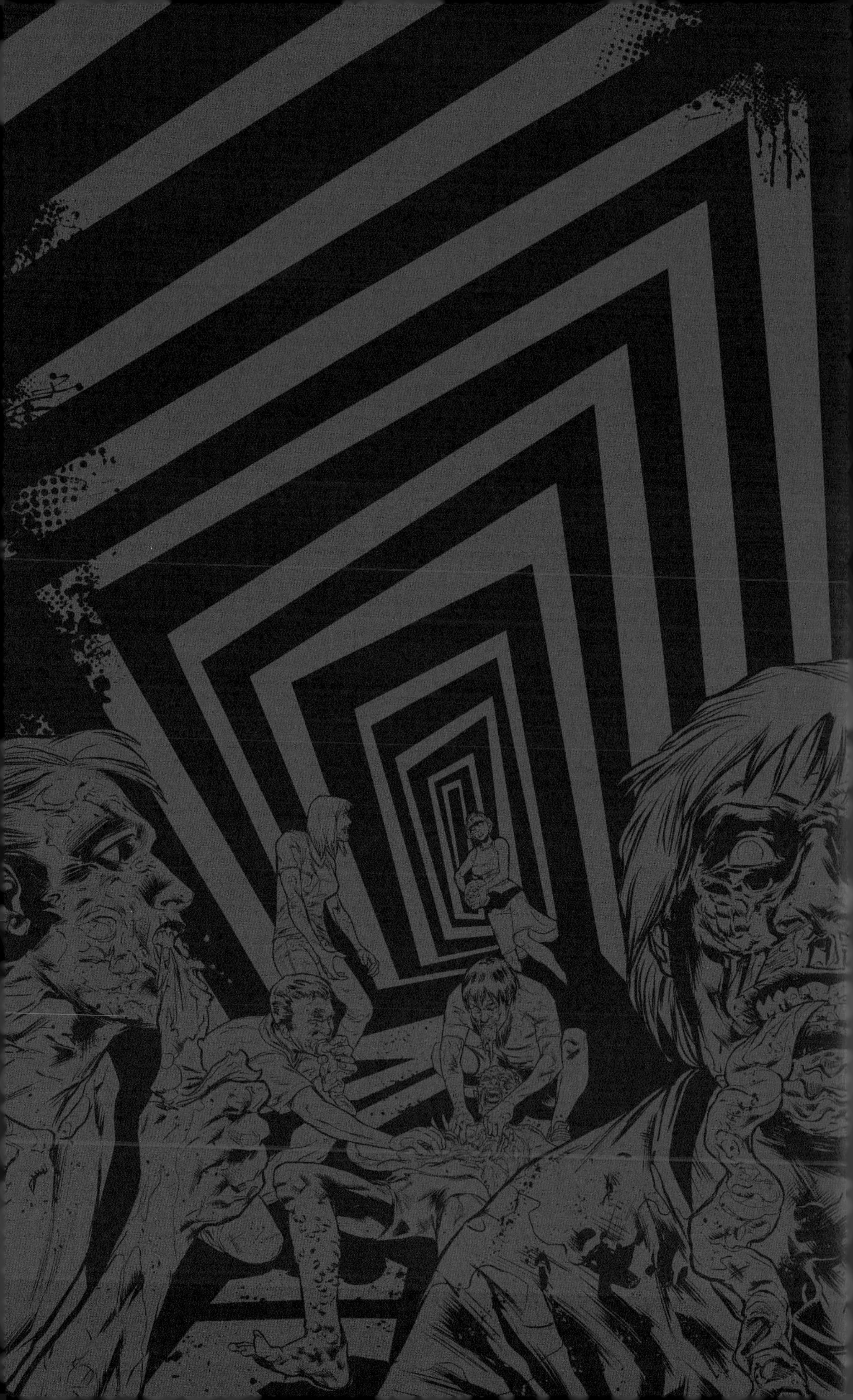

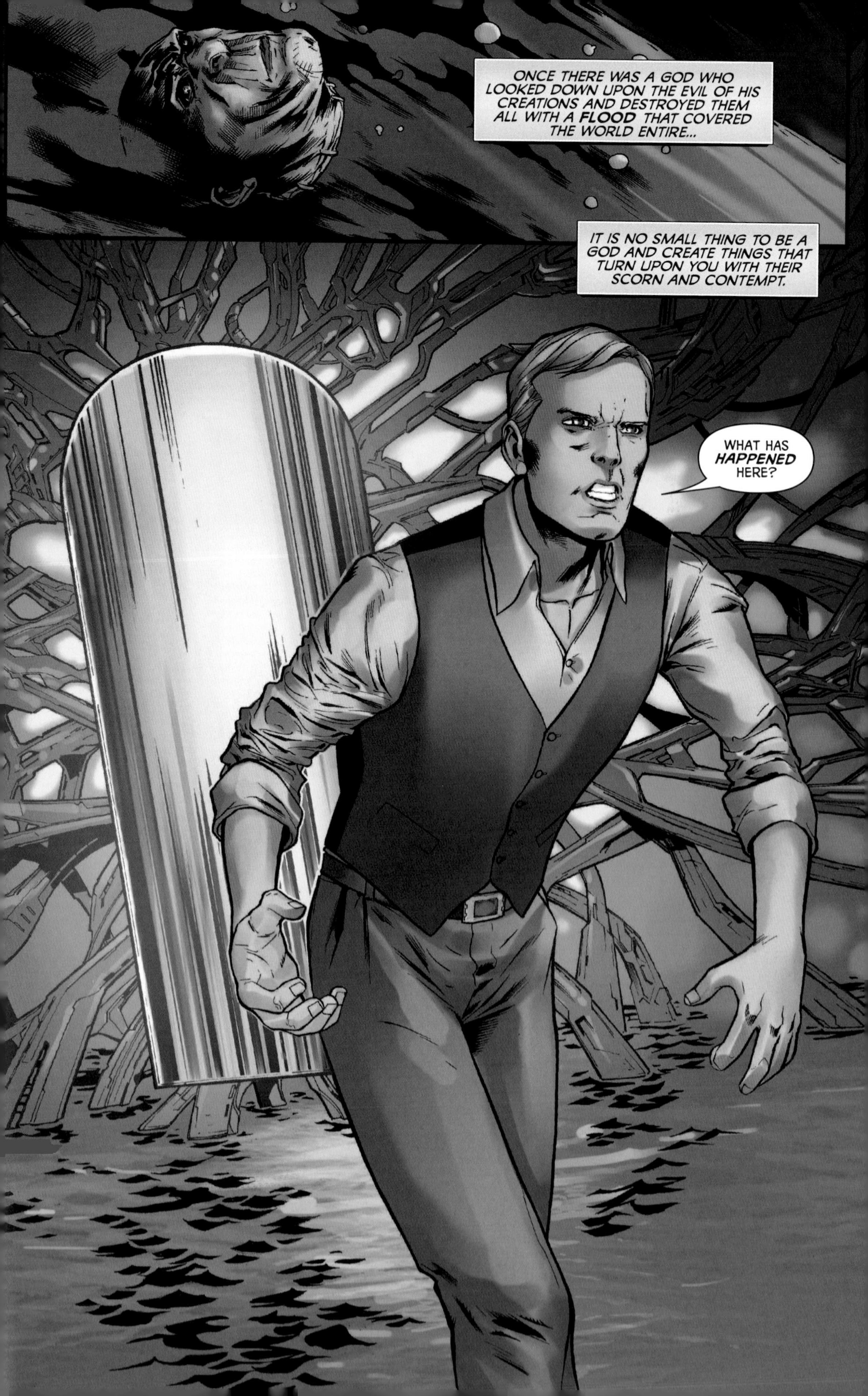
ONCE THERE WAS A GOD WHO LOOKED DOWN UPON THE EVIL OF HIS CREATIONS AND DESTROYED THEM ALL WITH A FLOOD THAT COVERED THE WORLD ENTIRE...
IT IS NO SMALL THING TO BE A GOD AND CREATE THINGS THAT TURN UPON YOU WITH THEIR SCORN AND CONTEMPT.
WHAT HAS HAPPENED HERE?

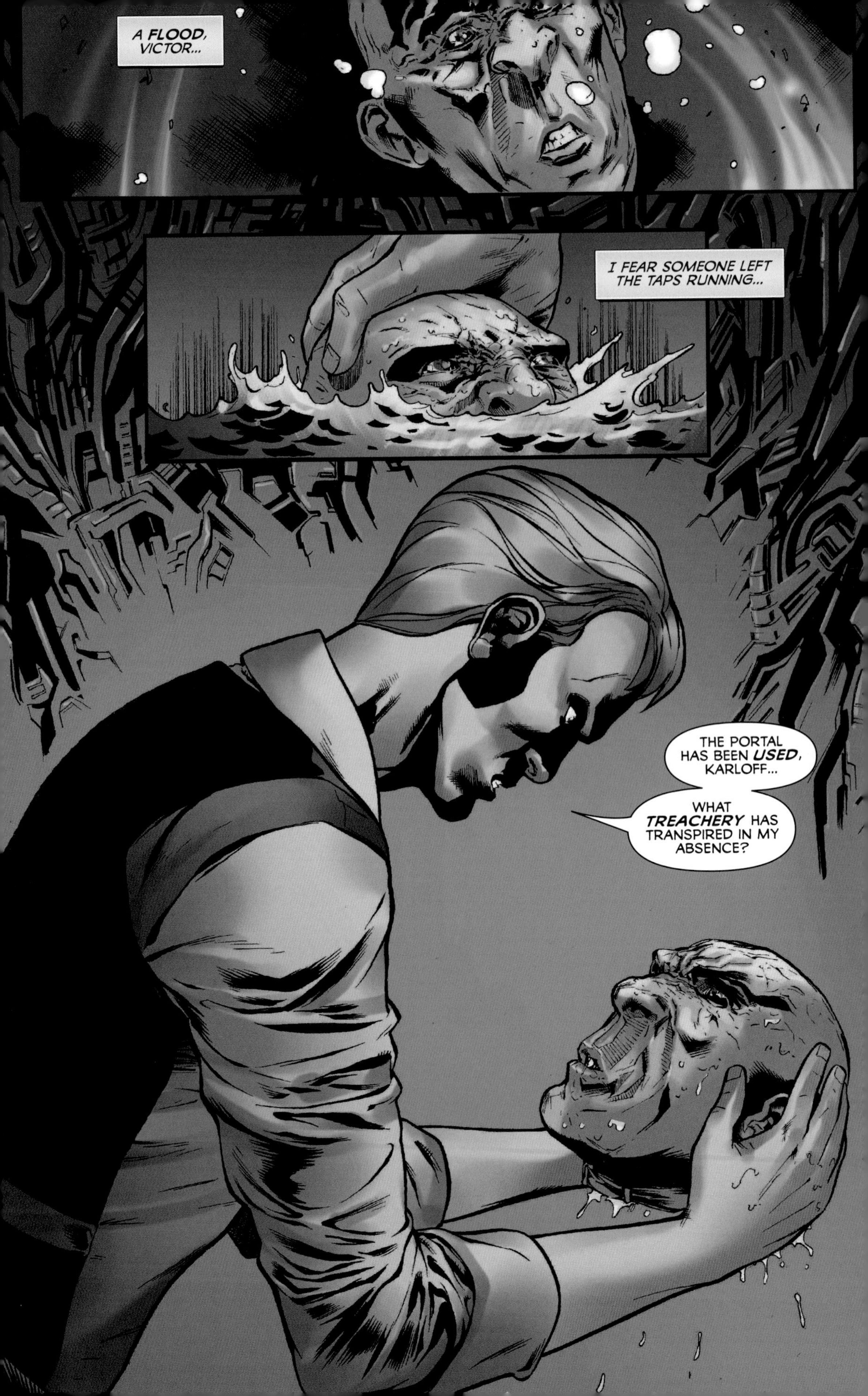

A FLOOD, VICTOR...
I FEAR SOMEONE LEFT THE TAPS RUNNING...
THE PORTAL HAS BEEN USED, KARLOFF...
WHAT TREACHERY HAS TRANSPIRED IN MY ABSENCE?

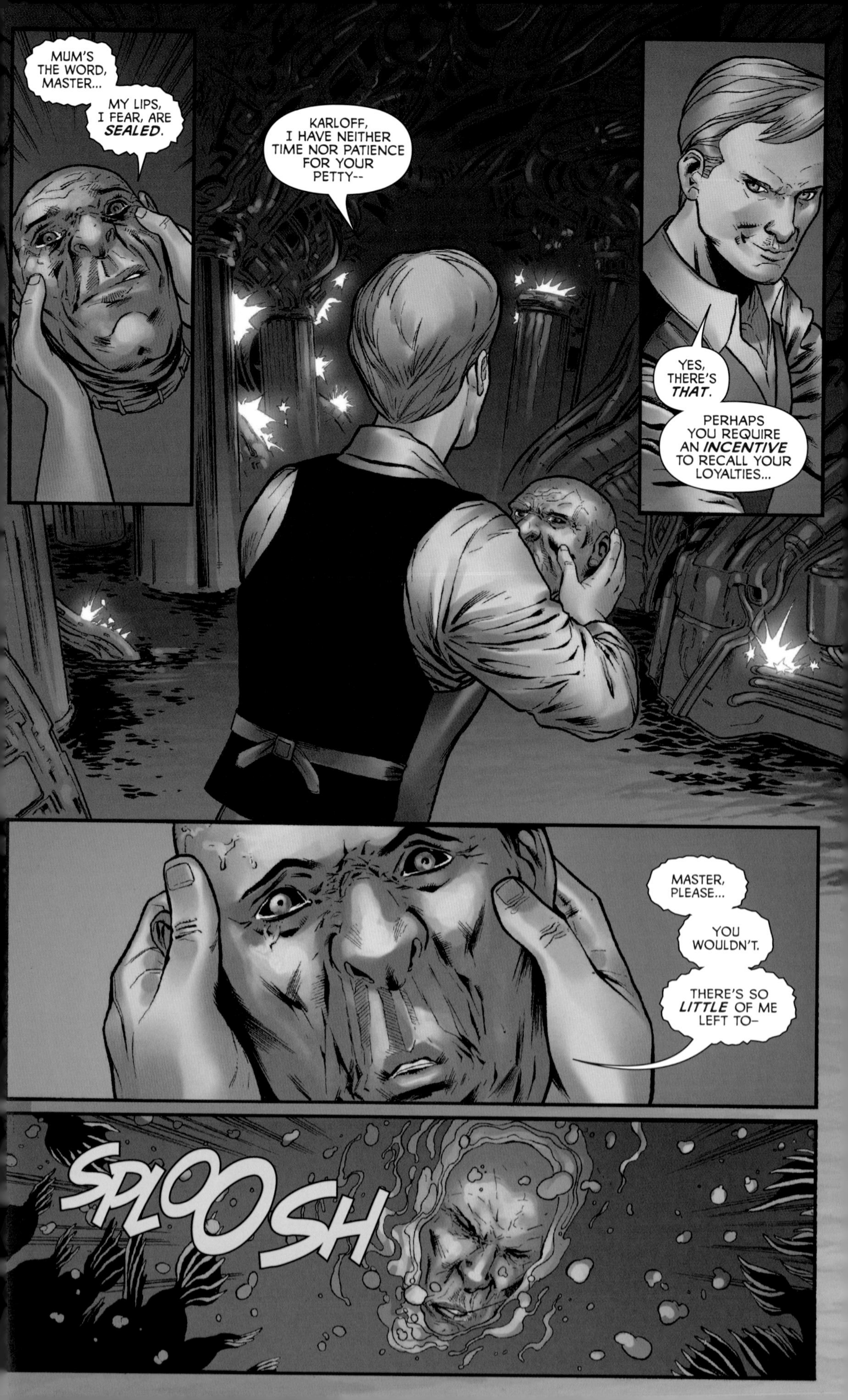
MUM'S THE WORD, MASTER...
MY LIPS, I FEAR, ARE *SEALED*.
KARLOFF, I HAVE NEITHER TIME NOR PATIENCE FOR YOUR PETTY--
YES, THERE'S *THAT*.
PERHAPS YOU REQUIRE AN *INCENTIVE* TO RECALL YOUR LOYALTIES...
MASTER, PLEASE...
YOU WOULDN'T.
THERE'S SO *LITTLE* OF ME LEFT TO–
SPLOOSH

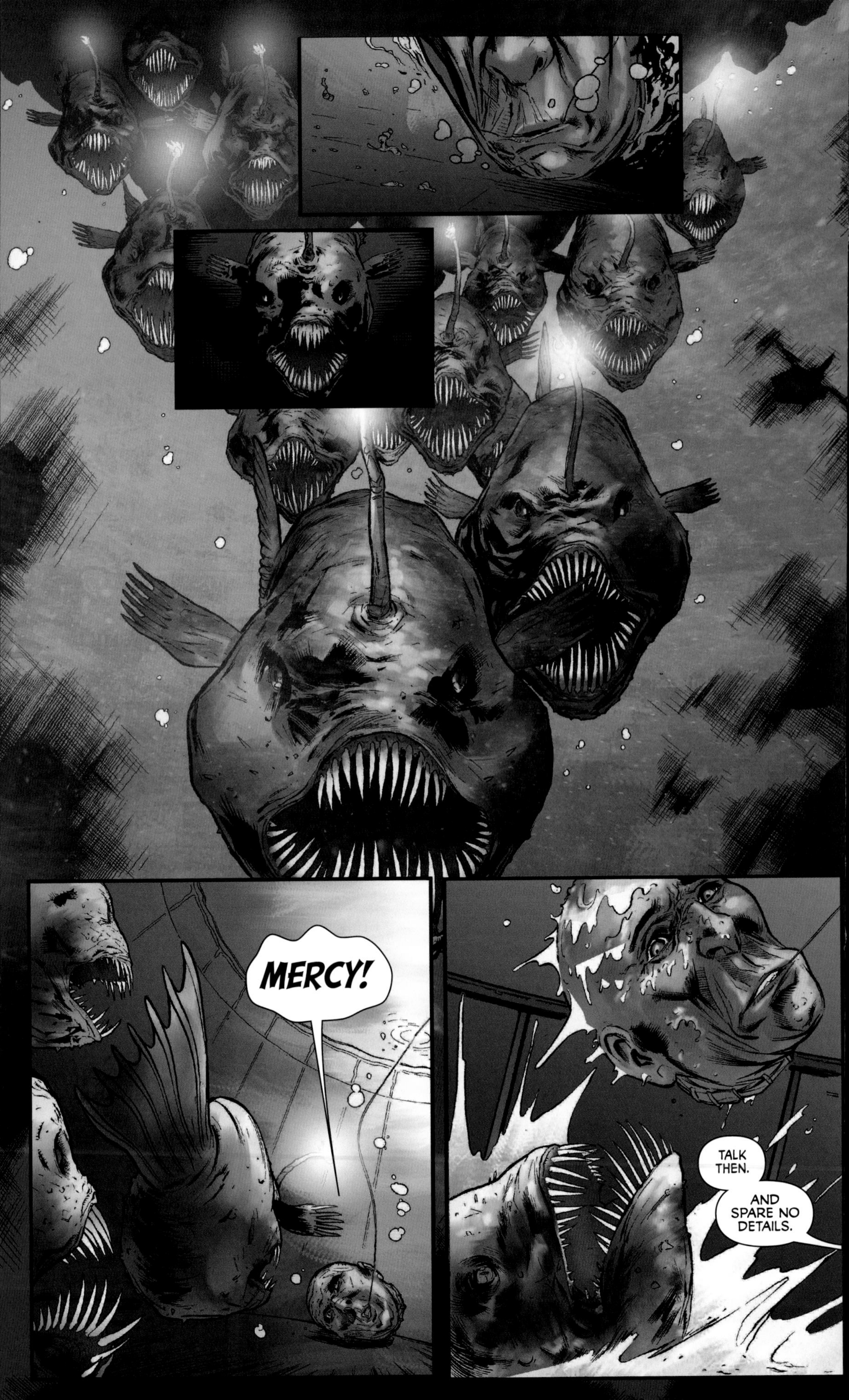
MERCY!
TALK THEN.
AND SPARE NO DETAILS.

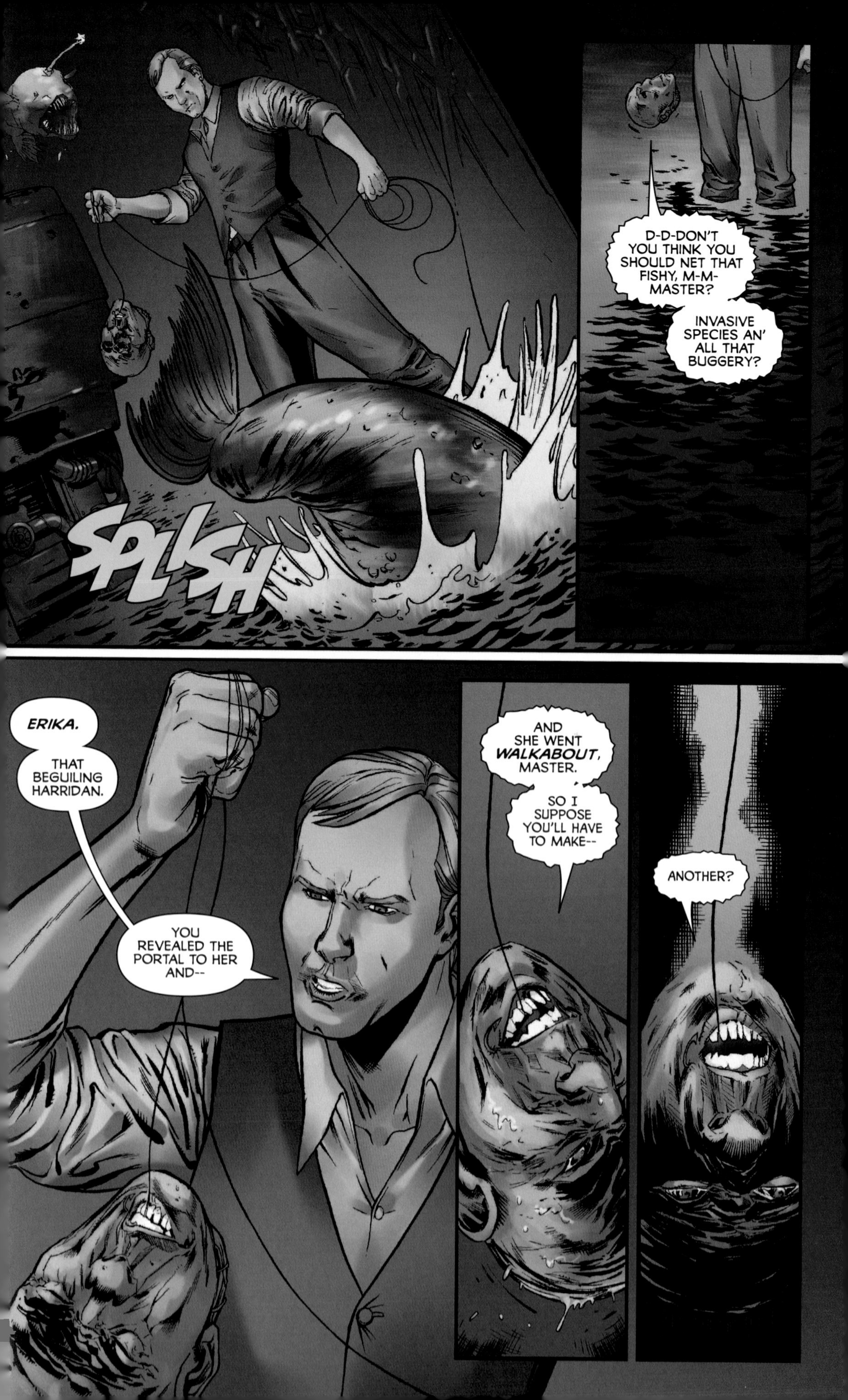
D-D-DON'T YOU THINK YOU SHOULD NET THAT FISHY, M-M-MASTER?
INVASIVE SPECIES AN' ALL THAT BUGGERY?
SPLISH
ERIKA.
THAT BEGUILING HARRIDAN.
YOU REVEALED THE PORTAL TO HER AND--
AND SHE WENT WALKABOUT, MASTER.
SO I SUPPOSE YOU'LL HAVE TO MAKE--
ANOTHER?

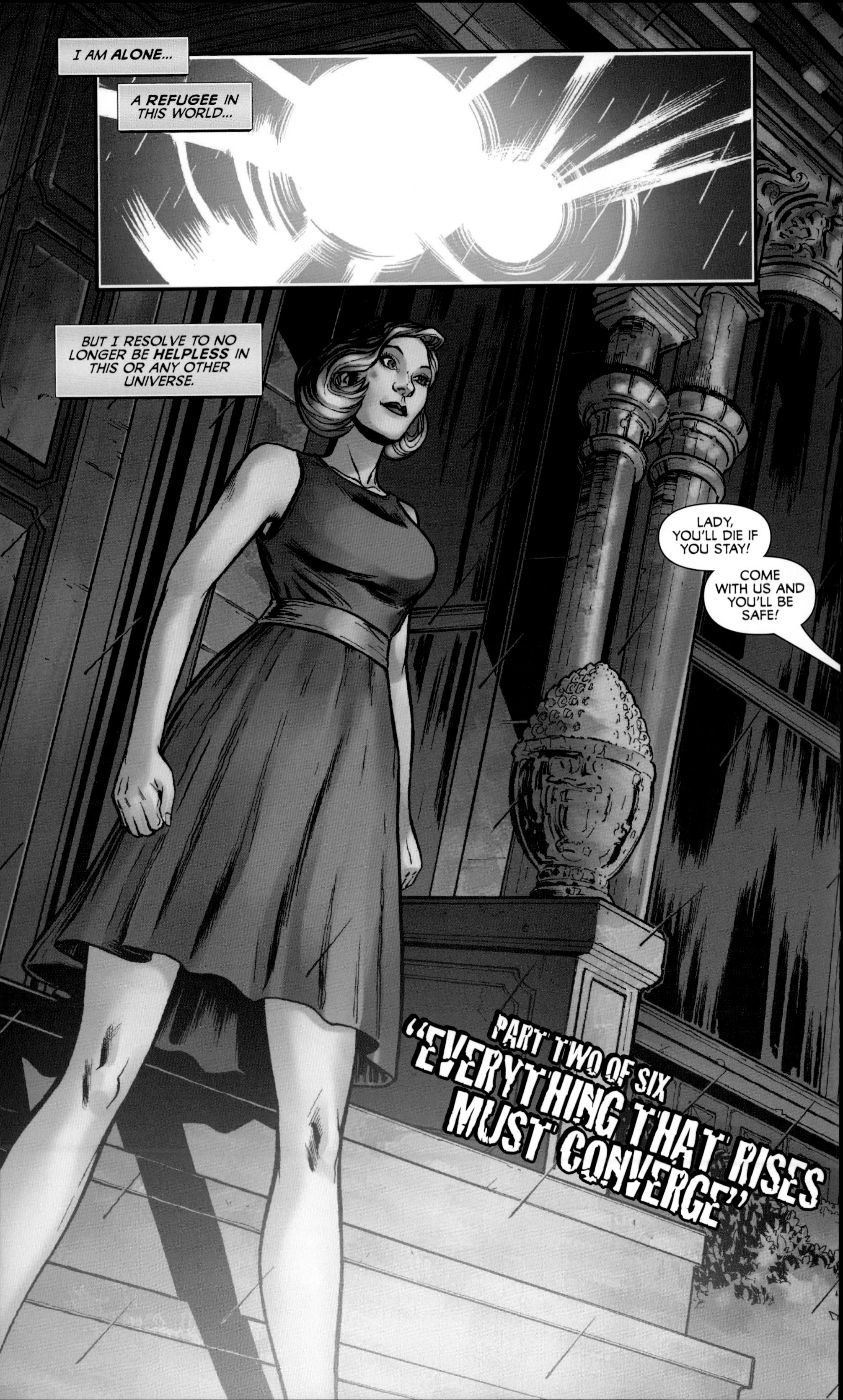
I AM ALONE...
A REFUGEE IN THIS WORLD...
BUT I RESOLVE TO NO LONGER BE HELPLESS IN THIS OR ANY OTHER UNIVERSE.
LADY, YOU'LL DIE IF YOU STAY!
COME WITH US AND YOU'LL BE SAFE!
PART TWO OF SIX
"EVERYTHING THAT RISES MUST CONVERGE"

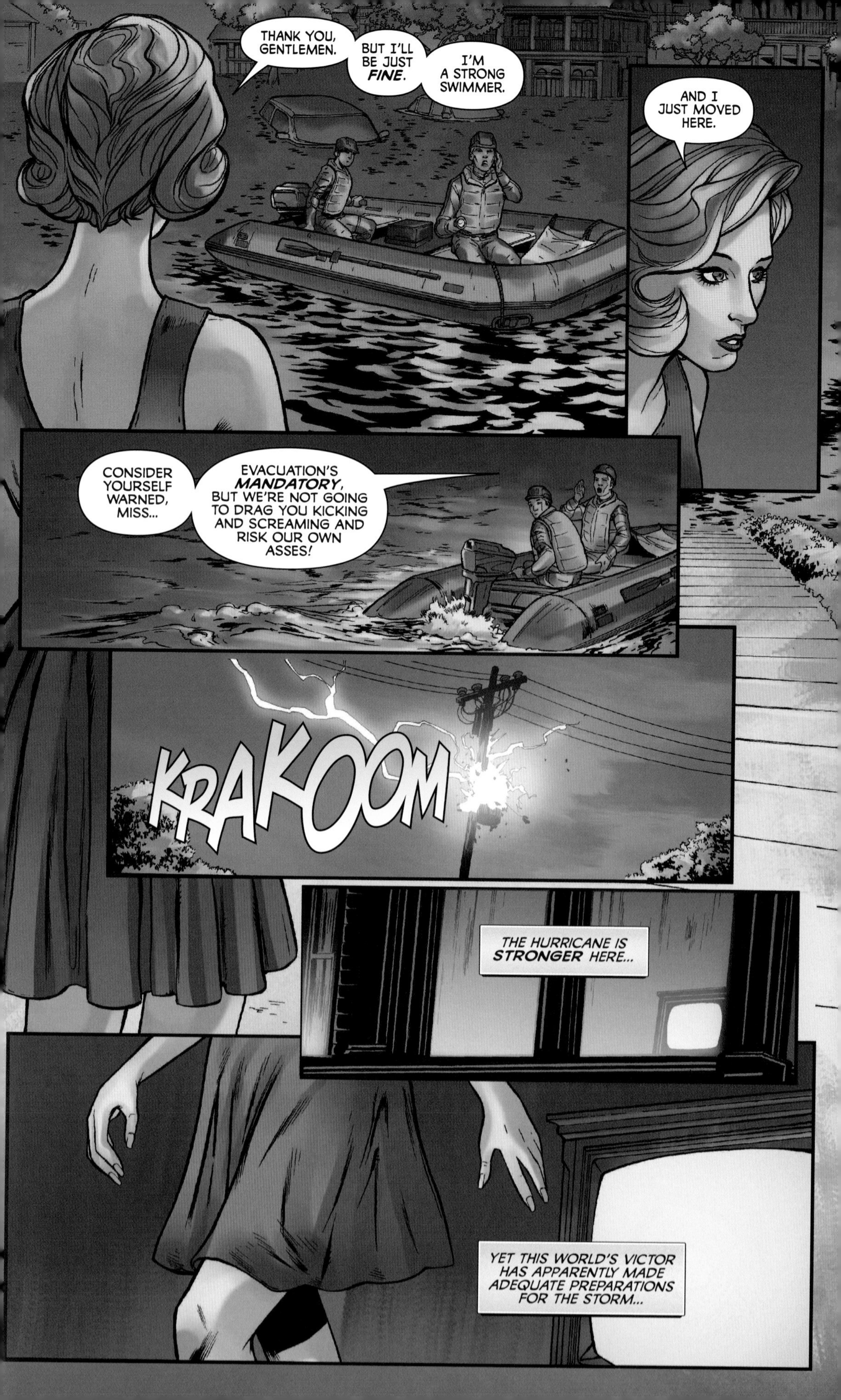
THANK YOU, GENTLEMEN.
BUT I'LL BE JUST FINE.
I'M A STRONG SWIMMER.
AND I JUST MOVED HERE.
CONSIDER YOURSELF WARNED, MISS...
EVACUATION'S MANDATORY, BUT WE'RE NOT GOING TO DRAG YOU KICKING AND SCREAMING AND RISK OUR OWN ASSES!
KRAKOOM
THE HURRICANE IS STRONGER HERE...
YET THIS WORLD'S VICTOR HAS APPARENTLY MADE ADEQUATE PREPARATIONS FOR THE STORM...

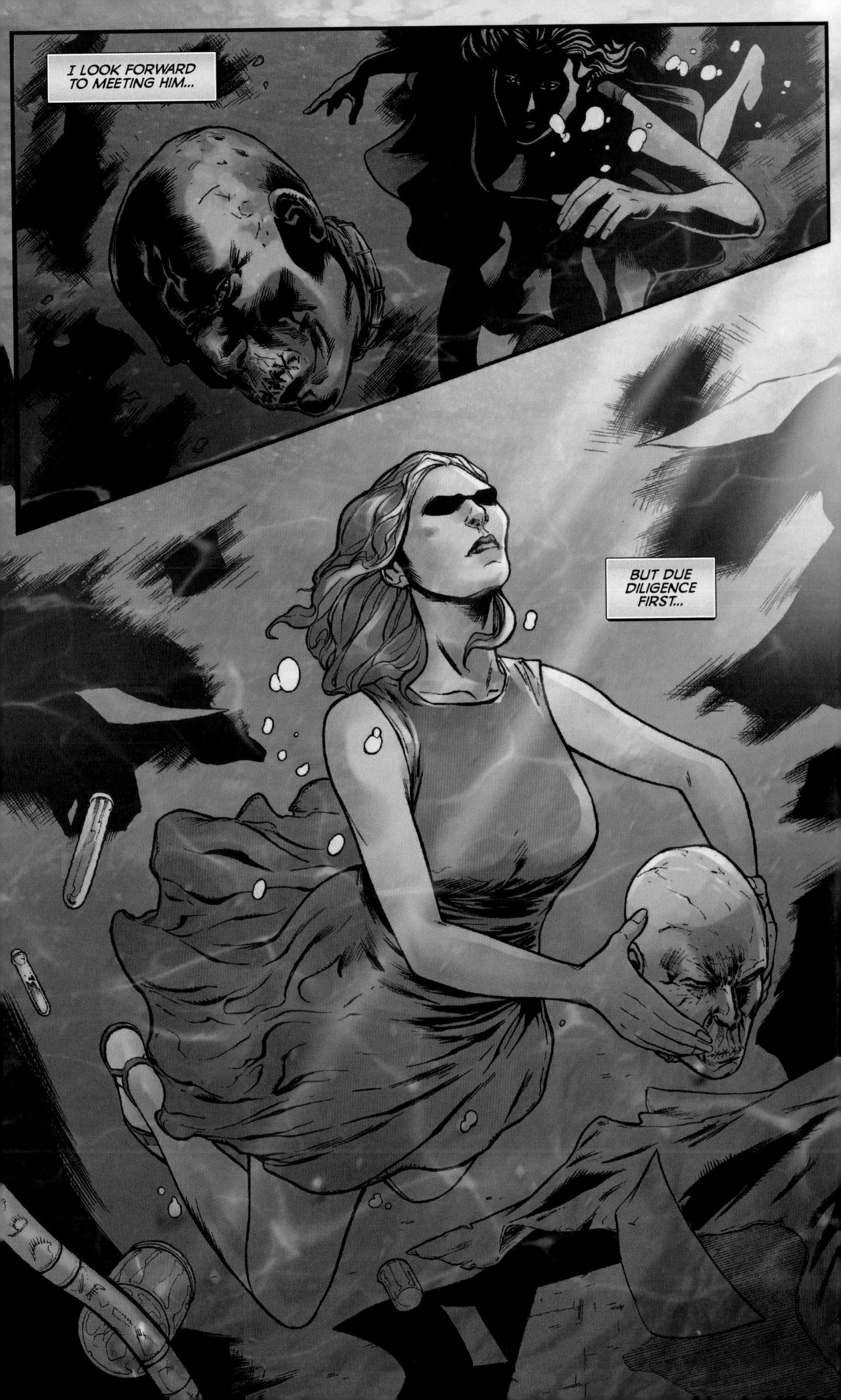
I LOOK FORWARD TO MEETING HIM...
BUT DUE DILIGENCE FIRST...

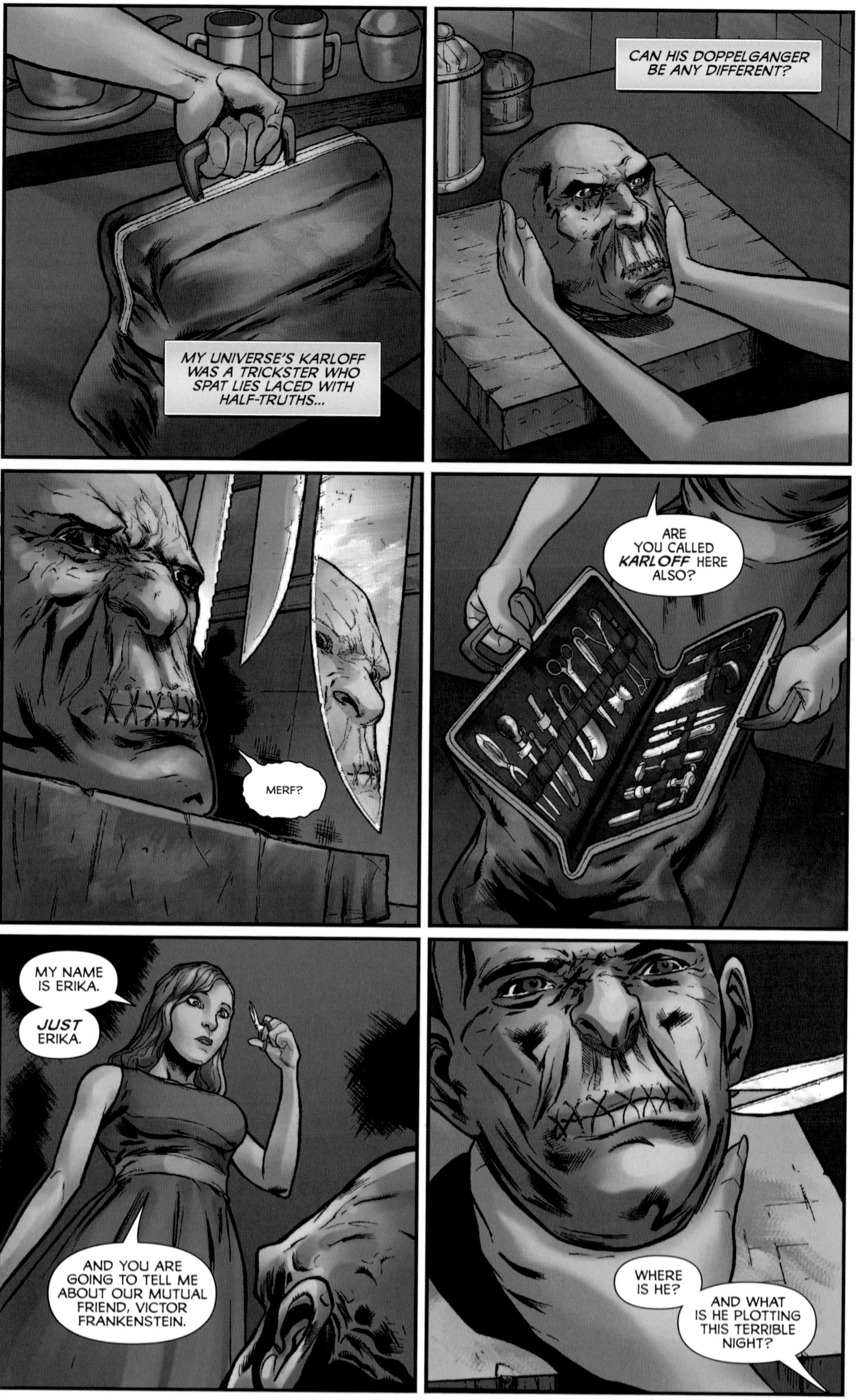
MY UNIVERSE'S KARLOFF WAS A TRICKSTER WHO SPAT LIES LACED WITH HALF-TRUTHS...
CAN HIS DOPPELGANGER BE ANY DIFFERENT?
MERF?
ARE YOU CALLED KARLOFF HERE ALSO?
MY NAME IS ERIKA.
JUST ERIKA.
AND YOU ARE GOING TO TELL ME ABOUT OUR MUTUAL FRIEND, VICTOR FRANKENSTEIN.
WHERE IS HE?
AND WHAT IS HE PLOTTING THIS TERRIBLE NIGHT?

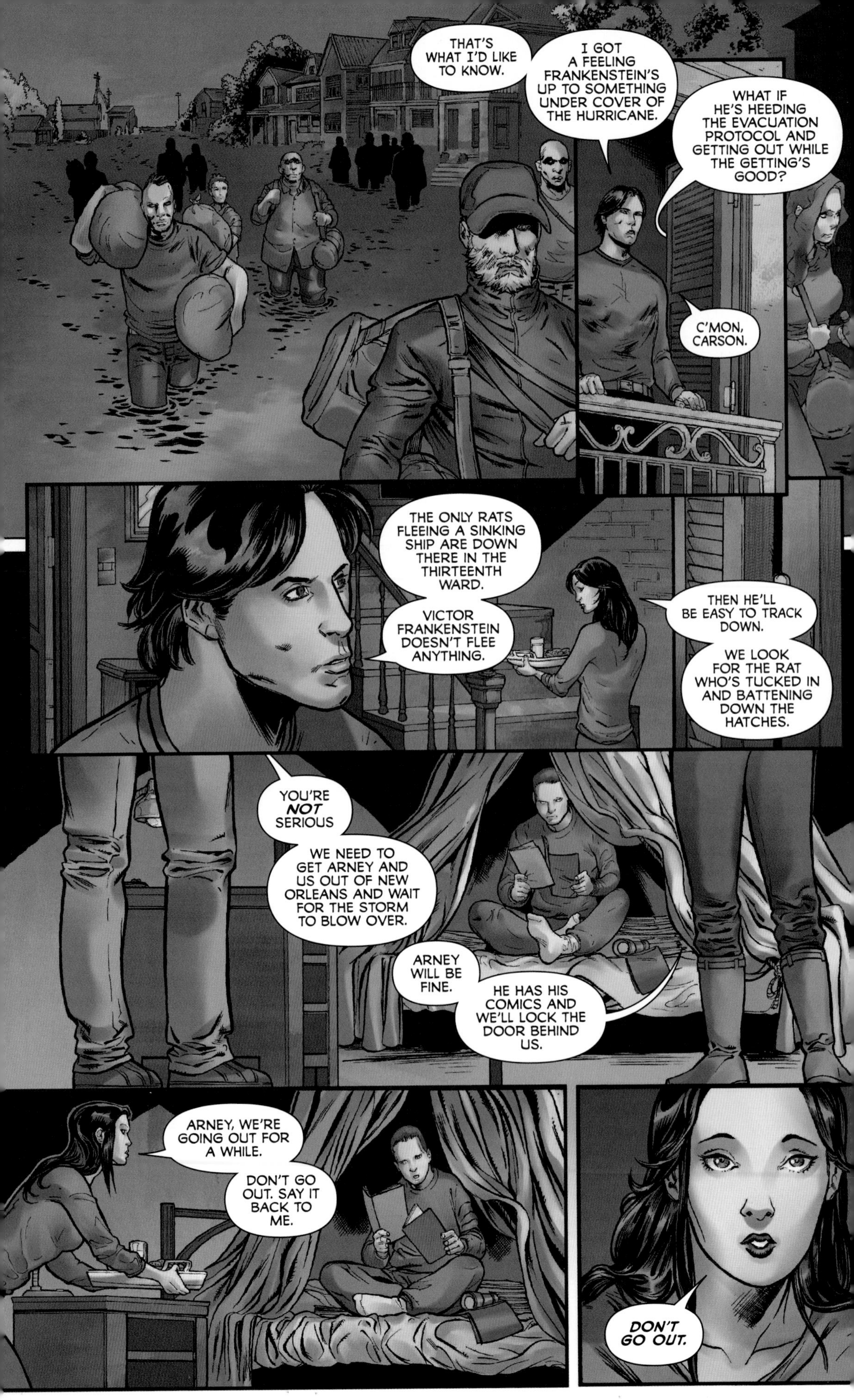
THAT'S WHAT I'D LIKE TO KNOW.
I GOT A FEELING FRANKENSTEIN'S UP TO SOMETHING UNDER COVER OF THE HURRICANE.
WHAT IF HE'S HEEDING THE EVACUATION PROTOCOL AND GETTING OUT WHILE THE GETTING'S GOOD?
C'MON, CARSON.
THE ONLY RATS FLEEING A SINKING SHIP ARE DOWN THERE IN THE THIRTEENTH WARD.
VICTOR FRANKENSTEIN DOESN'T FLEE ANYTHING.
THEN HE'LL BE EASY TO TRACK DOWN.
WE LOOK FOR THE RAT WHO'S TUCKED IN AND BATTENING DOWN THE HATCHES.
YOU'RE ***NOT*** SERIOUS
WE NEED TO GET ARNEY AND US OUT OF NEW ORLEANS AND WAIT FOR THE STORM TO BLOW OVER.
ARNEY WILL BE FINE.
HE HAS HIS COMICS AND WE'LL LOCK THE DOOR BEHIND US.
ARNEY, WE'RE GOING OUT FOR A WHILE.
DON'T GO OUT. SAY IT BACK TO ME.
DON'T GO OUT.

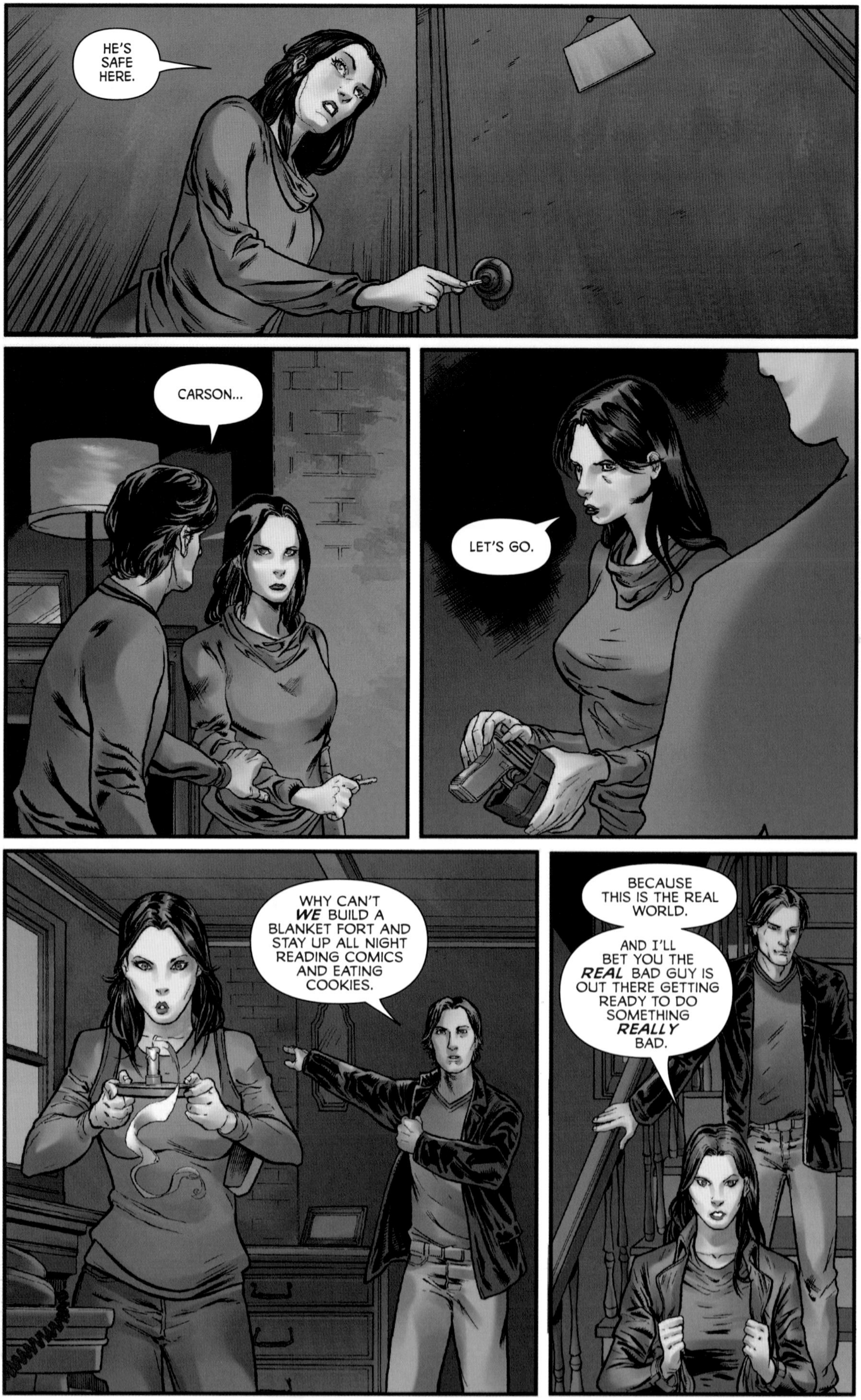
HE'S SAFE HERE.
CARSON...
LET'S GO.
WHY CAN'T *WE* BUILD A BLANKET FORT AND STAY UP ALL NIGHT READING COMICS AND EATING COOKIES.
BECAUSE THIS IS THE REAL WORLD.
AND I'LL BET YOU THE *REAL* BAD GUY IS OUT THERE GETTING READY TO DO SOMETHING *REALLY* BAD.

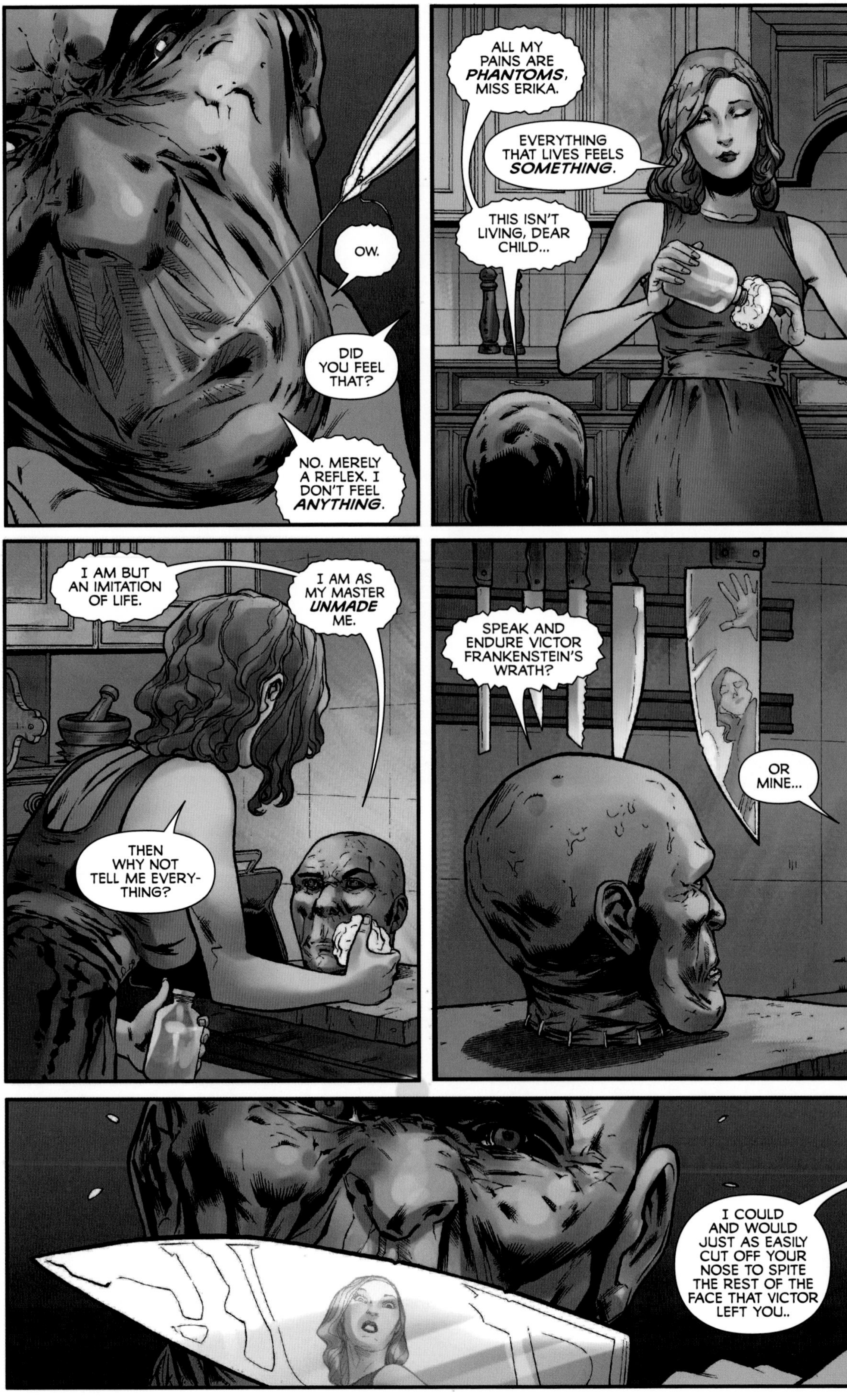
OW.
DID YOU FEEL THAT?
NO. MERELY A REFLEX. I DON'T FEEL ***ANYTHING***.
ALL MY PAINS ARE ***PHANTOMS***, MISS ERIKA.
EVERYTHING THAT LIVES FEELS ***SOMETHING***.
THIS ISN'T LIVING, DEAR CHILD...
I AM BUT AN IMITATION OF LIFE.
I AM AS MY MASTER ***UNMADE*** ME.
THEN WHY NOT TELL ME EVERY-THING?
SPEAK AND ENDURE VICTOR FRANKENSTEIN'S WRATH?
OR MINE...
I COULD AND WOULD JUST AS EASILY CUT OFF YOUR NOSE TO SPITE THE REST OF THE FACE THAT VICTOR LEFT YOU..

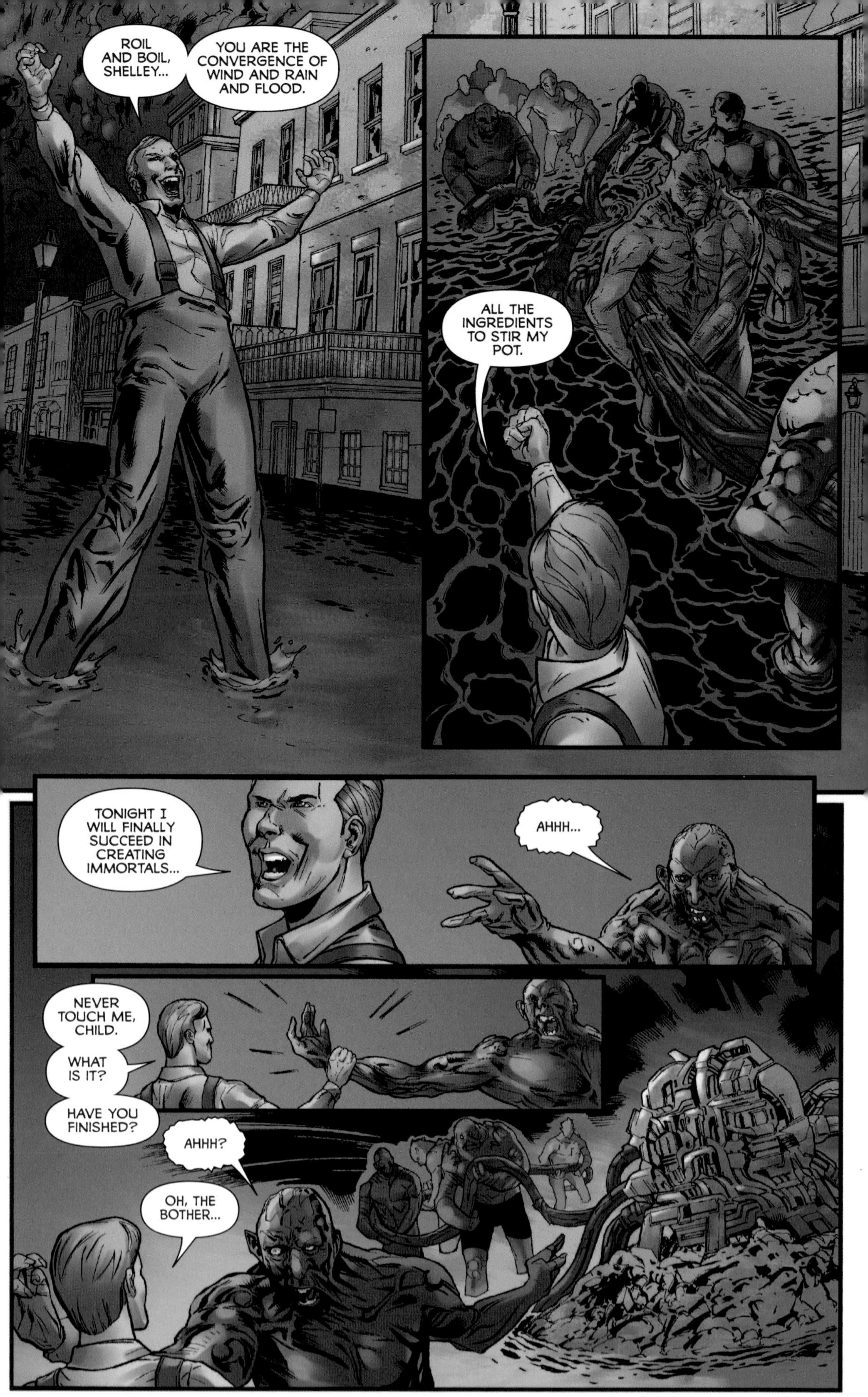
ROIL AND BOIL, SHELLEY...
YOU ARE THE CONVERGENCE OF WIND AND RAIN AND FLOOD.
ALL THE INGREDIENTS TO STIR MY POT.
TONIGHT I WILL FINALLY SUCCEED IN CREATING IMMORTALS...
AHHH...
NEVER TOUCH ME, CHILD.
WHAT IS IT?
HAVE YOU FINISHED?
AHHH?
OH, THE BOTHER...

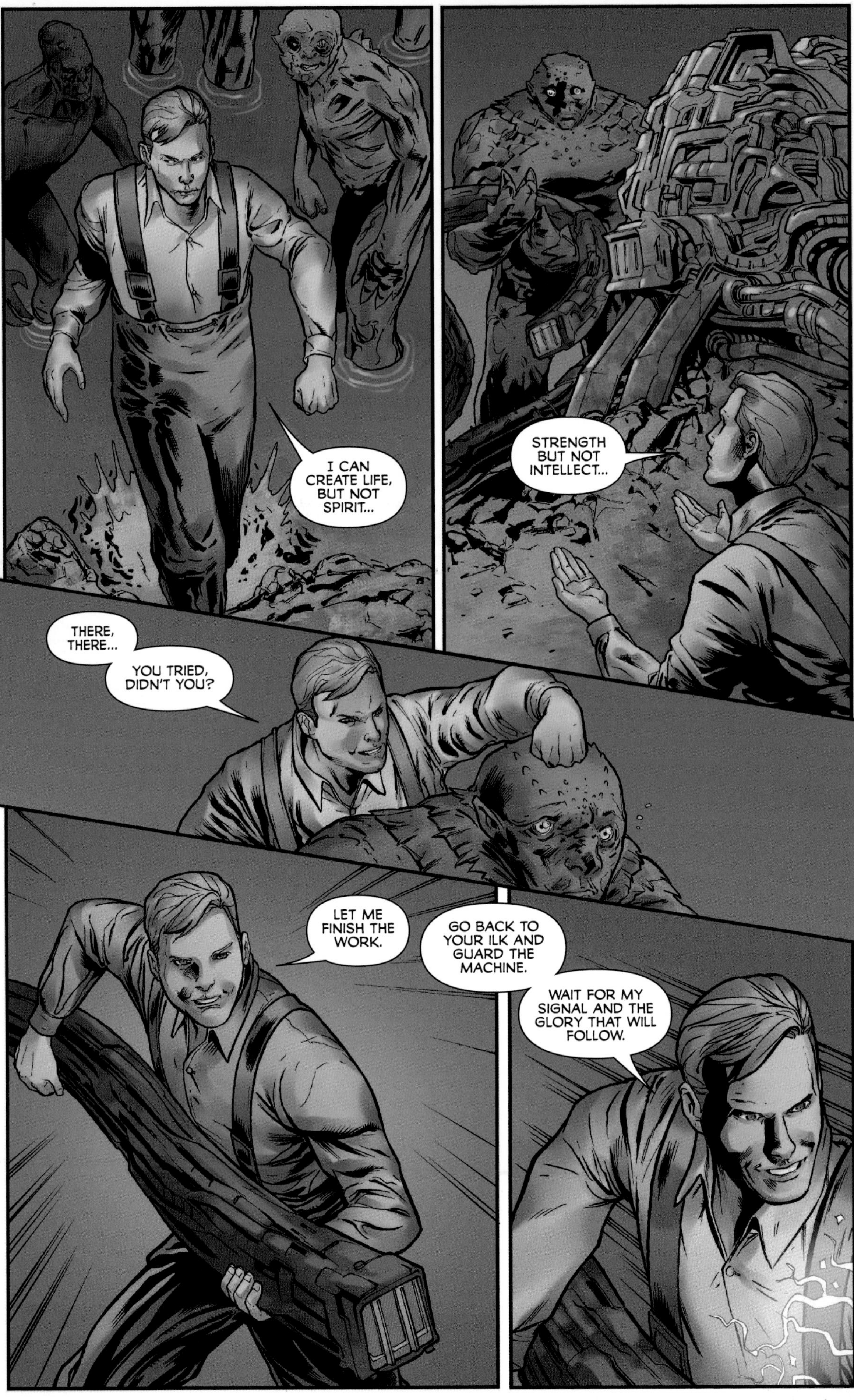
I CAN CREATE LIFE, BUT NOT SPIRIT...
STRENGTH BUT NOT INTELLECT...
THERE, THERE...
YOU TRIED, DIDN'T YOU?
LET ME FINISH THE WORK.
GO BACK TO YOUR ILK AND GUARD THE MACHINE.
WAIT FOR MY SIGNAL AND THE GLORY THAT WILL FOLLOW.

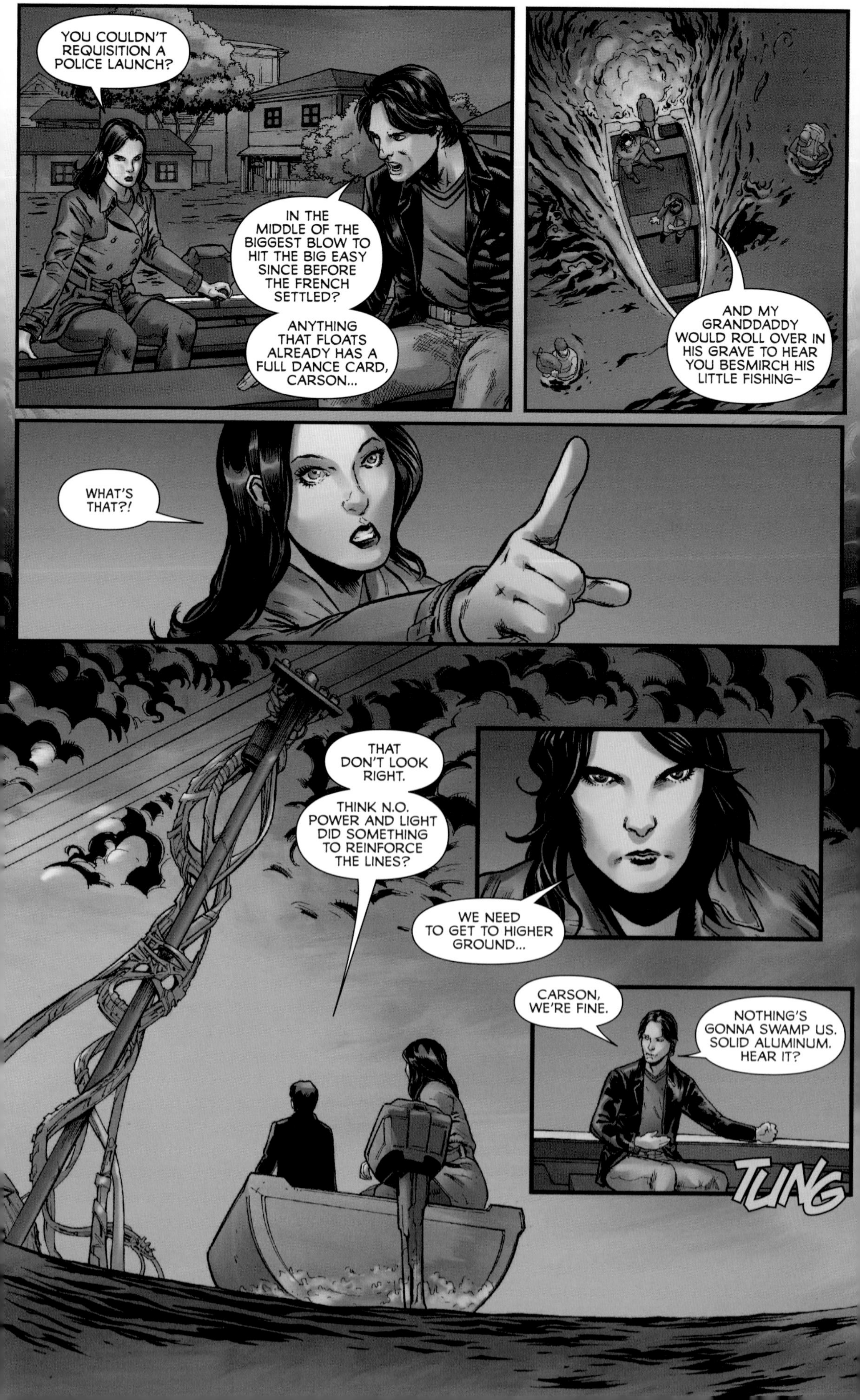
YOU COULDN'T REQUISITION A POLICE LAUNCH?
IN THE MIDDLE OF THE BIGGEST BLOW TO HIT THE BIG EASY SINCE BEFORE THE FRENCH SETTLED?
ANYTHING THAT FLOATS ALREADY HAS A FULL DANCE CARD, CARSON...
AND MY GRANDDADDY WOULD ROLL OVER IN HIS GRAVE TO HEAR YOU BESMIRCH HIS LITTLE FISHING–
WHAT'S THAT?!
THAT DON'T LOOK RIGHT.
THINK N.O. POWER AND LIGHT DID SOMETHING TO REINFORCE THE LINES?
WE NEED TO GET TO HIGHER GROUND...
CARSON, WE'RE FINE.
NOTHING'S GONNA SWAMP US. SOLID ALUMINUM. HEAR IT?
TUNG

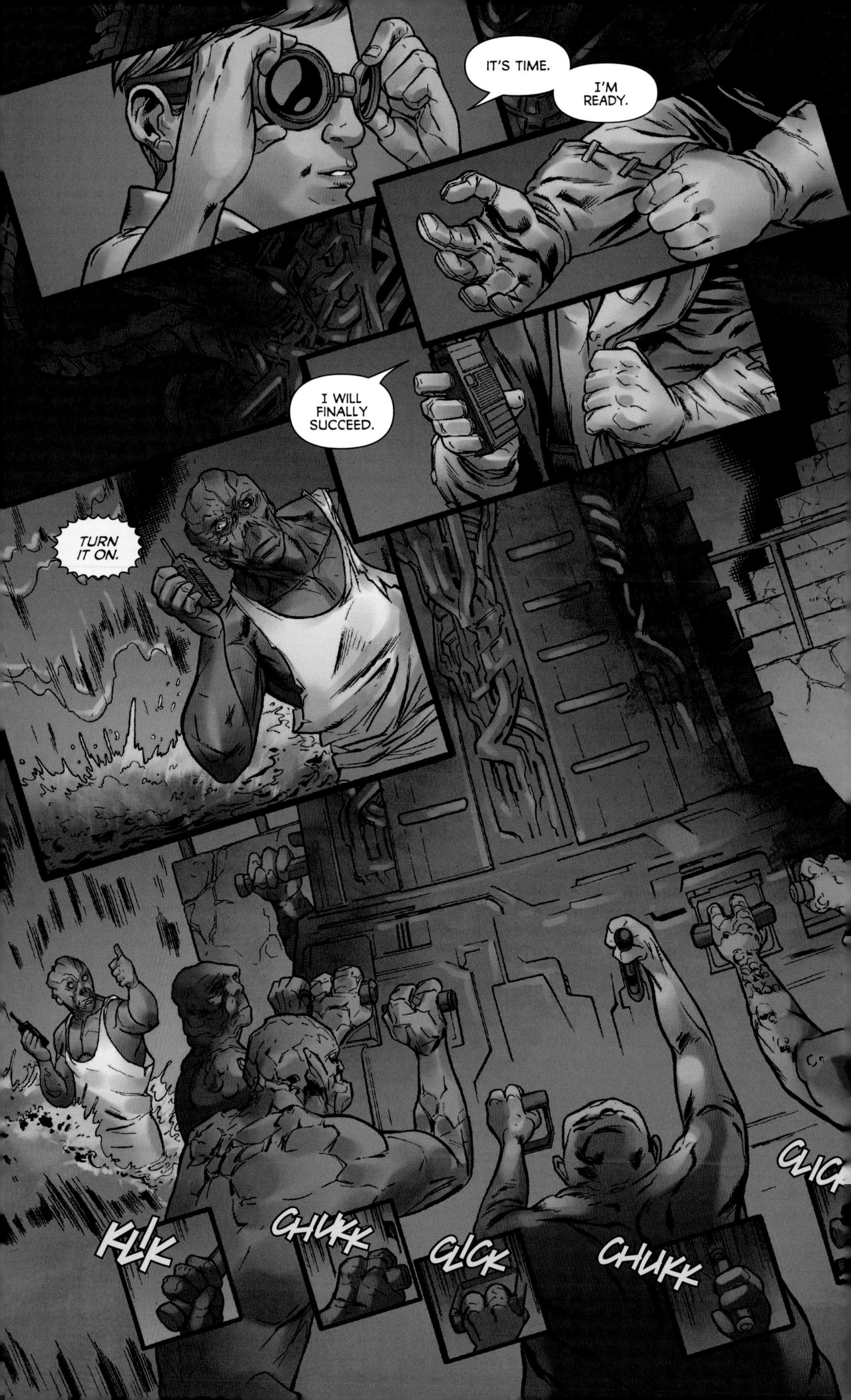
IT'S TIME.
I'M READY.
I WILL FINALLY SUCCEED.
TURN IT ON.
CLICK
KLIK
CHUKK
CLICK
CHUKK

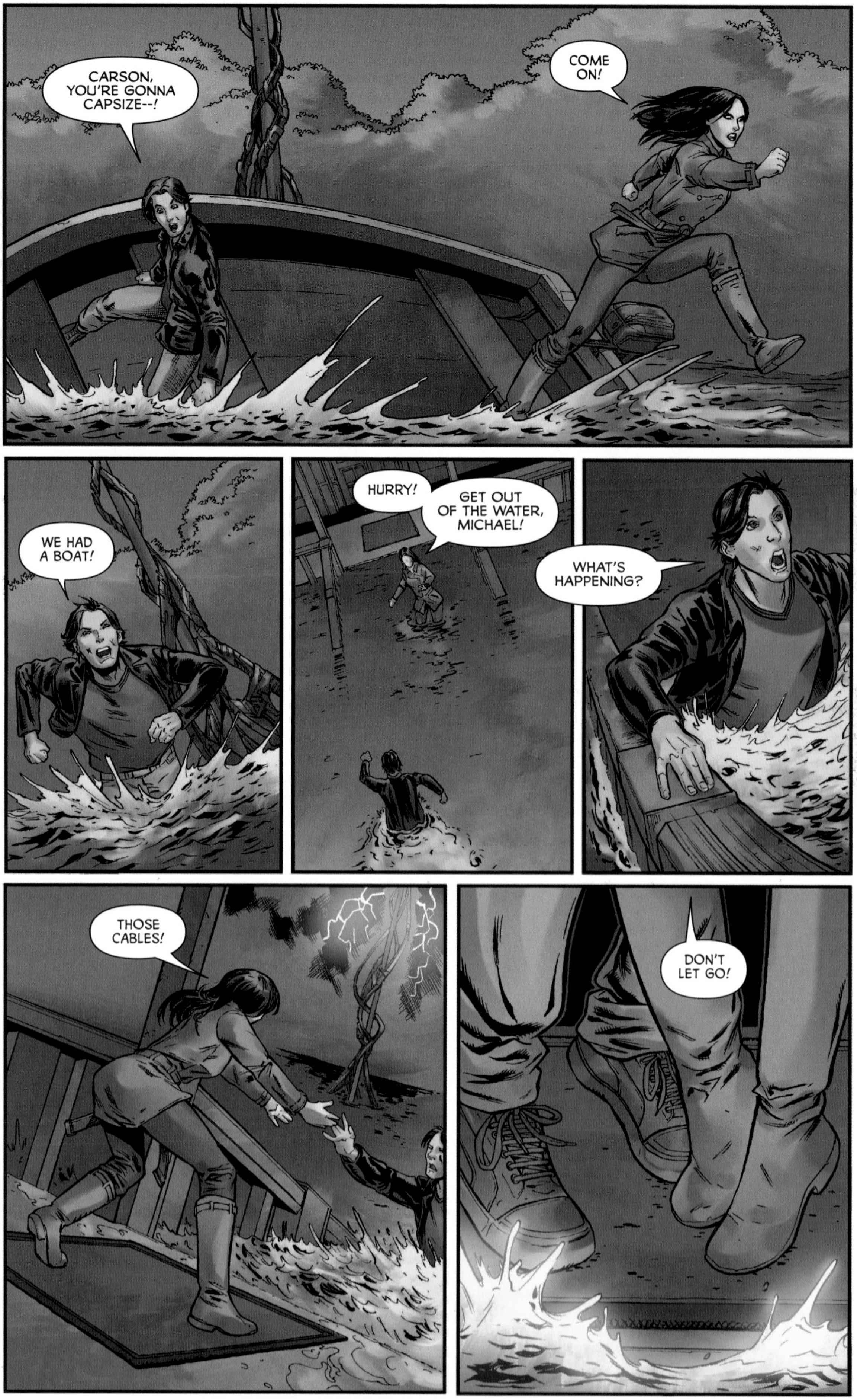
CARSON, YOU'RE GONNA CAPSIZE--!
COME ON!
WE HAD A BOAT!
HURRY!
GET OUT OF THE WATER, MICHAEL!
WHAT'S HAPPENING?
THOSE CABLES!
DON'T LET GO!

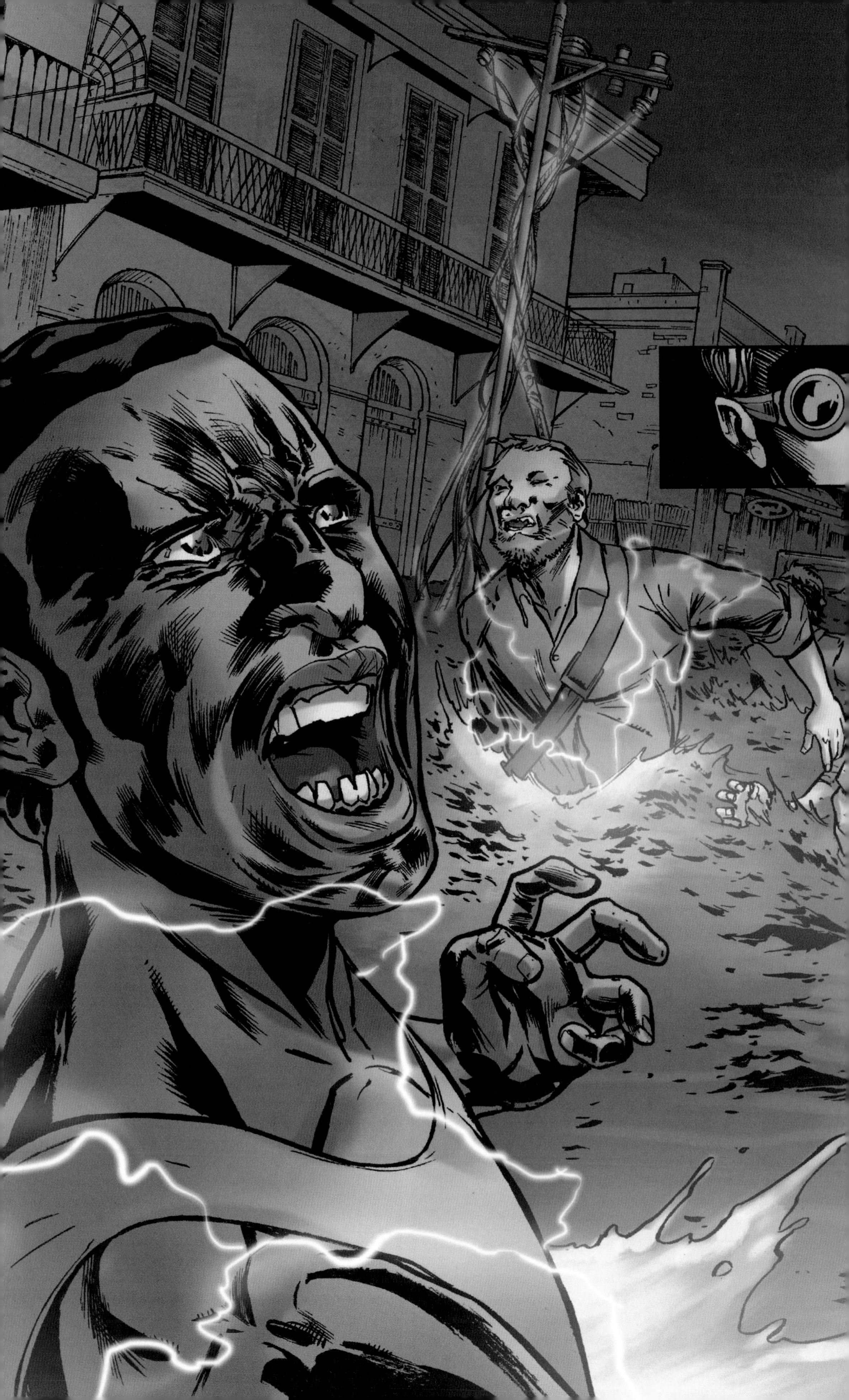

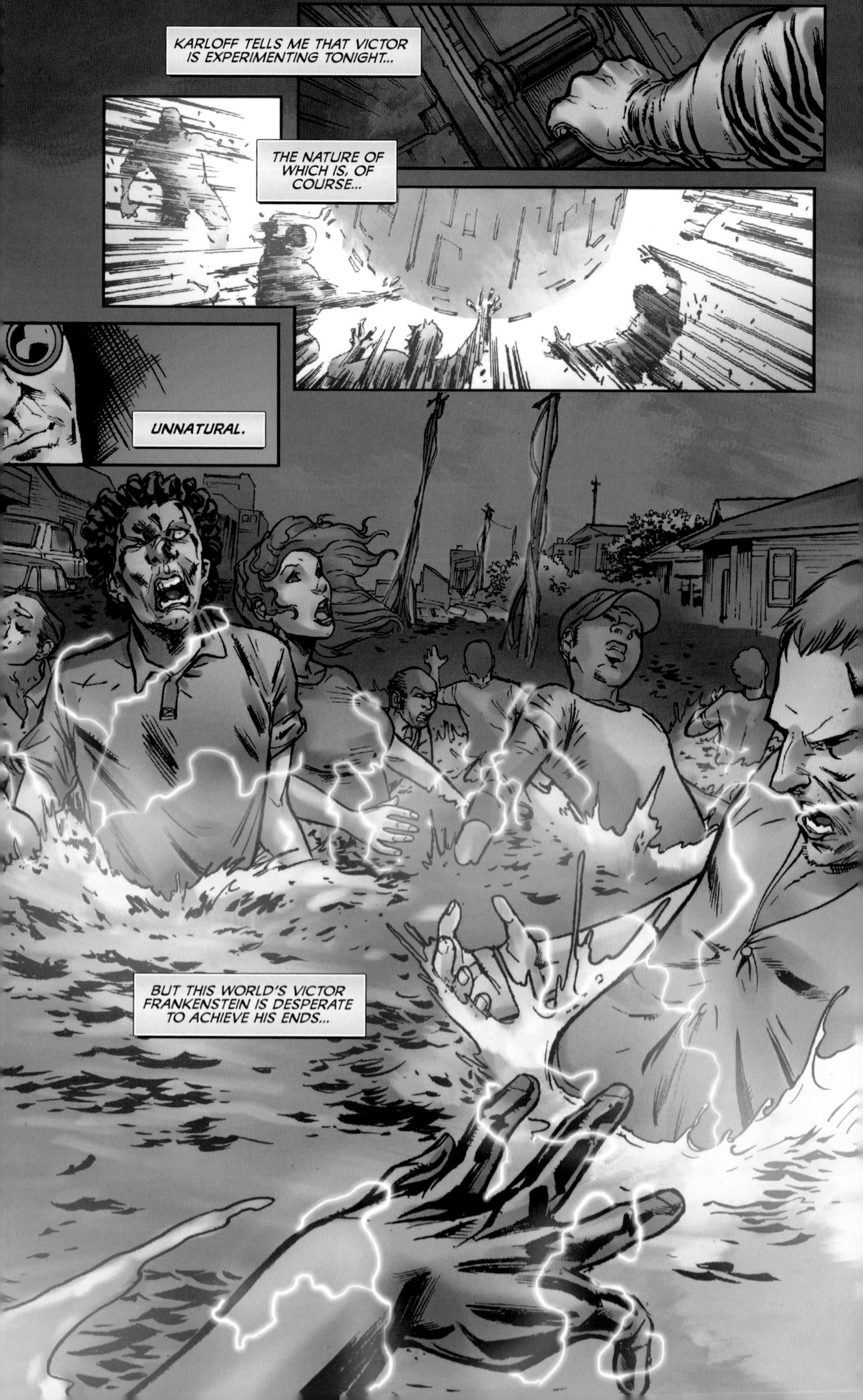
KARLOFF TELLS ME THAT VICTOR IS EXPERIMENTING TONIGHT...
THE NATURE OF WHICH IS, OF COURSE...
UNNATURAL.
BUT THIS WORLD'S VICTOR FRANKENSTEIN IS DESPERATE TO ACHIEVE HIS ENDS...

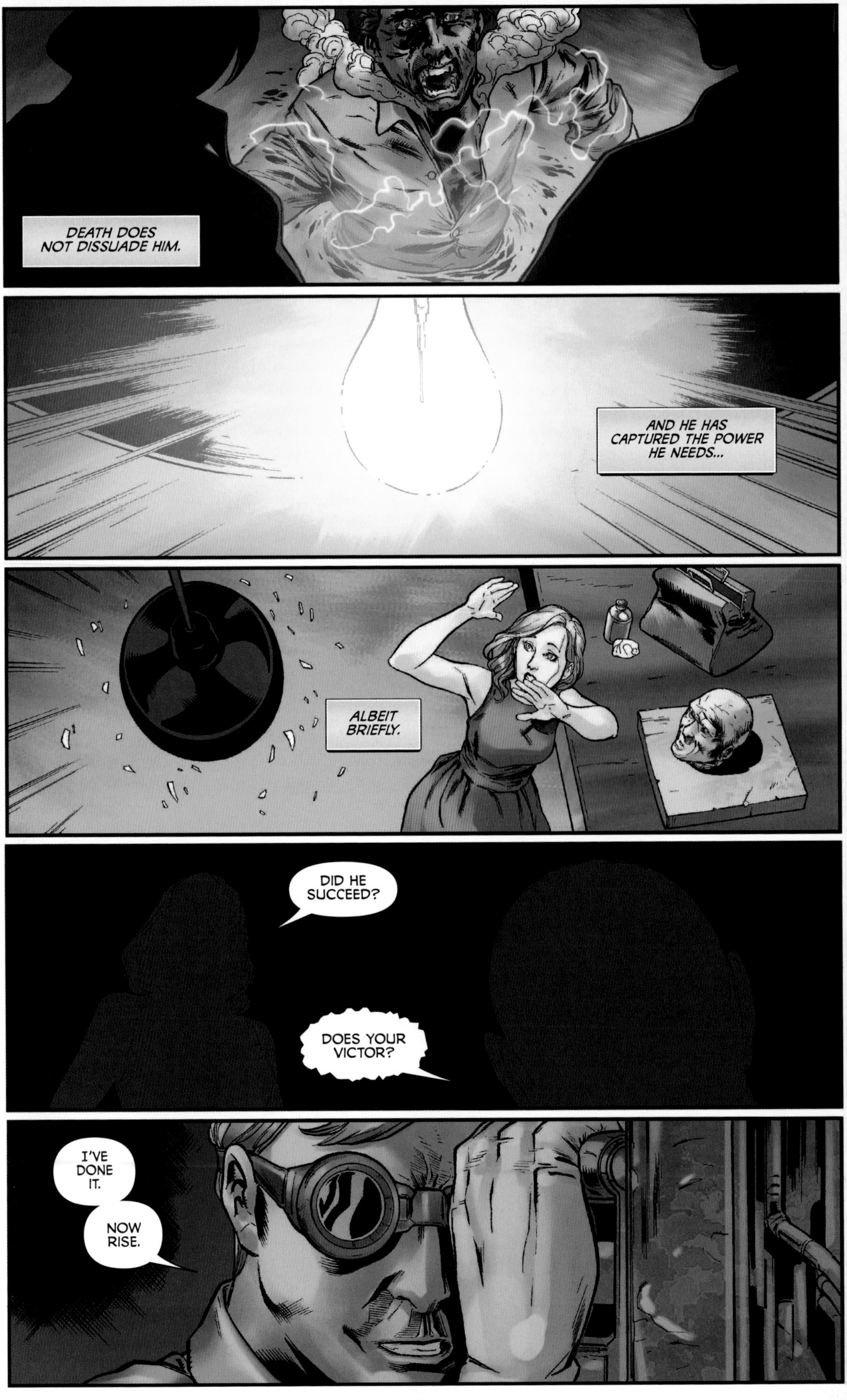
DEATH DOES NOT DISSUADE HIM.
AND HE HAS CAPTURED THE POWER HE NEEDS...
ALBEIT BRIEFLY.
DID HE SUCCEED?
DOES YOUR VICTOR?
I'VE DONE IT.
NOW RISE.

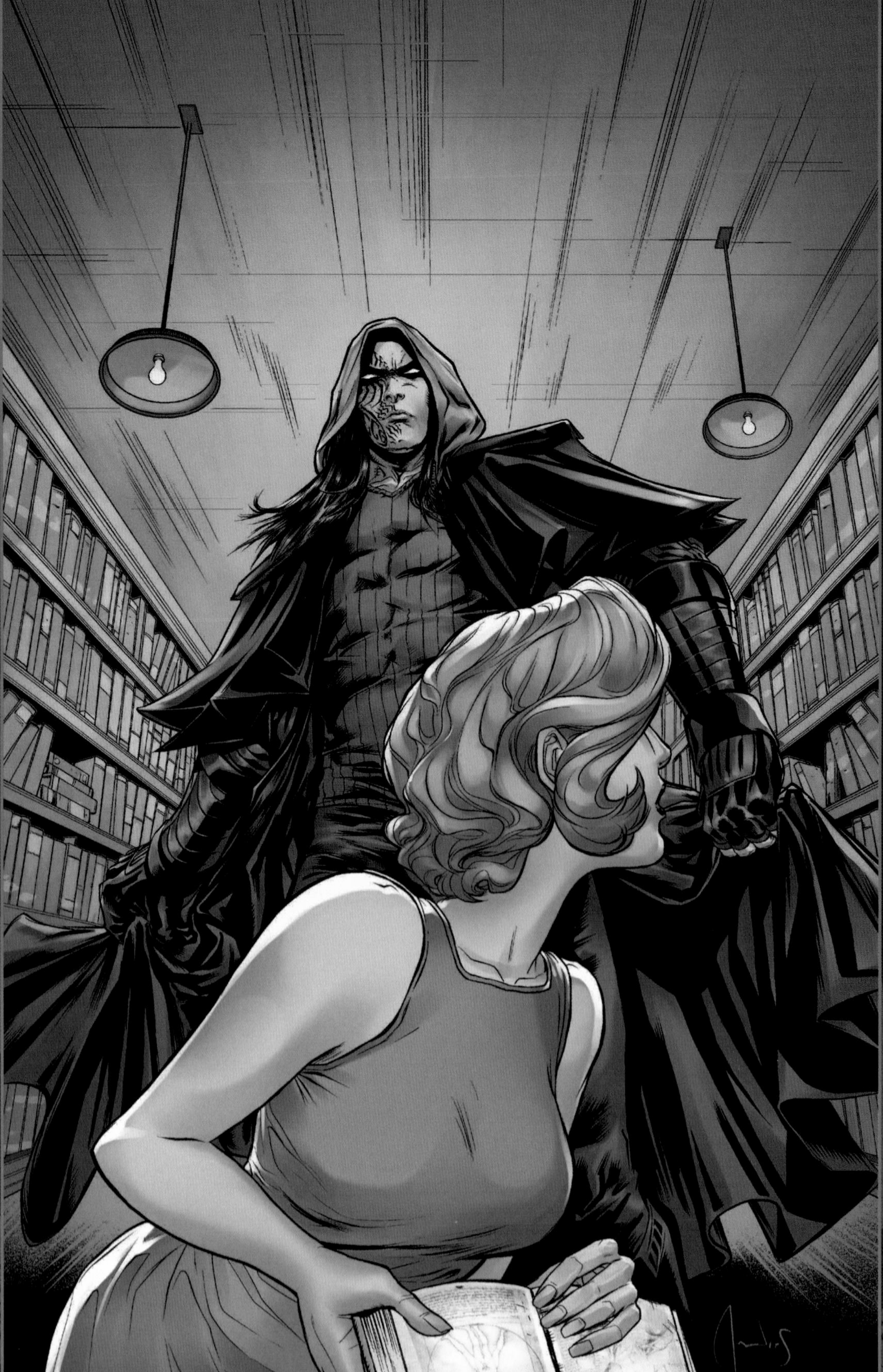

ISSUE THREE COVER
ART BY ANDRES PONCE COLORS BY MOHAN

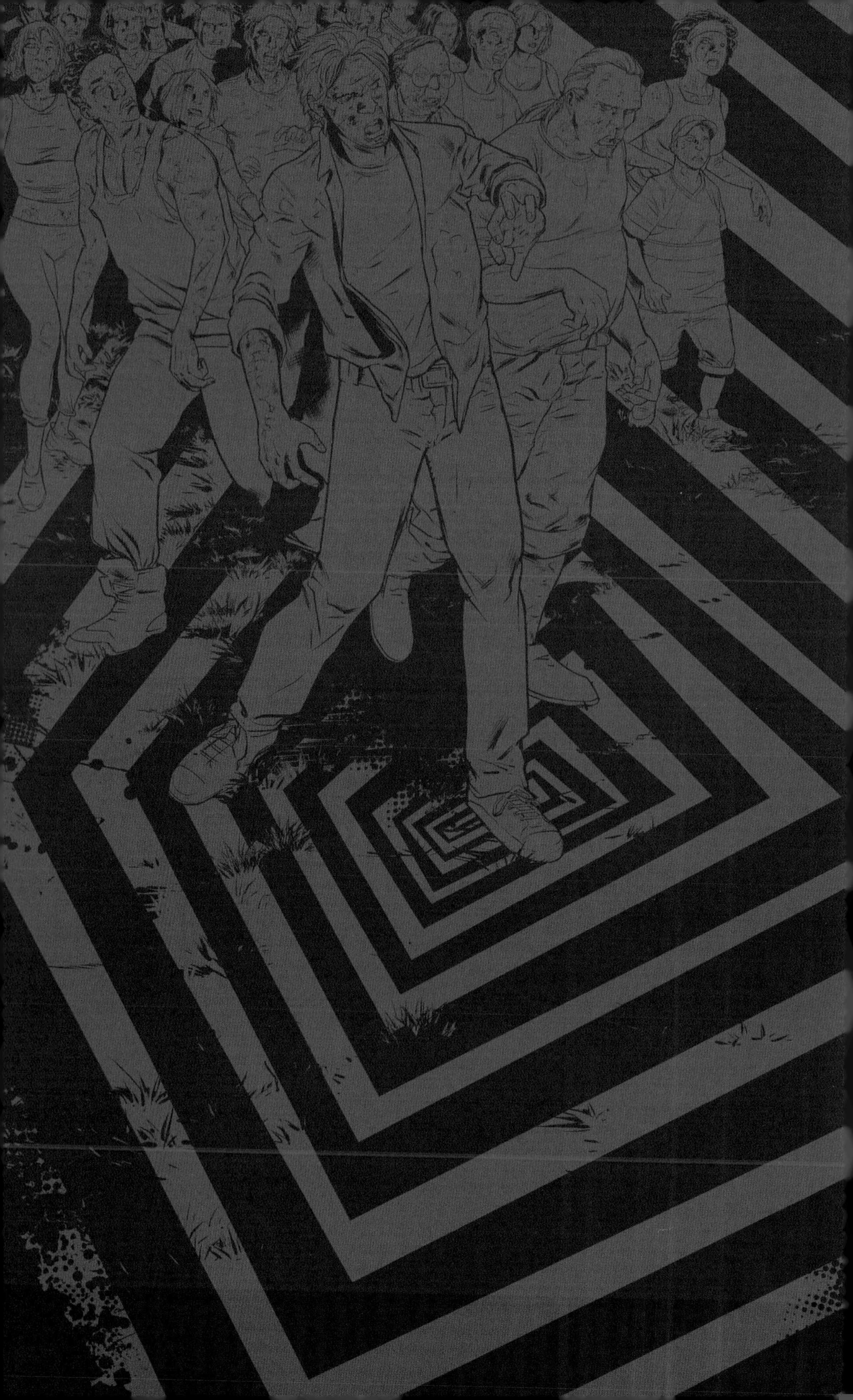

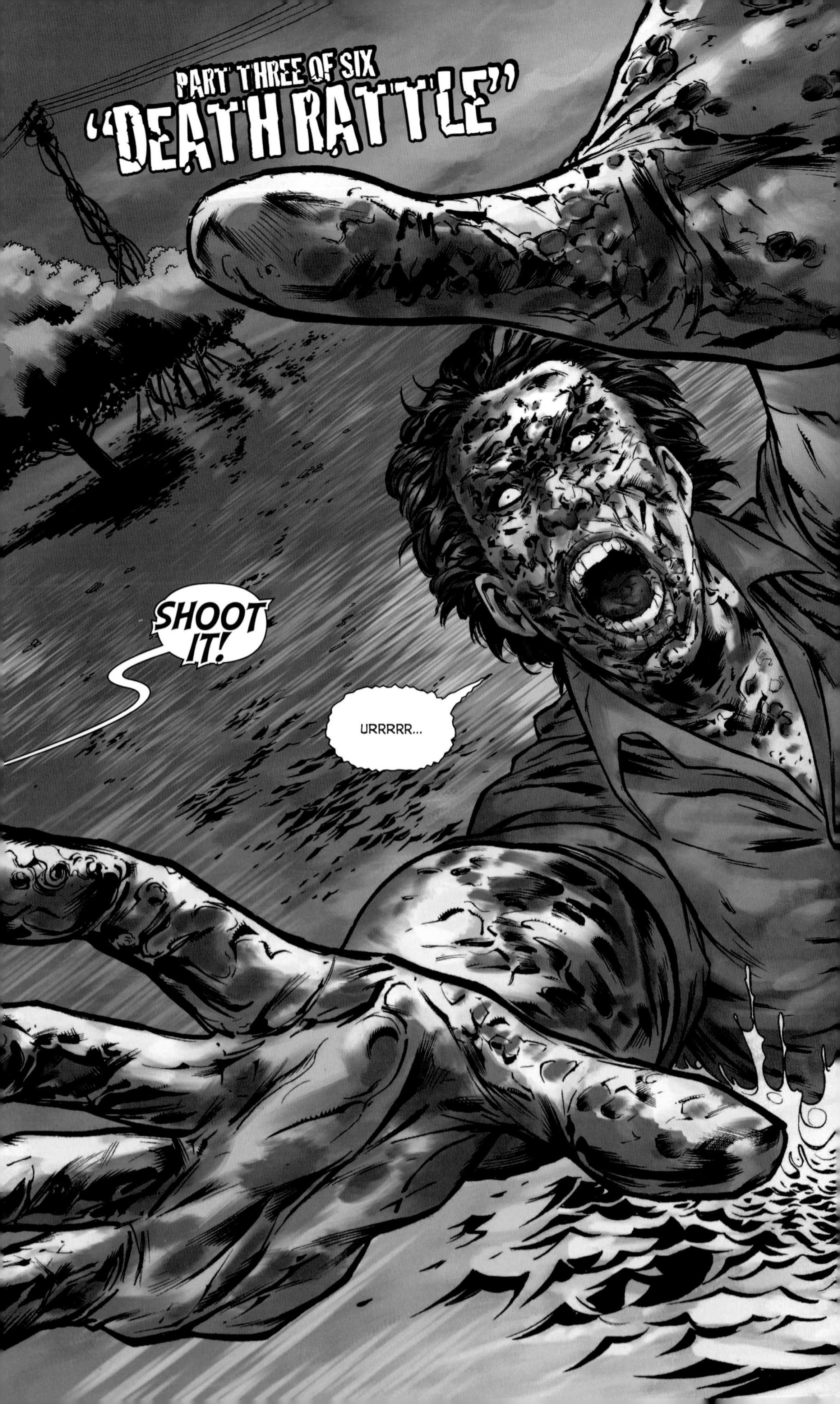
PART THREE OF SIX
"DEATH RATTLE"
SHOOT IT!
URRRRR...

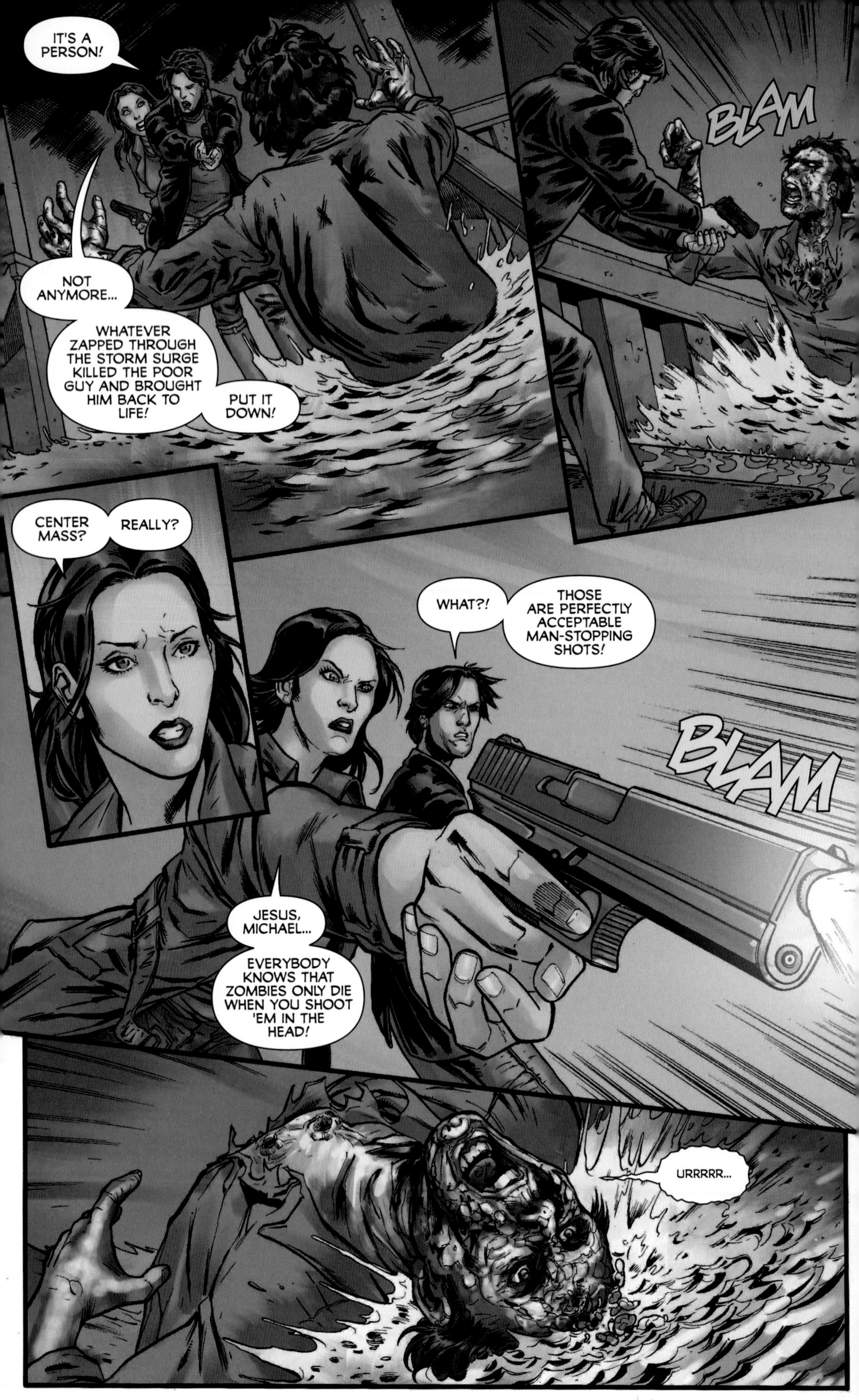
IT'S A PERSON!
NOT ANYMORE...
WHATEVER ZAPPED THROUGH THE STORM SURGE KILLED THE POOR GUY AND BROUGHT HIM BACK TO LIFE!
PUT IT DOWN!
BLAM
CENTER MASS?
REALLY?
WHAT?!
THOSE ARE PERFECTLY ACCEPTABLE MAN-STOPPING SHOTS!
BLAM
JESUS, MICHAEL...
EVERYBODY KNOWS THAT ZOMBIES ONLY DIE WHEN YOU SHOOT 'EM IN THE HEAD!
URRRRR...

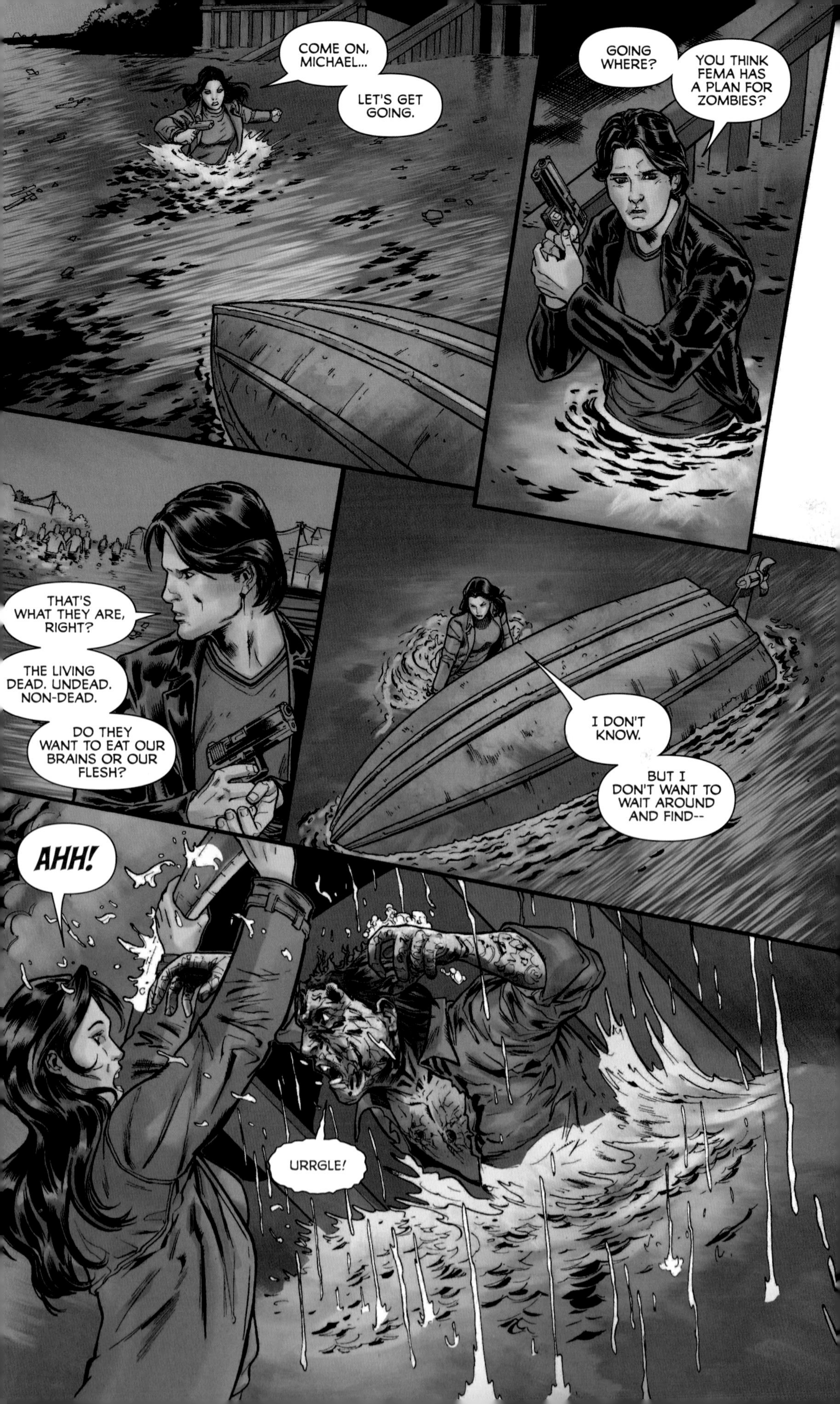

COME ON, MICHAEL...
LET'S GET GOING.
GOING WHERE?
YOU THINK FEMA HAS A PLAN FOR ZOMBIES?
THAT'S WHAT THEY ARE, RIGHT?
THE LIVING DEAD. UNDEAD. NON-DEAD.
DO THEY WANT TO EAT OUR BRAINS OR OUR FLESH?
I DON'T KNOW.
BUT I DON'T WANT TO WAIT AROUND AND FIND--
AHH!
URRGLE!

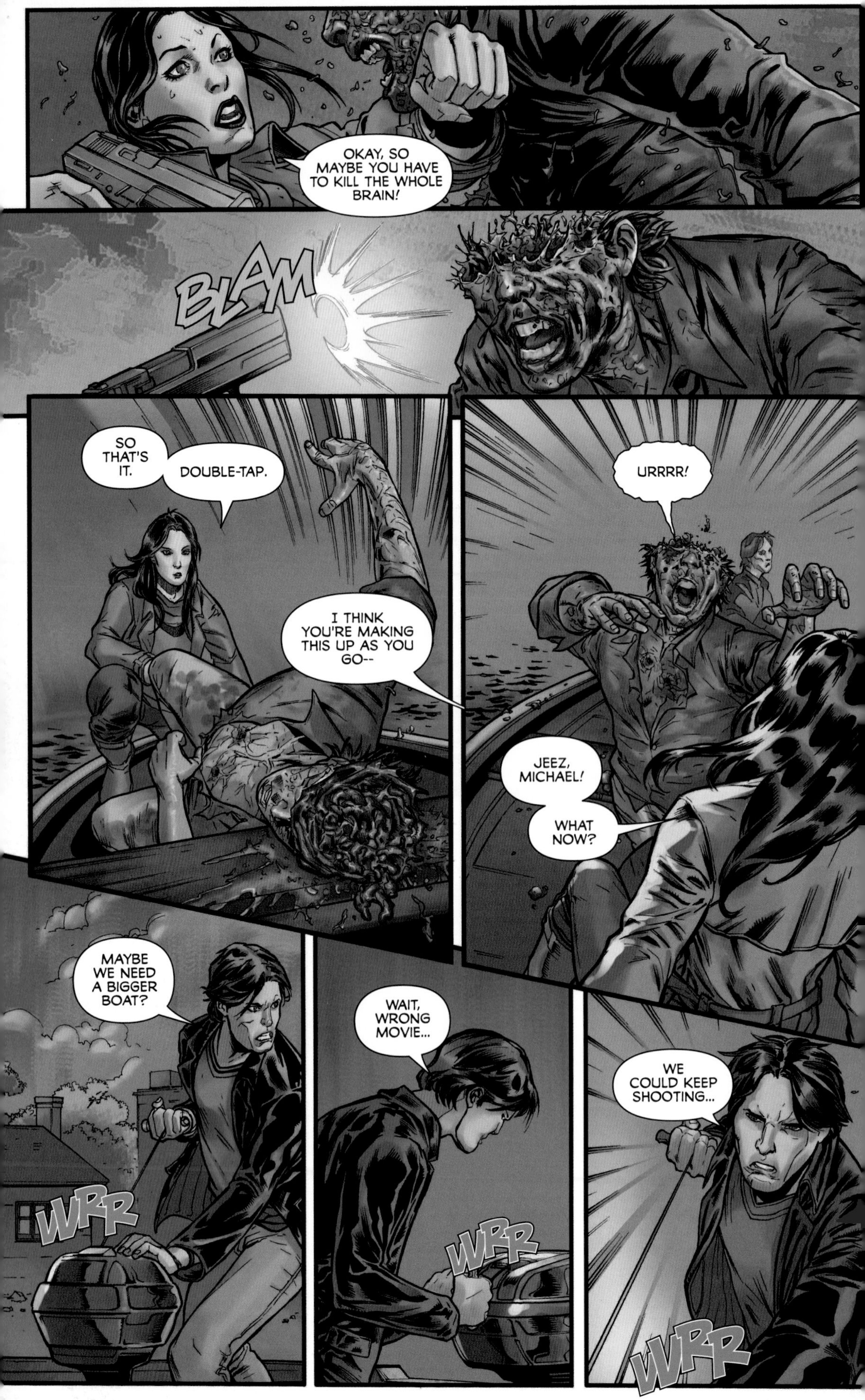

OKAY, SO MAYBE YOU HAVE TO KILL THE WHOLE BRAIN!
BLAM
SO THAT'S IT.
DOUBLE-TAP.
I THINK YOU'RE MAKING THIS UP AS YOU GO--
URRRR!
JEEZ, MICHAEL!
WHAT NOW?
MAYBE WE NEED A BIGGER BOAT?
WRR
WAIT, WRONG MOVIE...
WRR
WE COULD KEEP SHOOTING...
WRR

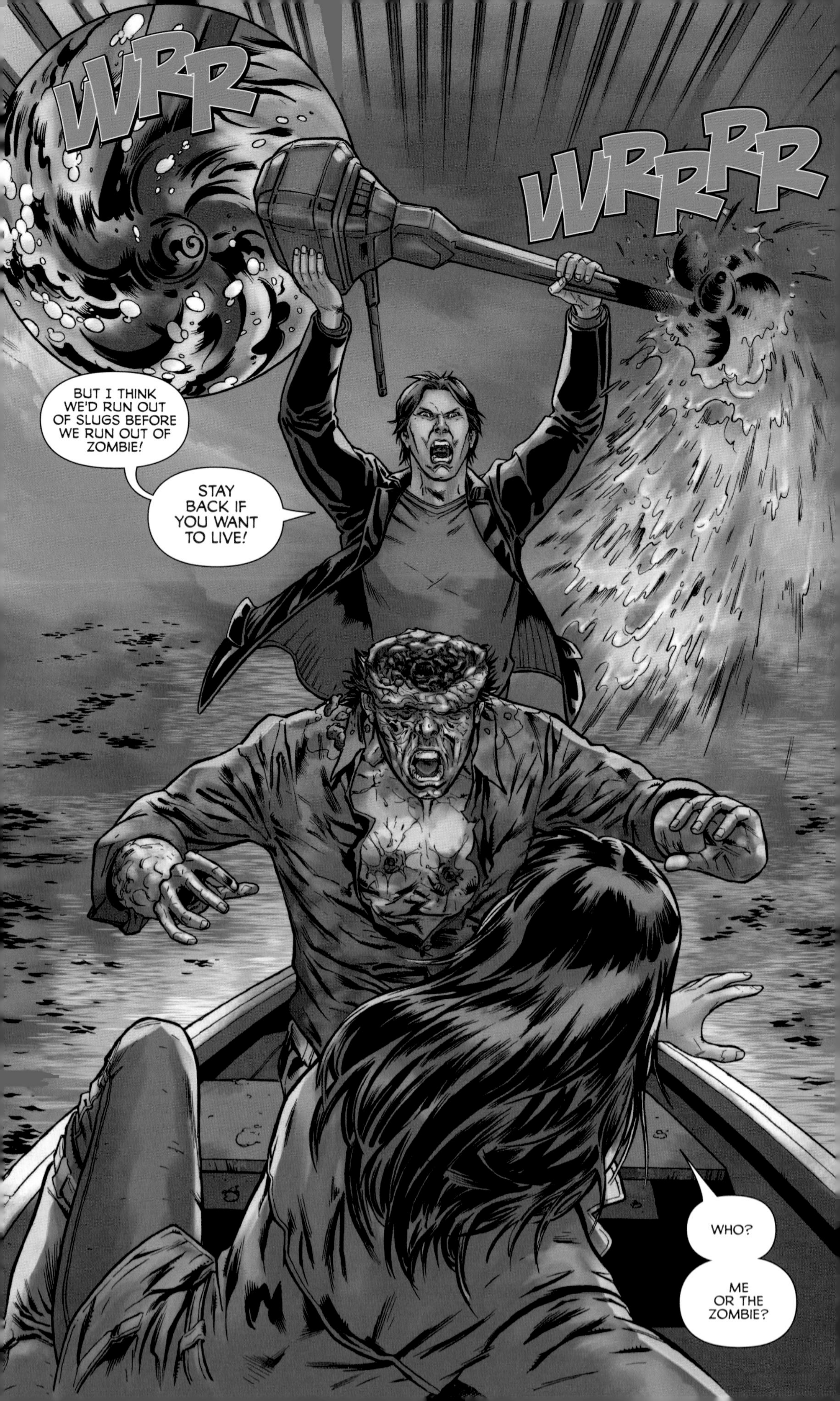
WRR
WRRRR
BUT I THINK WE'D RUN OUT OF SLUGS BEFORE WE RUN OUT OF ZOMBIE!
STAY BACK IF YOU WANT TO LIVE!
WHO?
ME OR THE ZOMBIE?

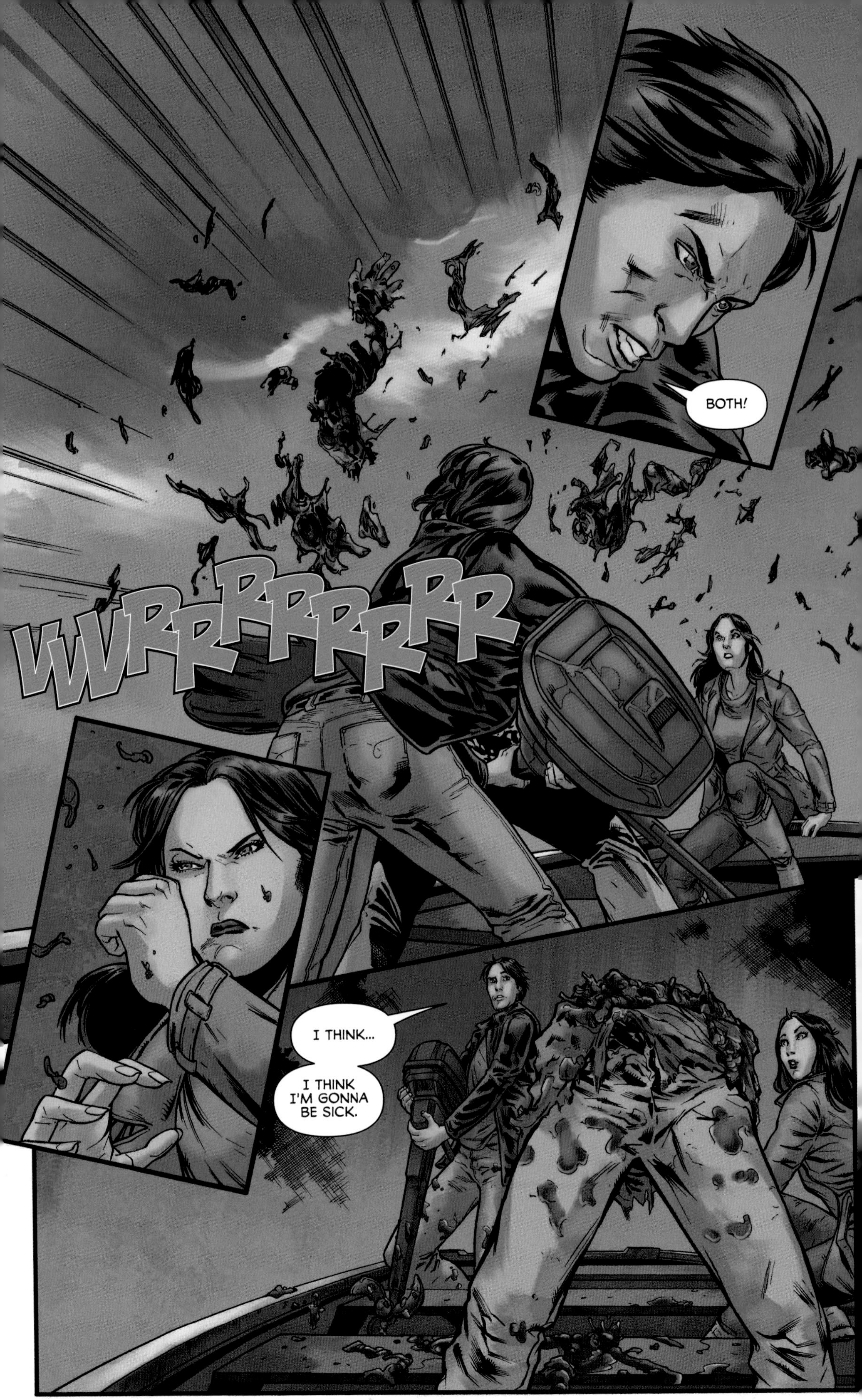
BOTH!
WWRRRRRRRR
I THINK...
I THINK I'M GONNA BE SICK.

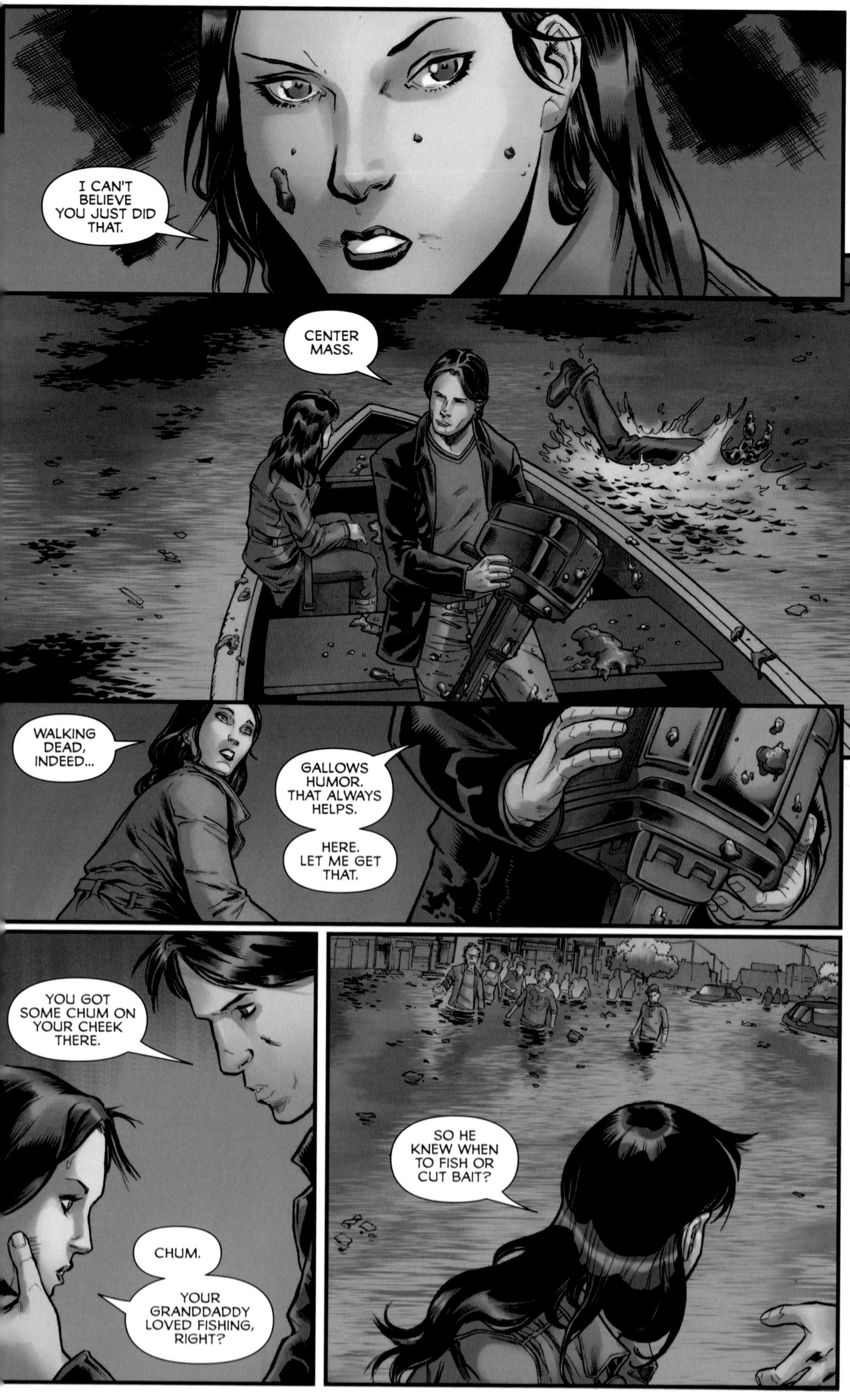
I CAN'T BELIEVE YOU JUST DID THAT.
CENTER MASS.
WALKING DEAD, INDEED...
GALLOWS HUMOR. THAT ALWAYS HELPS.
HERE. LET ME GET THAT.
YOU GOT SOME CHUM ON YOUR CHEEK THERE.
CHUM.
YOUR GRANDDADDY LOVED FISHING, RIGHT?
SO HE KNEW WHEN TO FISH OR CUT BAIT?

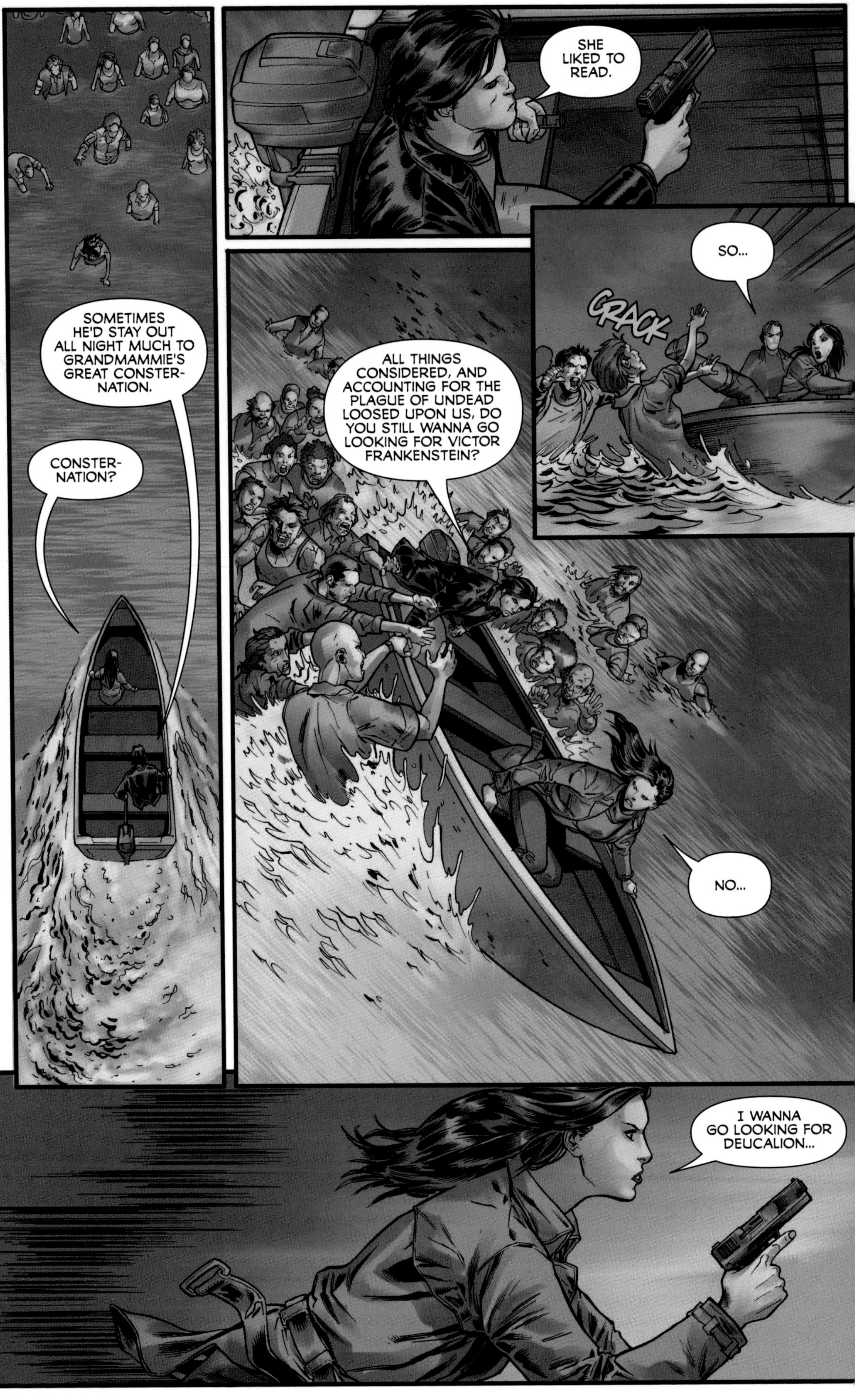
SHE LIKED TO READ.
SOMETIMES HE'D STAY OUT ALL NIGHT MUCH TO GRANDMAMMIE'S GREAT CONSTER-NATION.
CONSTER-NATION?
SO...
CRACK
ALL THINGS CONSIDERED, AND ACCOUNTING FOR THE PLAGUE OF UNDEAD LOOSED UPON US, DO YOU STILL WANNA GO LOOKING FOR VICTOR FRANKENSTEIN?
NO...
I WANNA GO LOOKING FOR DEUCALION...

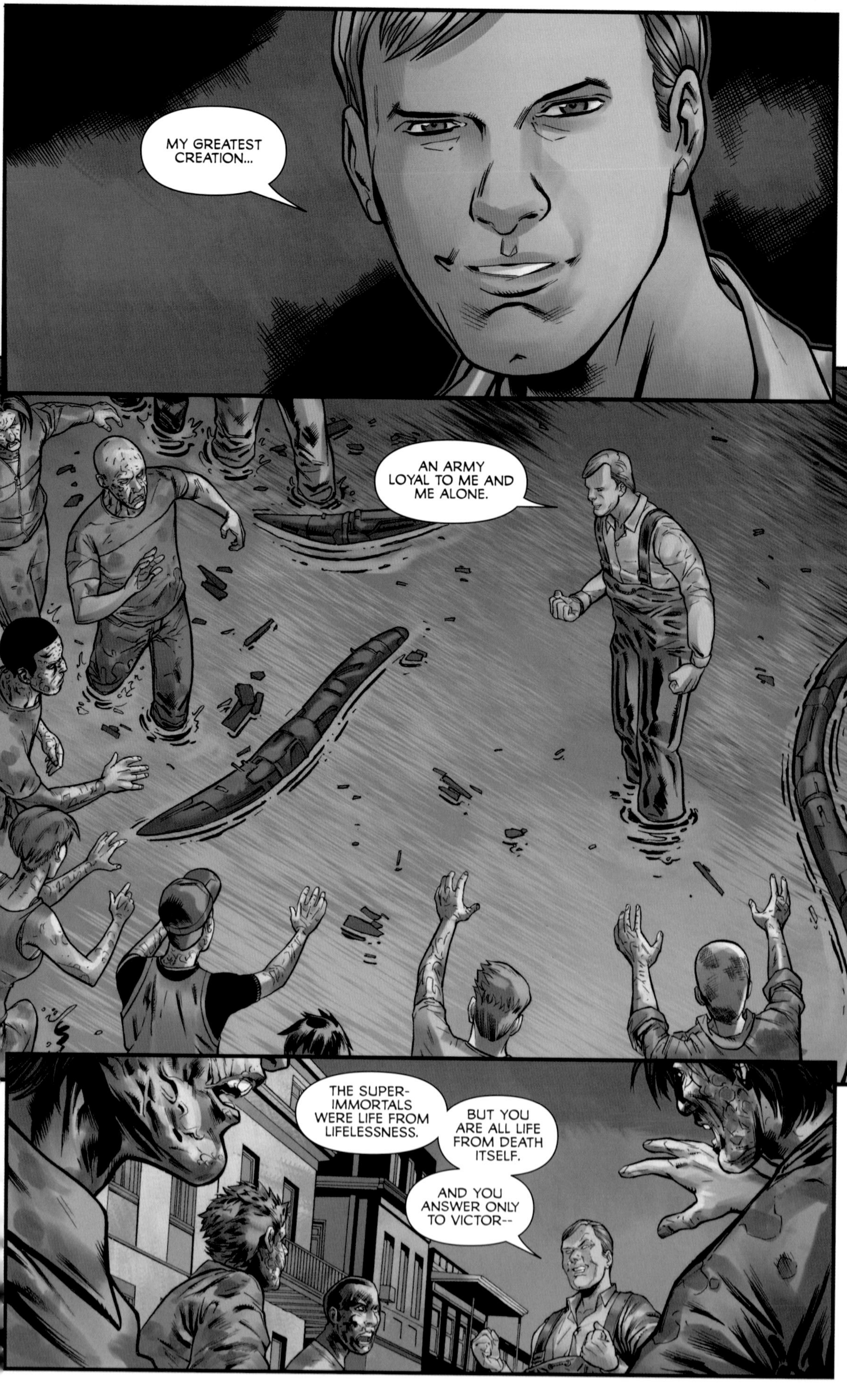
MY GREATEST CREATION...
AN ARMY LOYAL TO ME AND ME ALONE.
THE SUPER-IMMORTALS WERE LIFE FROM LIFELESSNESS.
BUT YOU ARE ALL LIFE FROM DEATH ITSELF.
AND YOU ANSWER ONLY TO VICTOR--

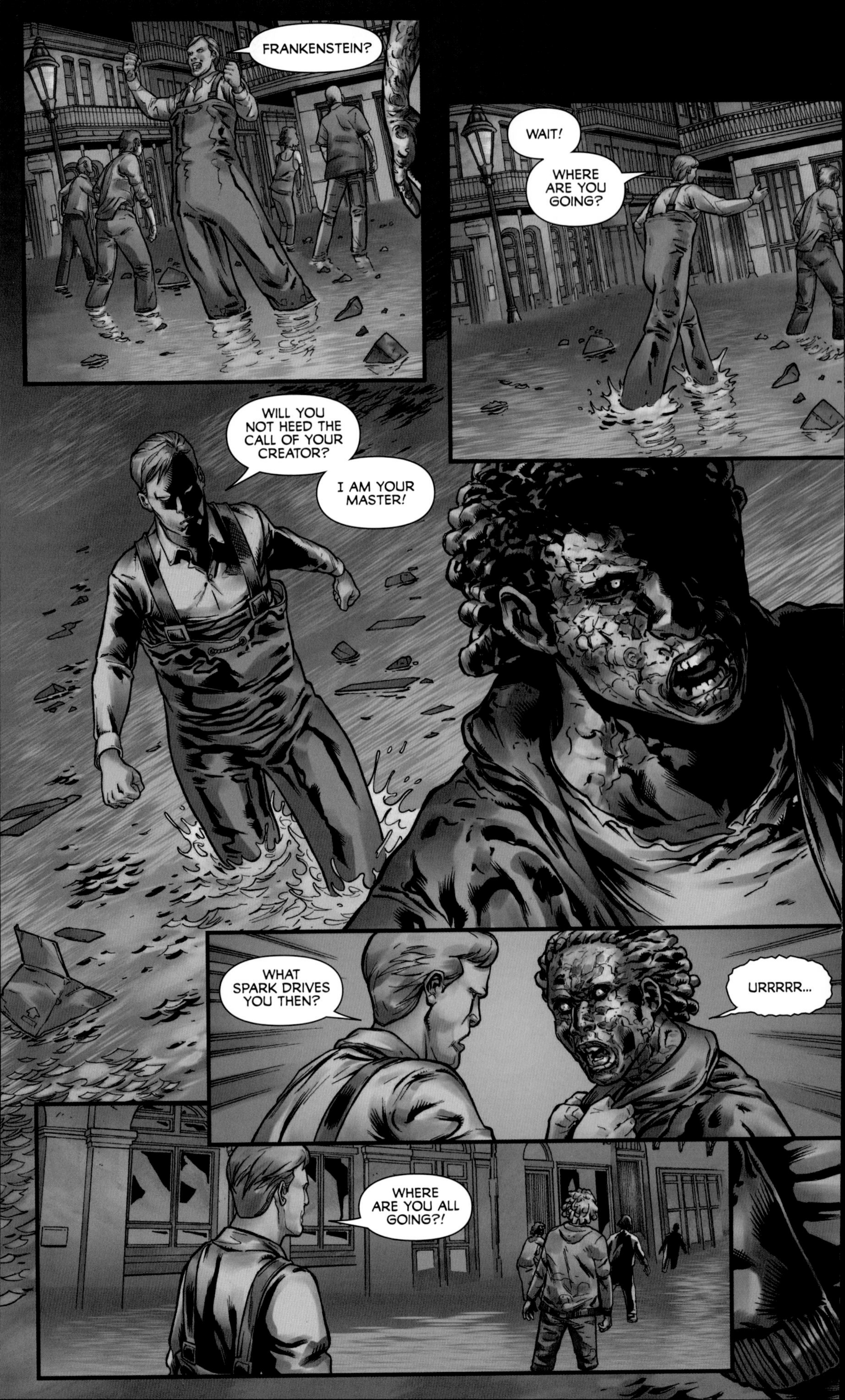
FRANKENSTEIN?
WAIT!
WHERE ARE YOU GOING?
WILL YOU NOT HEED THE CALL OF YOUR CREATOR?
I AM YOUR MASTER!
WHAT SPARK DRIVES YOU THEN?
URRRRR...
WHERE ARE YOU ALL GOING?!

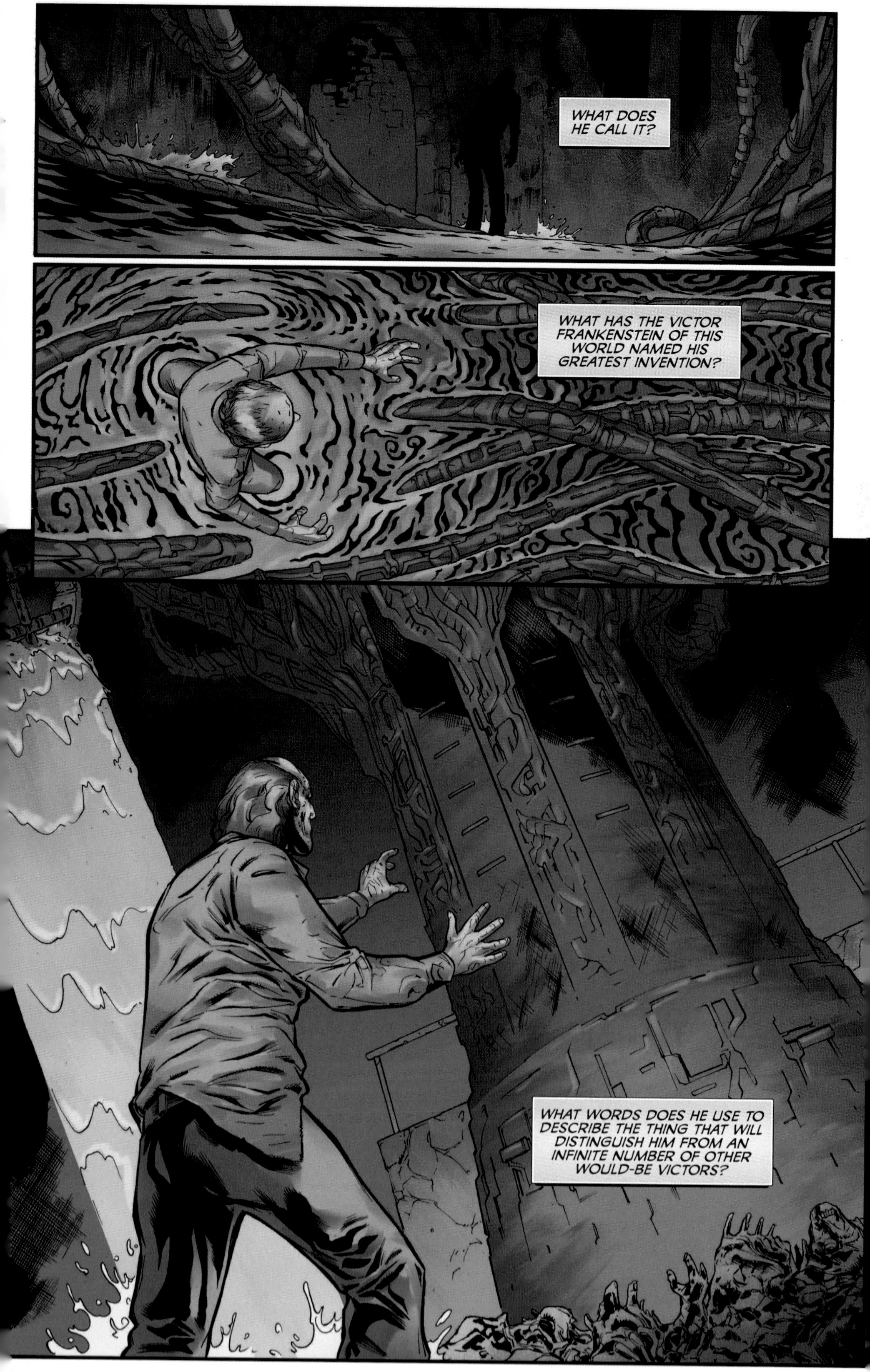
WHAT DOES HE CALL IT?
WHAT HAS THE VICTOR FRANKENSTEIN OF THIS WORLD NAMED HIS GREATEST INVENTION?
WHAT WORDS DOES HE USE TO DESCRIBE THE THING THAT WILL DISTINGUISH HIM FROM AN INFINITE NUMBER OF OTHER WOULD-BE VICTORS?

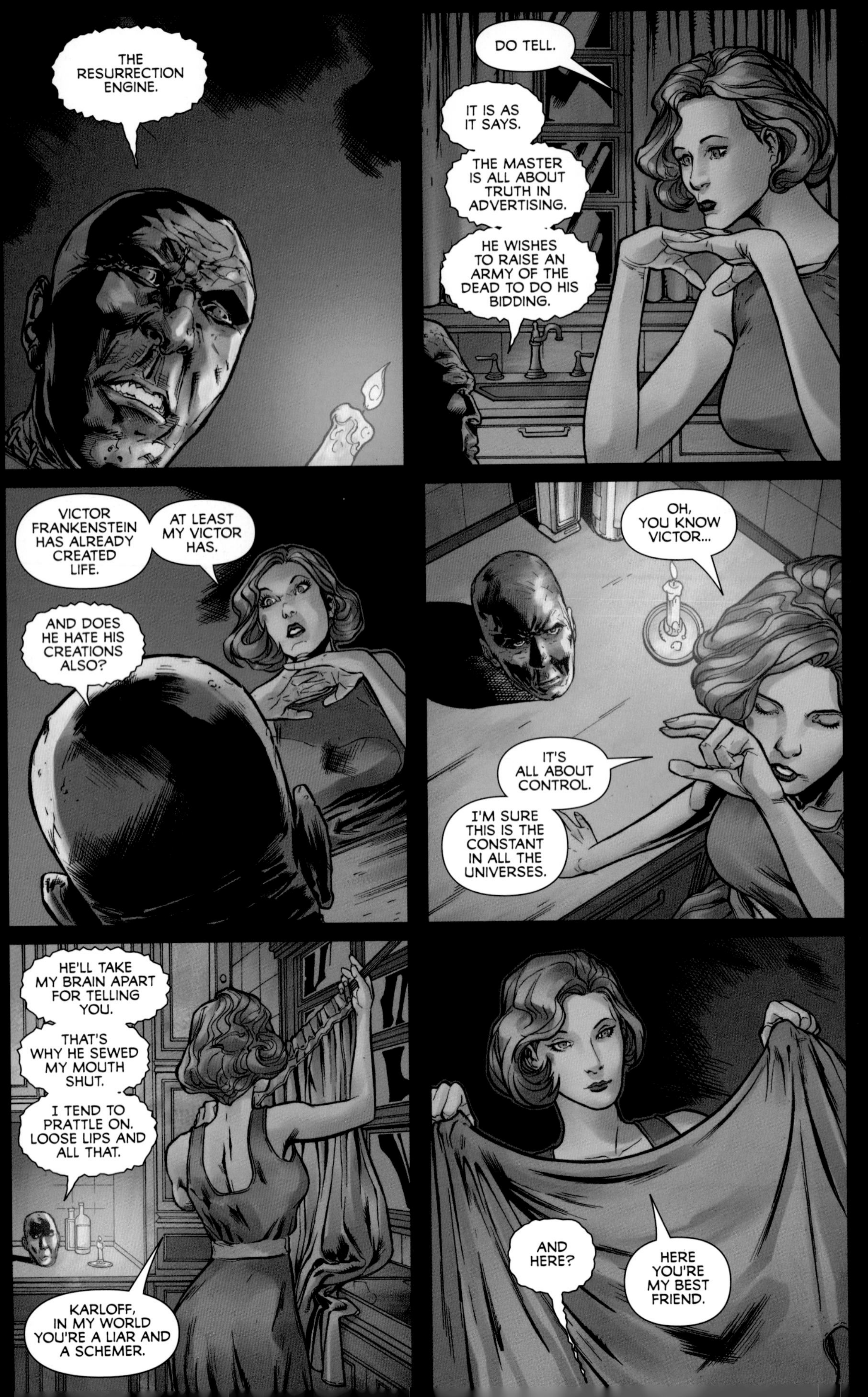
THE RESURRECTION ENGINE.
DO TELL.
IT IS AS IT SAYS.
THE MASTER IS ALL ABOUT TRUTH IN ADVERTISING.
HE WISHES TO RAISE AN ARMY OF THE DEAD TO DO HIS BIDDING.
VICTOR FRANKENSTEIN HAS ALREADY CREATED LIFE.
AT LEAST MY VICTOR HAS.
AND DOES HE HATE HIS CREATIONS ALSO?
OH, YOU KNOW VICTOR...
IT'S ALL ABOUT CONTROL.
I'M SURE THIS IS THE CONSTANT IN ALL THE UNIVERSES.
HE'LL TAKE MY BRAIN APART FOR TELLING YOU.
THAT'S WHY HE SEWED MY MOUTH SHUT.
I TEND TO PRATTLE ON. LOOSE LIPS AND ALL THAT.
KARLOFF, IN MY WORLD YOU'RE A LIAR AND A SCHEMER.
AND HERE?
HERE YOU'RE MY BEST FRIEND.

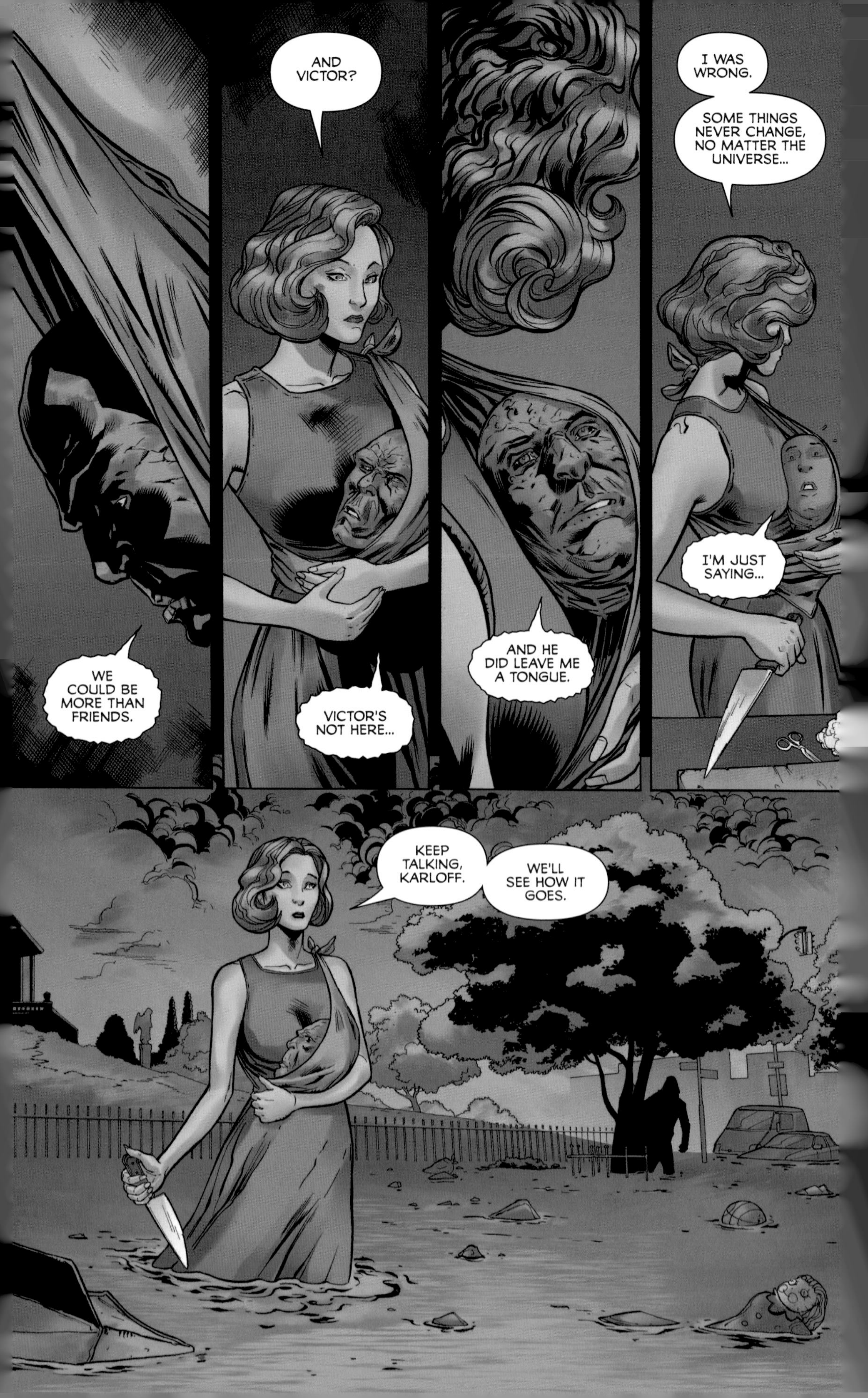
WE COULD BE MORE THAN FRIENDS.
AND VICTOR?
VICTOR'S NOT HERE...
AND HE DID LEAVE ME A TONGUE.
I WAS WRONG.
SOME THINGS NEVER CHANGE, NO MATTER THE UNIVERSE...
I'M JUST SAYING...
KEEP TALKING, KARLOFF.
WE'LL SEE HOW IT GOES.

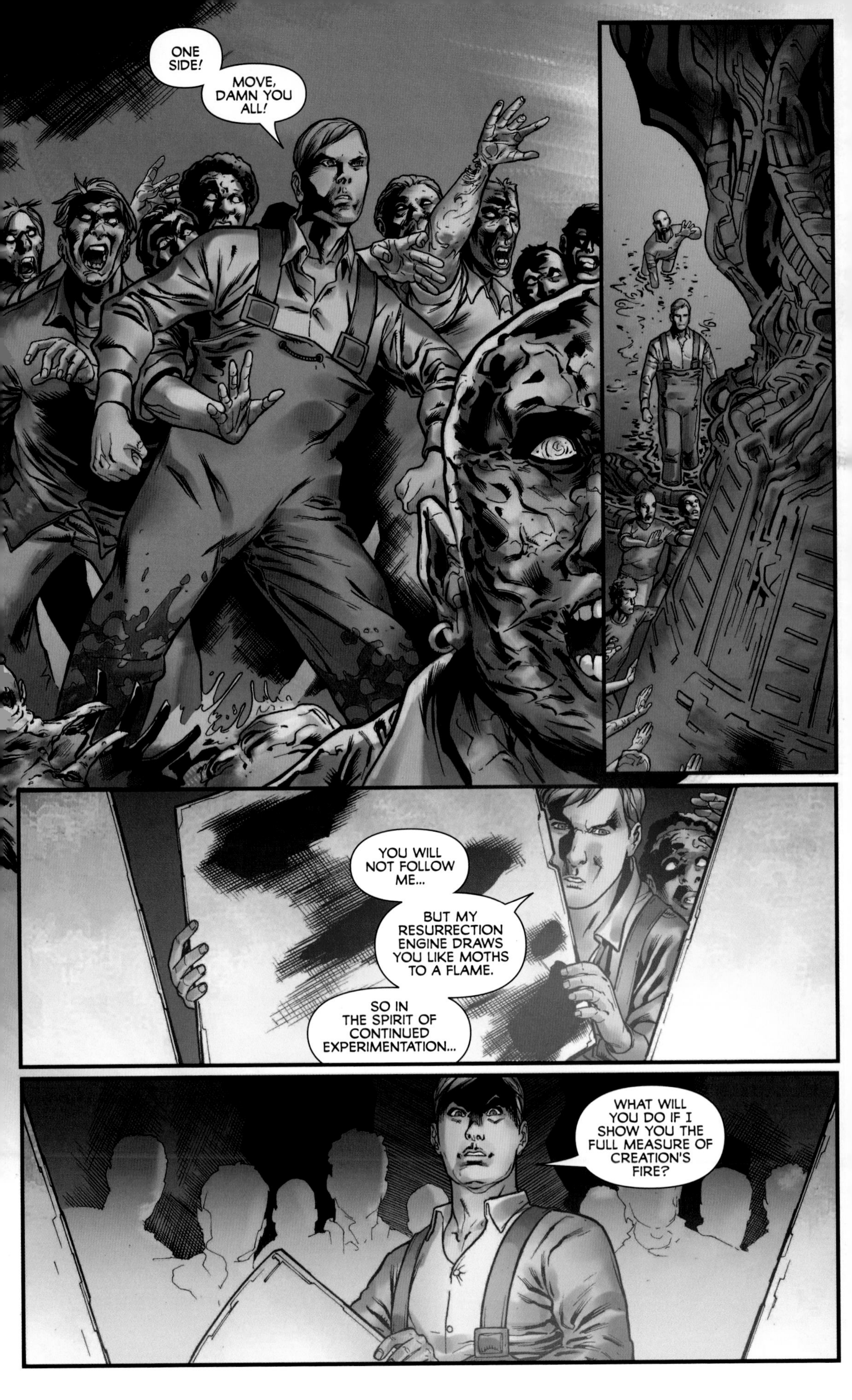

ONE SIDE!
MOVE, DAMN YOU ALL!
YOU WILL NOT FOLLOW ME...
BUT MY RESURRECTION ENGINE DRAWS YOU LIKE MOTHS TO A FLAME.
SO IN THE SPIRIT OF CONTINUED EXPERIMENTATION...
WHAT WILL YOU DO IF I SHOW YOU THE FULL MEASURE OF CREATION'S FIRE?

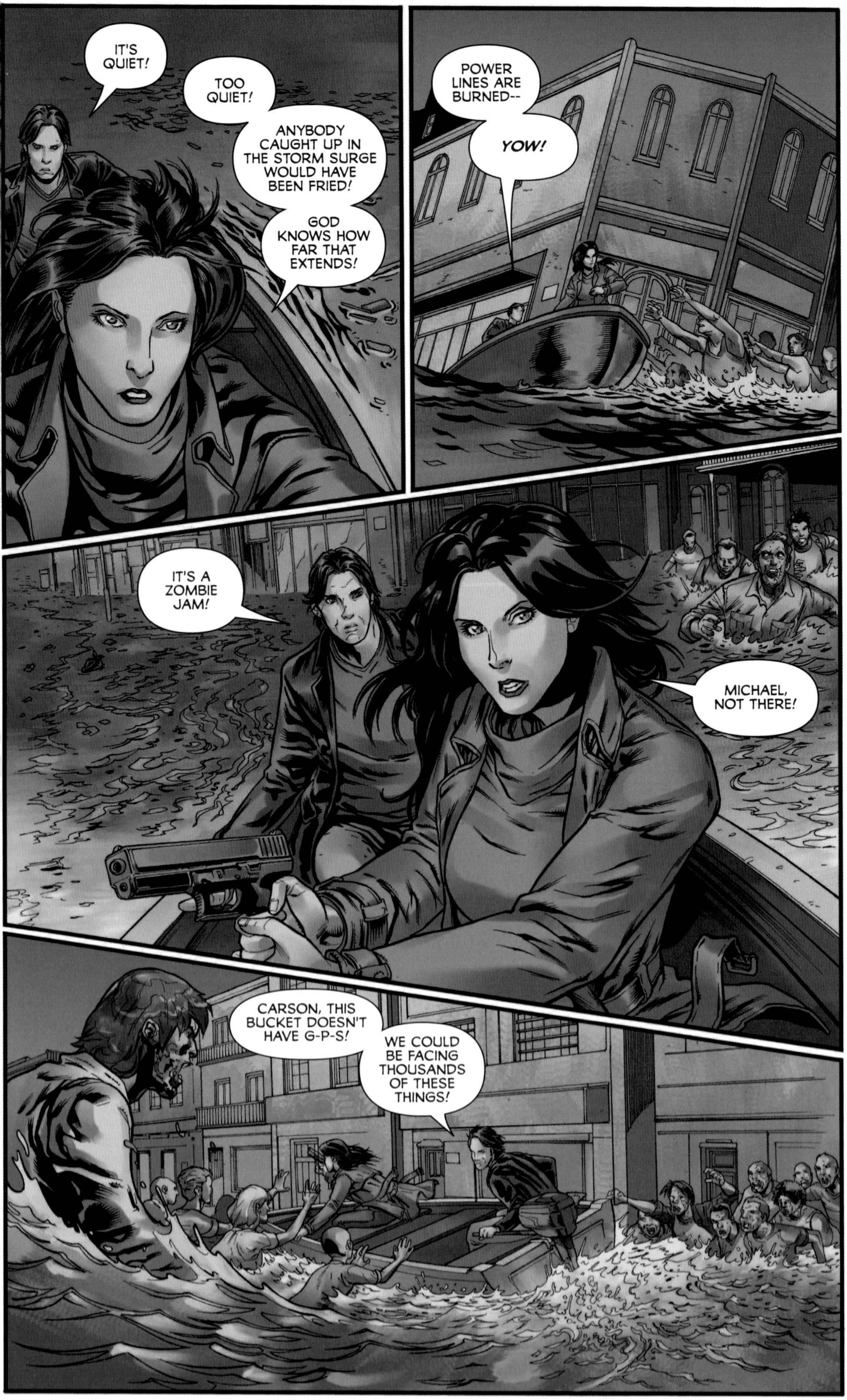
IT'S QUIET!
TOO QUIET!
ANYBODY CAUGHT UP IN THE STORM SURGE WOULD HAVE BEEN FRIED!
GOD KNOWS HOW FAR THAT EXTENDS!
POWER LINES ARE BURNED--
YOW!
IT'S A ZOMBIE JAM!
MICHAEL, NOT THERE!
CARSON, THIS BUCKET DOESN'T HAVE G-P-S!
WE COULD BE FACING THOUSANDS OF THESE THINGS!

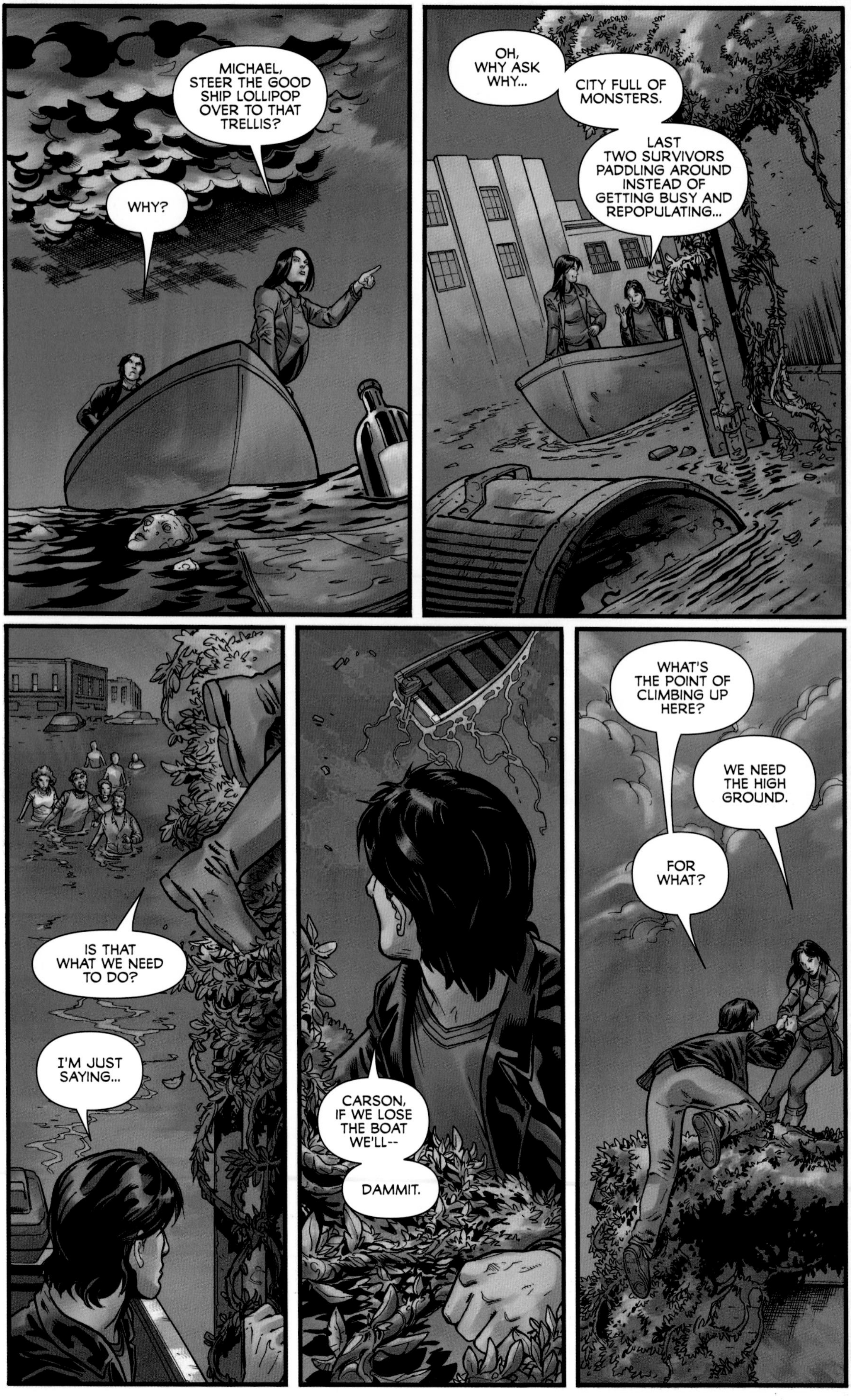
MICHAEL, STEER THE GOOD SHIP LOLLIPOP OVER TO THAT TRELLIS?
WHY?
OH, WHY ASK WHY...
CITY FULL OF MONSTERS.
LAST TWO SURVIVORS PADDLING AROUND INSTEAD OF GETTING BUSY AND REPOPULATING...
IS THAT WHAT WE NEED TO DO?
I'M JUST SAYING...
CARSON, IF WE LOSE THE BOAT WE'LL--
DAMMIT.
WHAT'S THE POINT OF CLIMBING UP HERE?
WE NEED THE HIGH GROUND.
FOR WHAT?

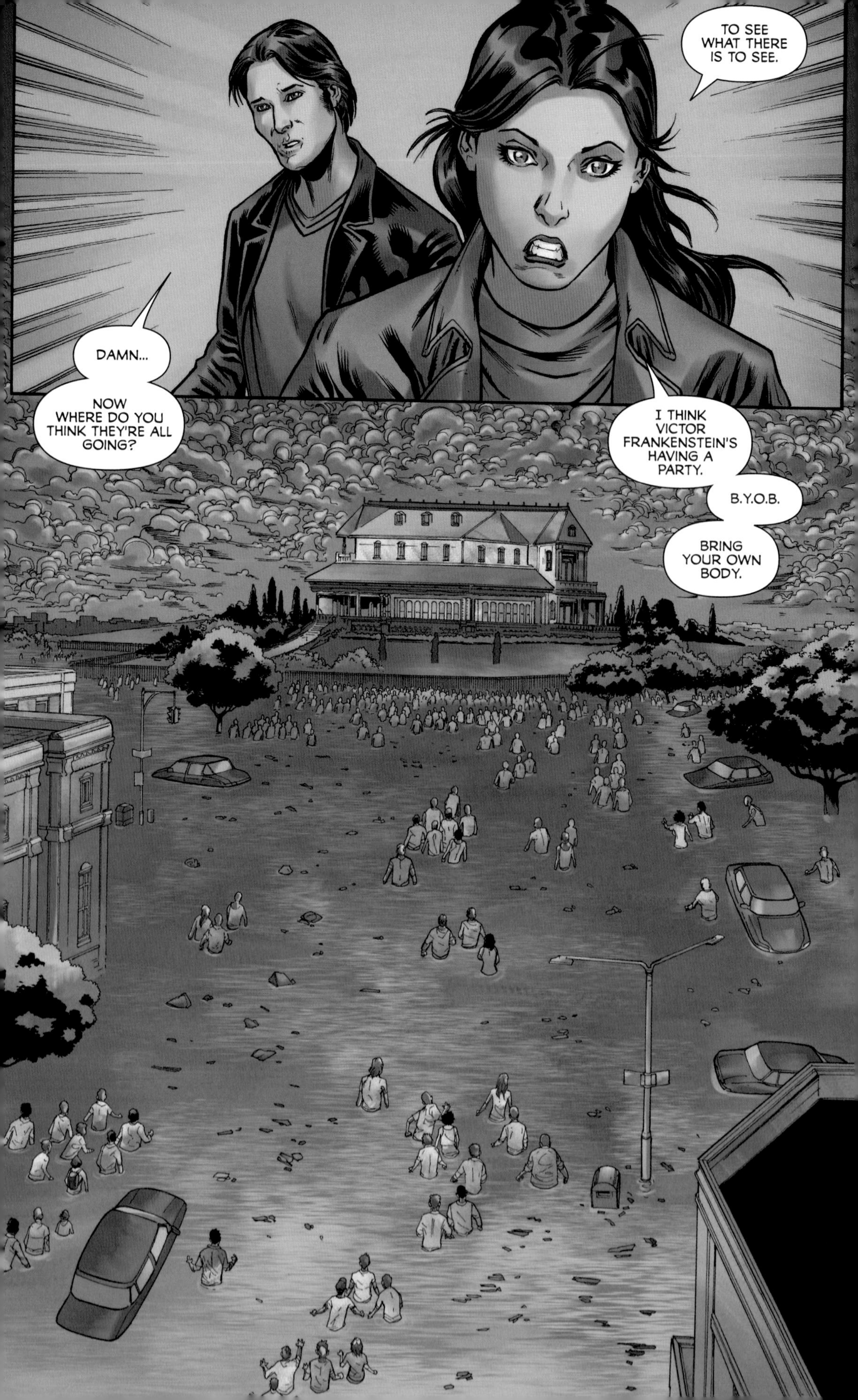
TO SEE WHAT THERE IS TO SEE.
DAMN...
NOW WHERE DO YOU THINK THEY'RE ALL GOING?
I THINK VICTOR FRANKENSTEIN'S HAVING A PARTY.
B.Y.O.B.
BRING YOUR OWN BODY.

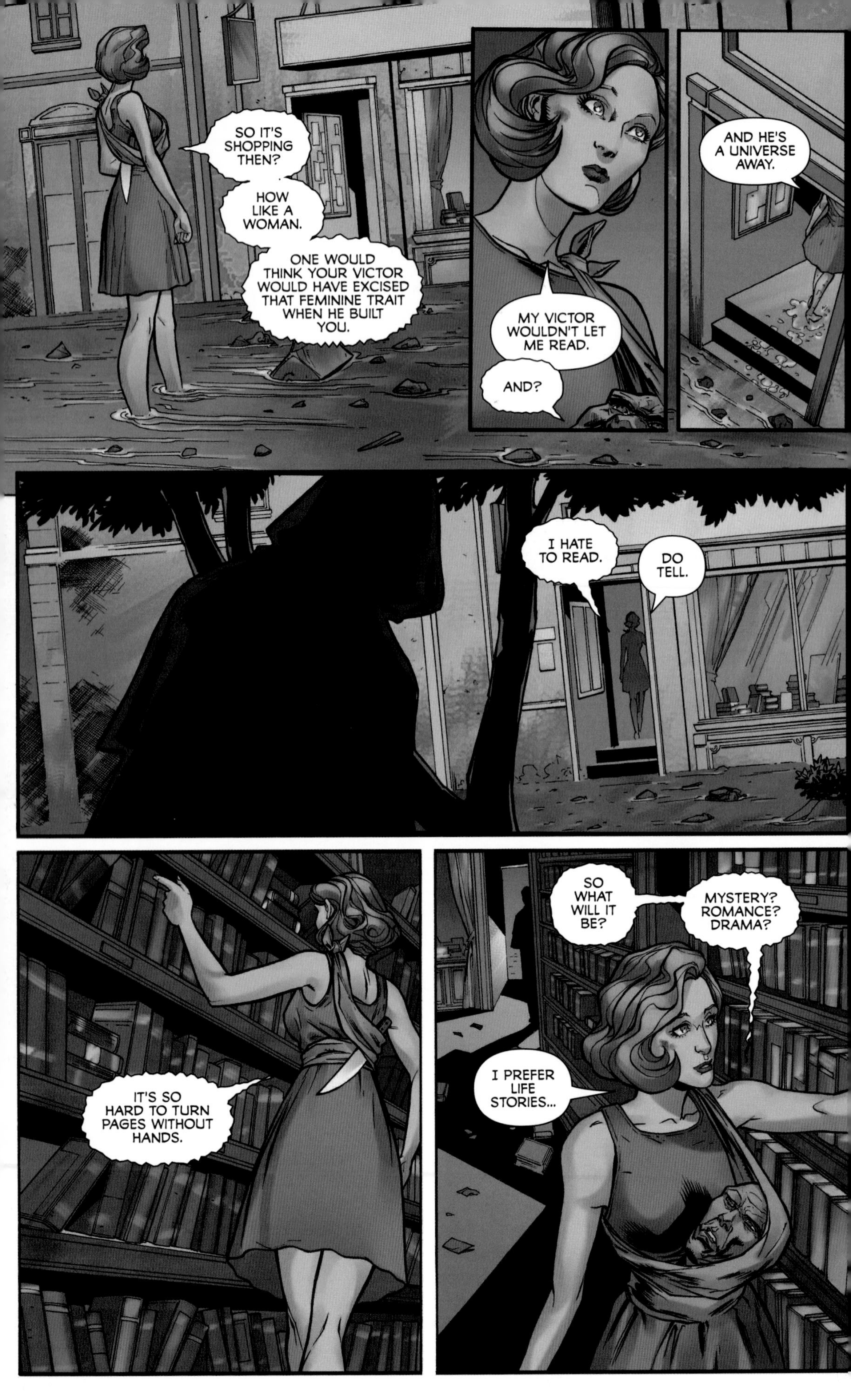
SO IT'S SHOPPING THEN?
HOW LIKE A WOMAN.
ONE WOULD THINK YOUR VICTOR WOULD HAVE EXCISED THAT FEMININE TRAIT WHEN HE BUILT YOU.
MY VICTOR WOULDN'T LET ME READ.
AND?
AND HE'S A UNIVERSE AWAY.
I HATE TO READ.
DO TELL.
IT'S SO HARD TO TURN PAGES WITHOUT HANDS.
SO WHAT WILL IT BE?
MYSTERY? ROMANCE? DRAMA?
I PREFER LIFE STORIES...

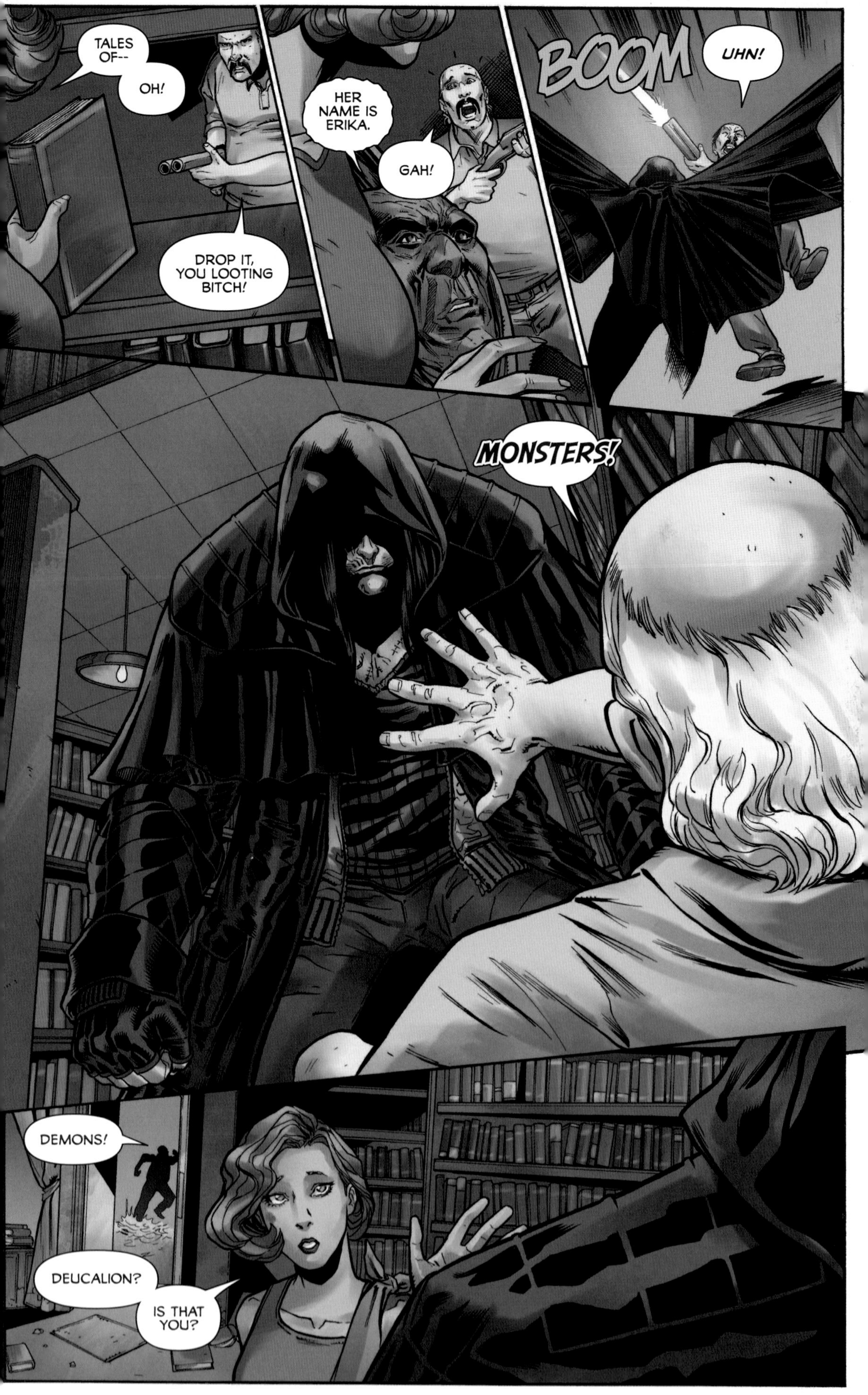
TALES OF--
OH!
DROP IT, YOU LOOTING BITCH!
HER NAME IS ERIKA.
GAH!
BOOM
UHN!
MONSTERS!
DEMONS!
DEUCALION?
IS THAT YOU?

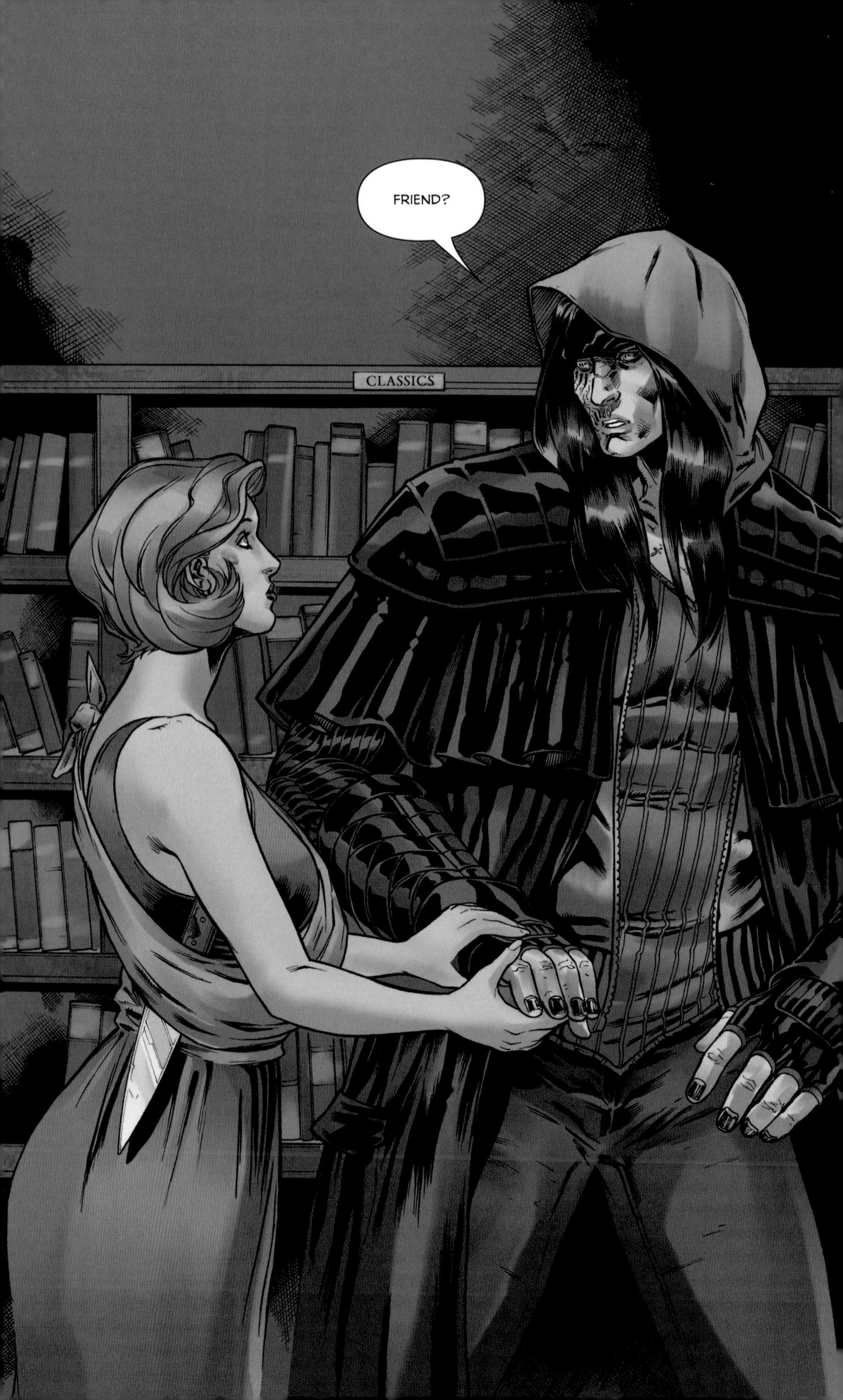
FRIEND?
CLASSICS

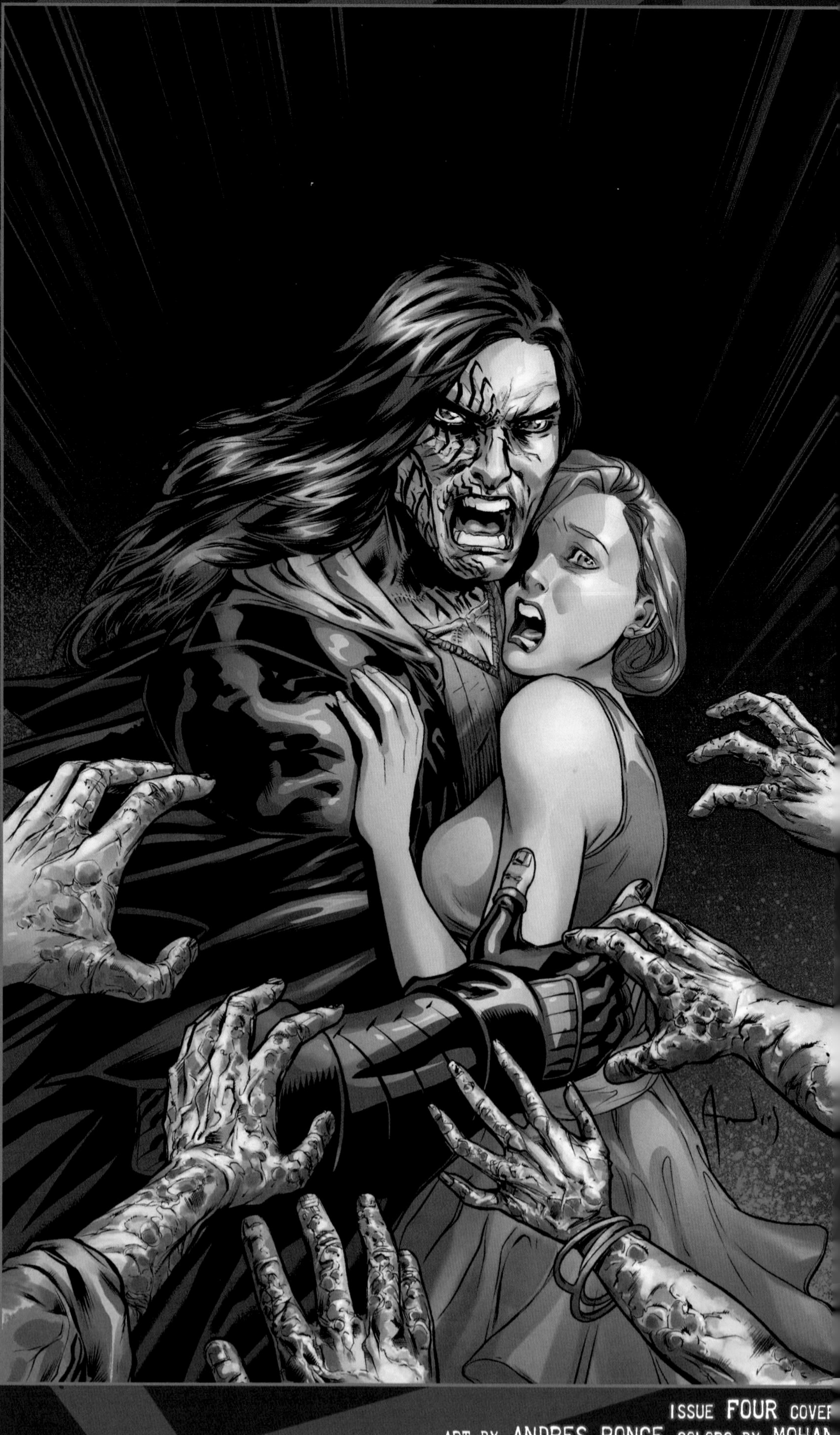

ISSUE FOUR COVER
ART BY ANDRES PONCE COLORS BY MOHAN

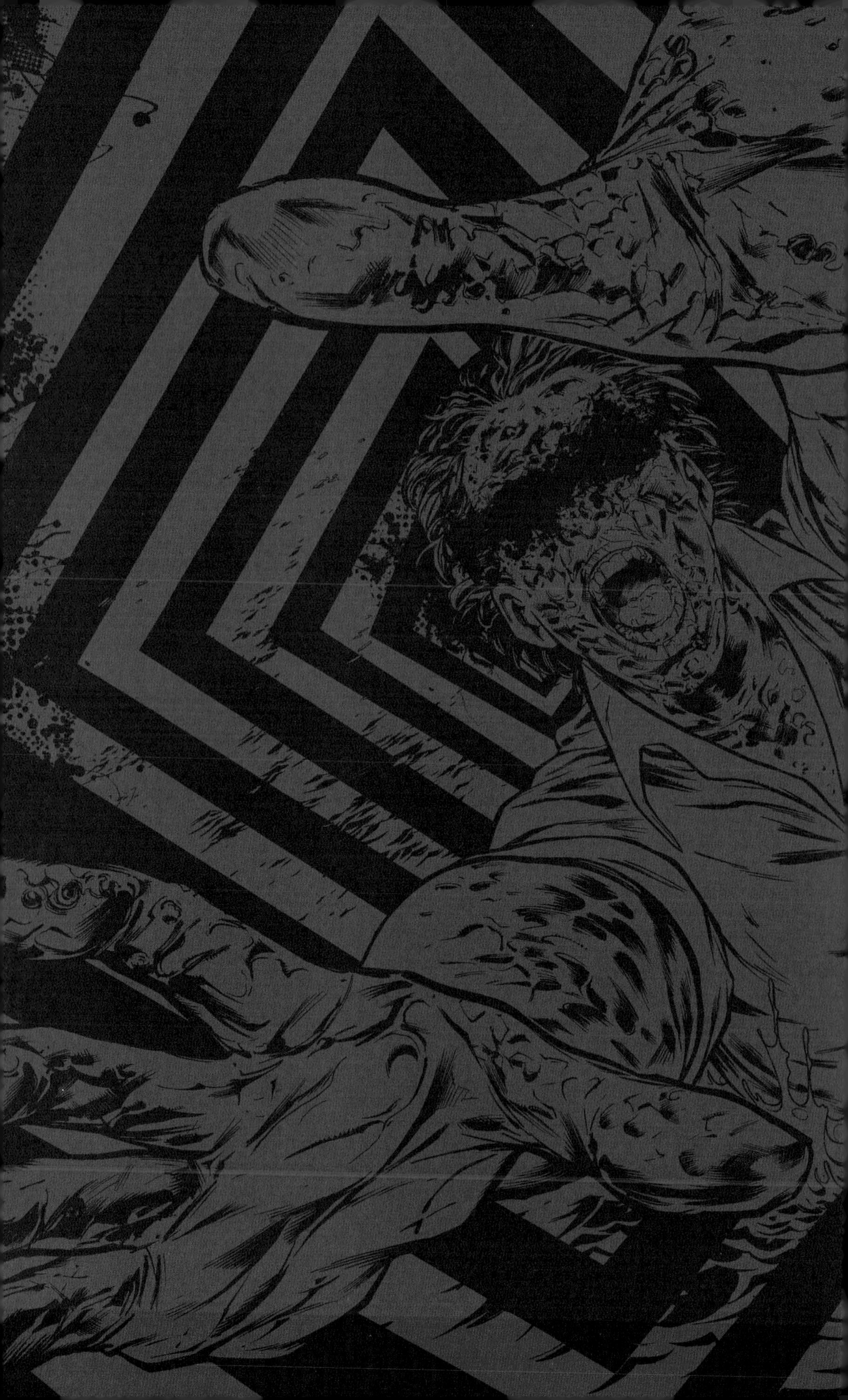

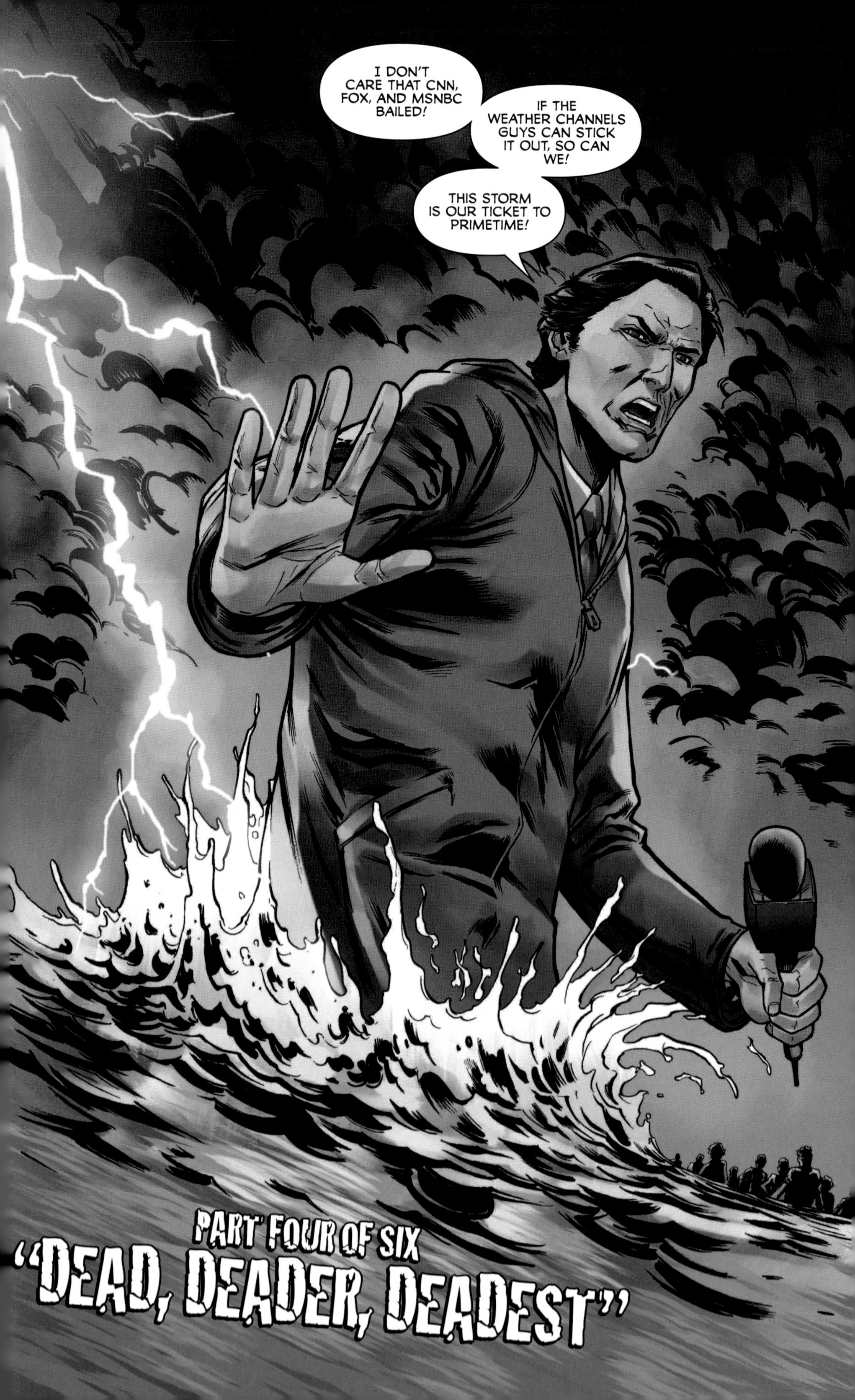
I DON'T CARE THAT CNN, FOX, AND MSNBC BAILED!
IF THE WEATHER CHANNELS GUYS CAN STICK IT OUT, SO CAN WE!
THIS STORM IS OUR TICKET TO PRIMETIME!
PART FOUR OF SIX
"DEAD, DEADER, DEADEST"

WE SHOULD BE HELPING REFUGEES, BRECK!

NOT ANGLING FOR A MURROW!

JUST ONE OR TWO MORE SHOTS AND WE CAN SHOW THE WORLD THAT FEMA CUT AND RAN TOO!

BROADCASTING THE TRUTH WILL *HELP* THESE PEOPLE!

SAYS THE GUY WHO CLAIMED HE WAS IMBEDDED WITH THE TROOPS IN ANBAR!

I WAS ON THE FRONT LINES--

OF THE *SUNDAE BAR* AT THE FORWARD OPERATING BASE!

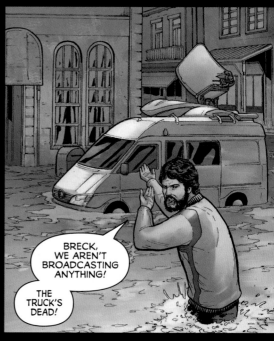

BRECK, WE AREN'T BROADCASTING ANYTHING!

THE TRUCK'S DEAD!

AND WE WILL BE TOO IF WE DON'T GET TO HIGHER GROUND!

I CAN FILM MYSELF...

GO! JUST GO!

CAMERA'S *AUTO-FOCUS* ANYWAY...

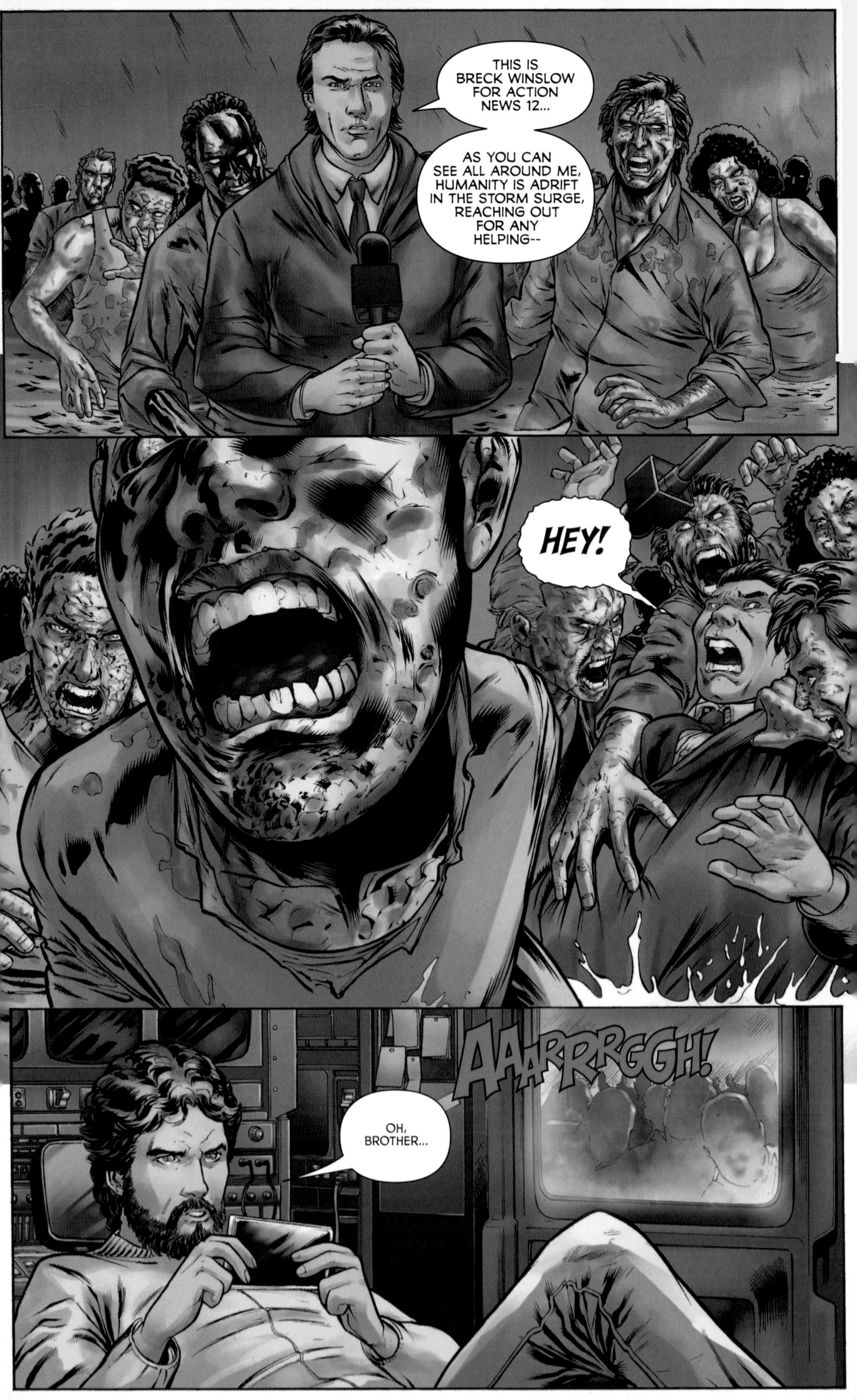
THIS IS BRECK WINSLOW FOR ACTION NEWS 12...
AS YOU CAN SEE ALL AROUND ME, HUMANITY IS ADRIFT IN THE STORM SURGE, REACHING OUT FOR ANY HELPING--
HEY!
AAARRRGGH!
OH, BROTHER...

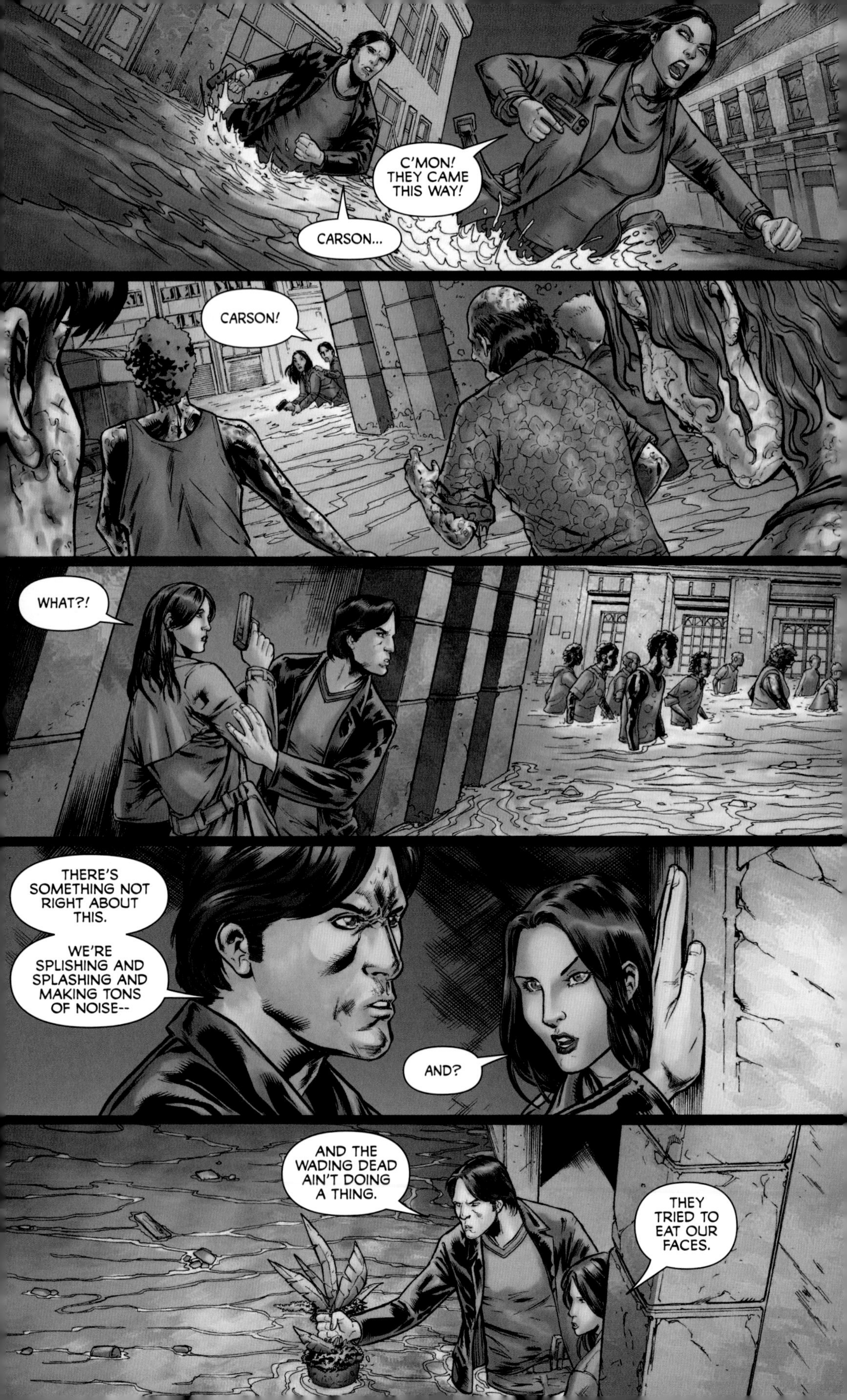
C'MON! THEY CAME THIS WAY!
CARSON...
CARSON!
WHAT?!
THERE'S SOMETHING NOT RIGHT ABOUT THIS.
WE'RE SPLISHING AND SPLASHING AND MAKING TONS OF NOISE--
AND?
AND THE WADING DEAD AIN'T DOING A THING.
THEY TRIED TO EAT OUR FACES.

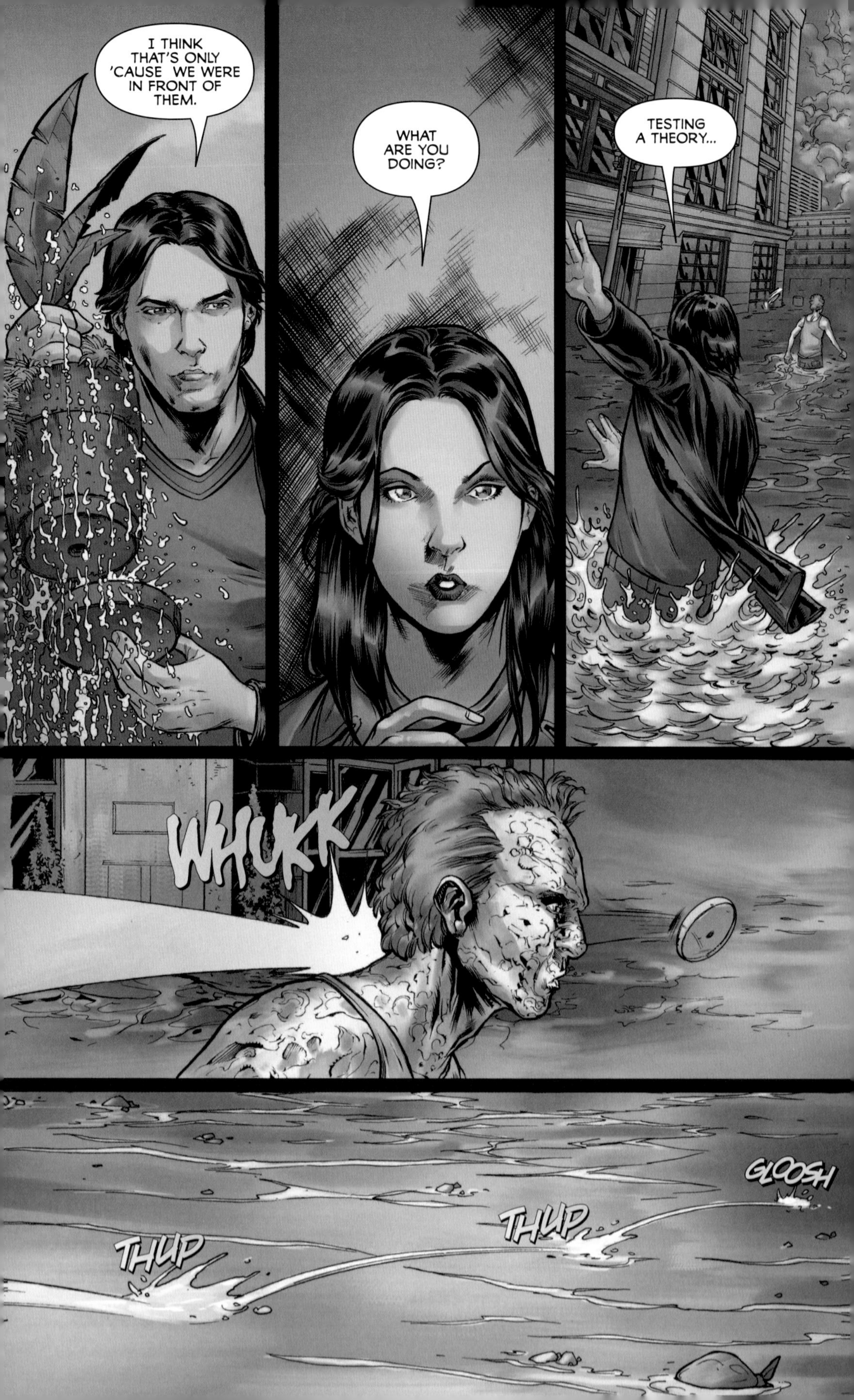
I THINK THAT'S ONLY 'CAUSE WE WERE IN FRONT OF THEM.
WHAT ARE YOU DOING?
TESTING A THEORY...
WHUKK
GLOOSH
THUP
THUP

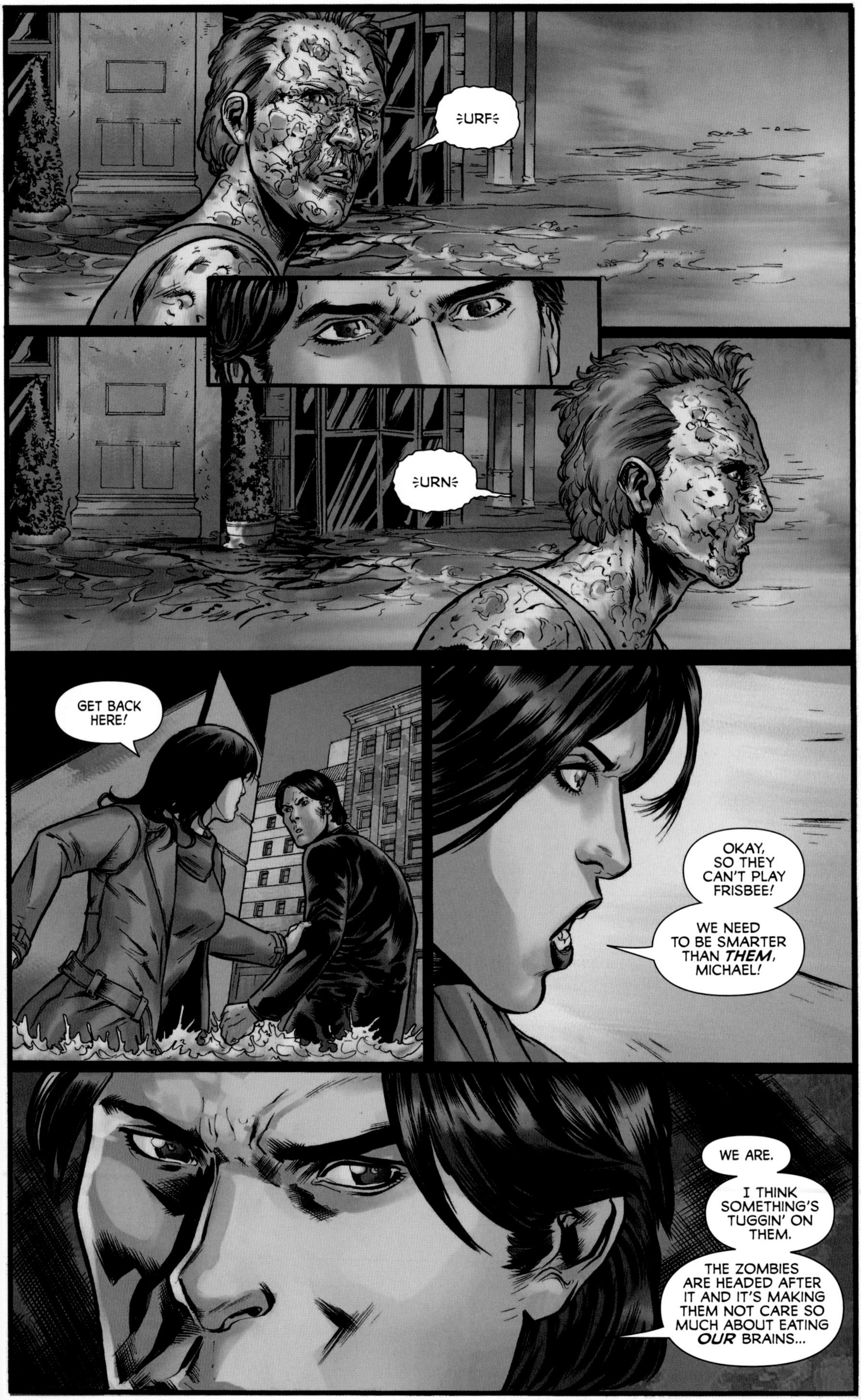
URF
URN
GET BACK HERE!
OKAY, SO THEY CAN'T PLAY FRISBEE!
WE NEED TO BE SMARTER THAN *THEM*, MICHAEL!
WE ARE.
I THINK SOMETHING'S TUGGIN' ON THEM.
THE ZOMBIES ARE HEADED AFTER IT AND IT'S MAKING THEM NOT CARE SO MUCH ABOUT EATING *OUR* BRAINS...

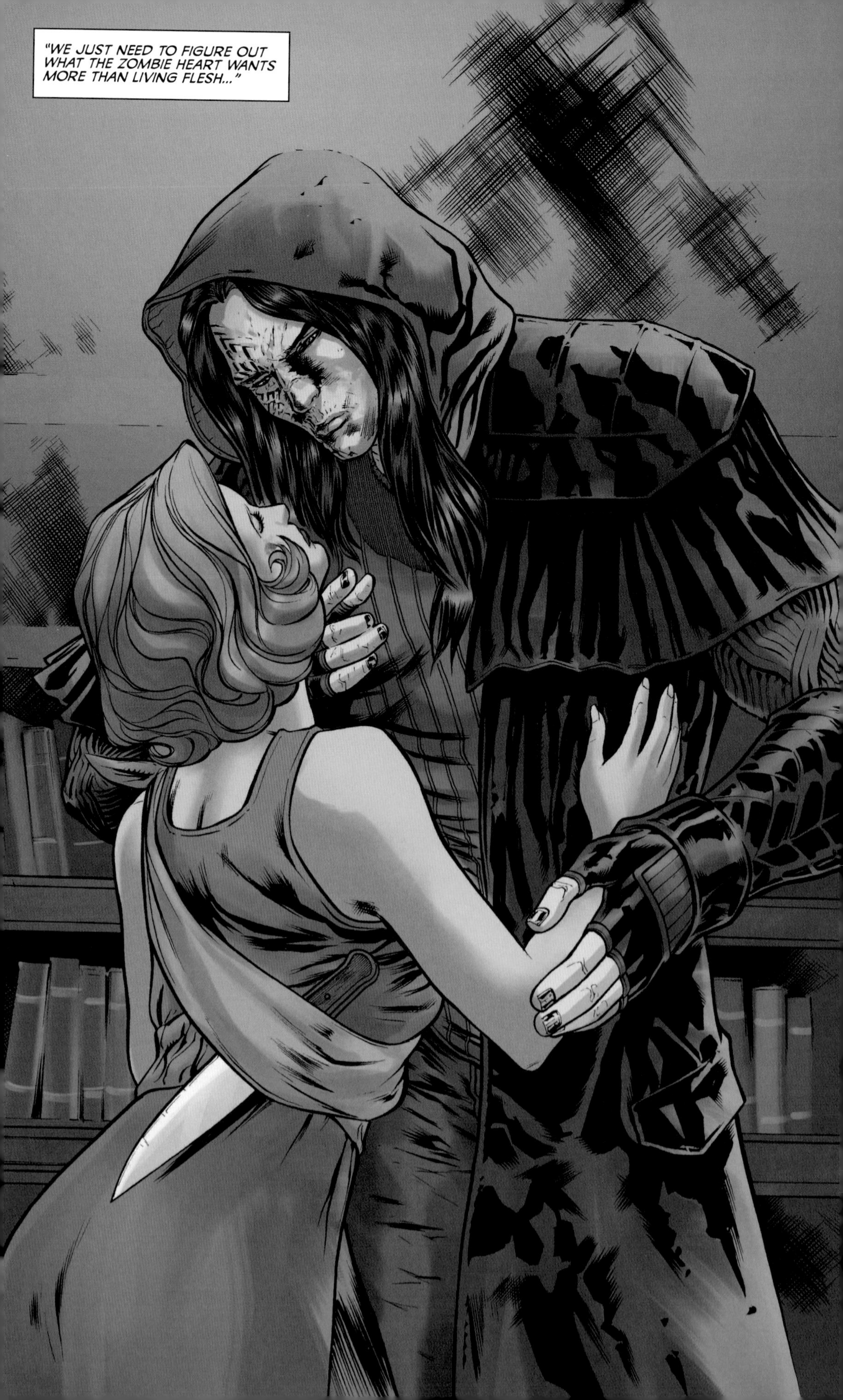
"WE JUST NEED TO FIGURE OUT WHAT THE ZOMBIE HEART WANTS MORE THAN LIVING FLESH..."

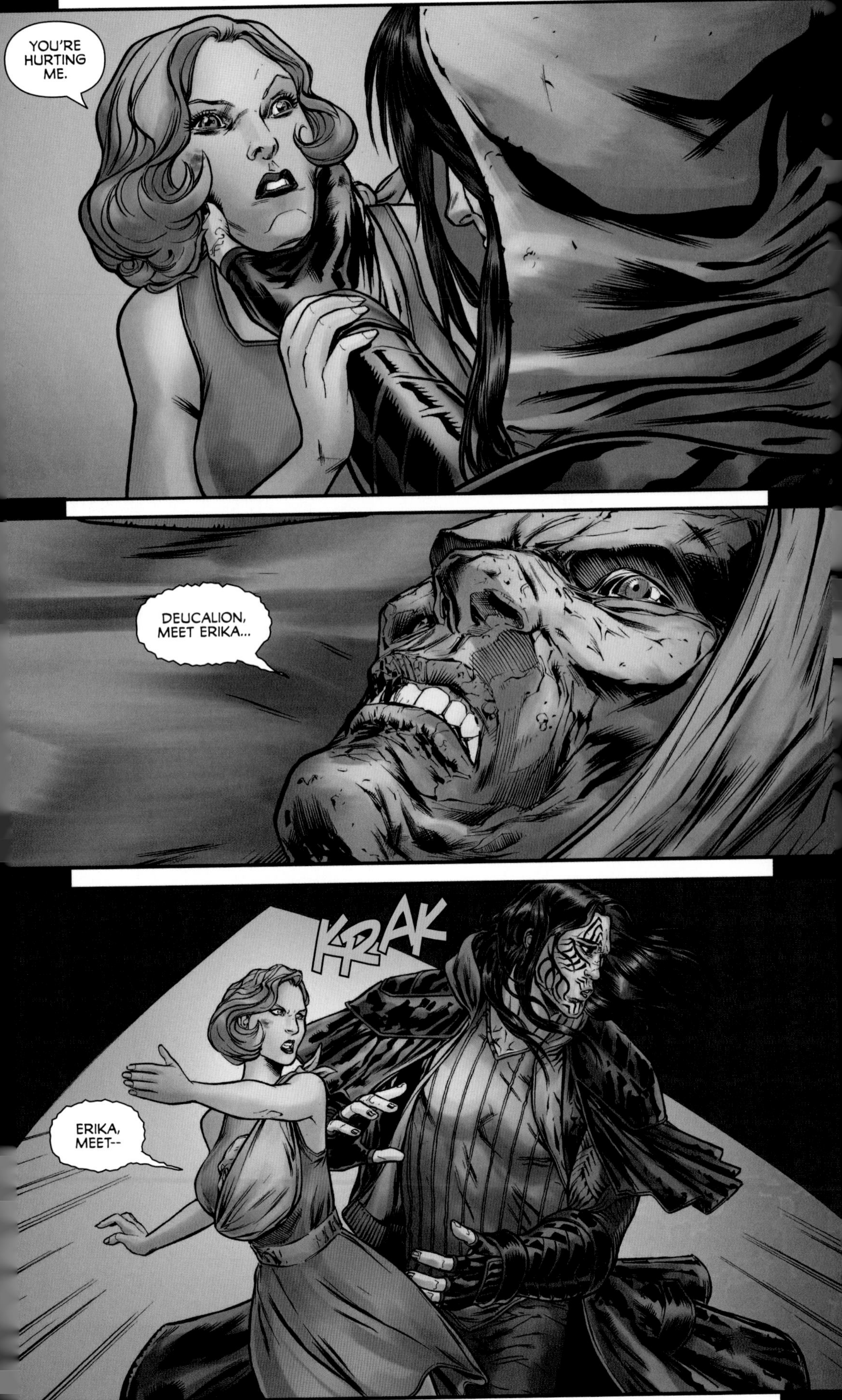

YOU'RE HURTING ME.
DEUCALION, MEET ERIKA...
KRAK
ERIKA, MEET--

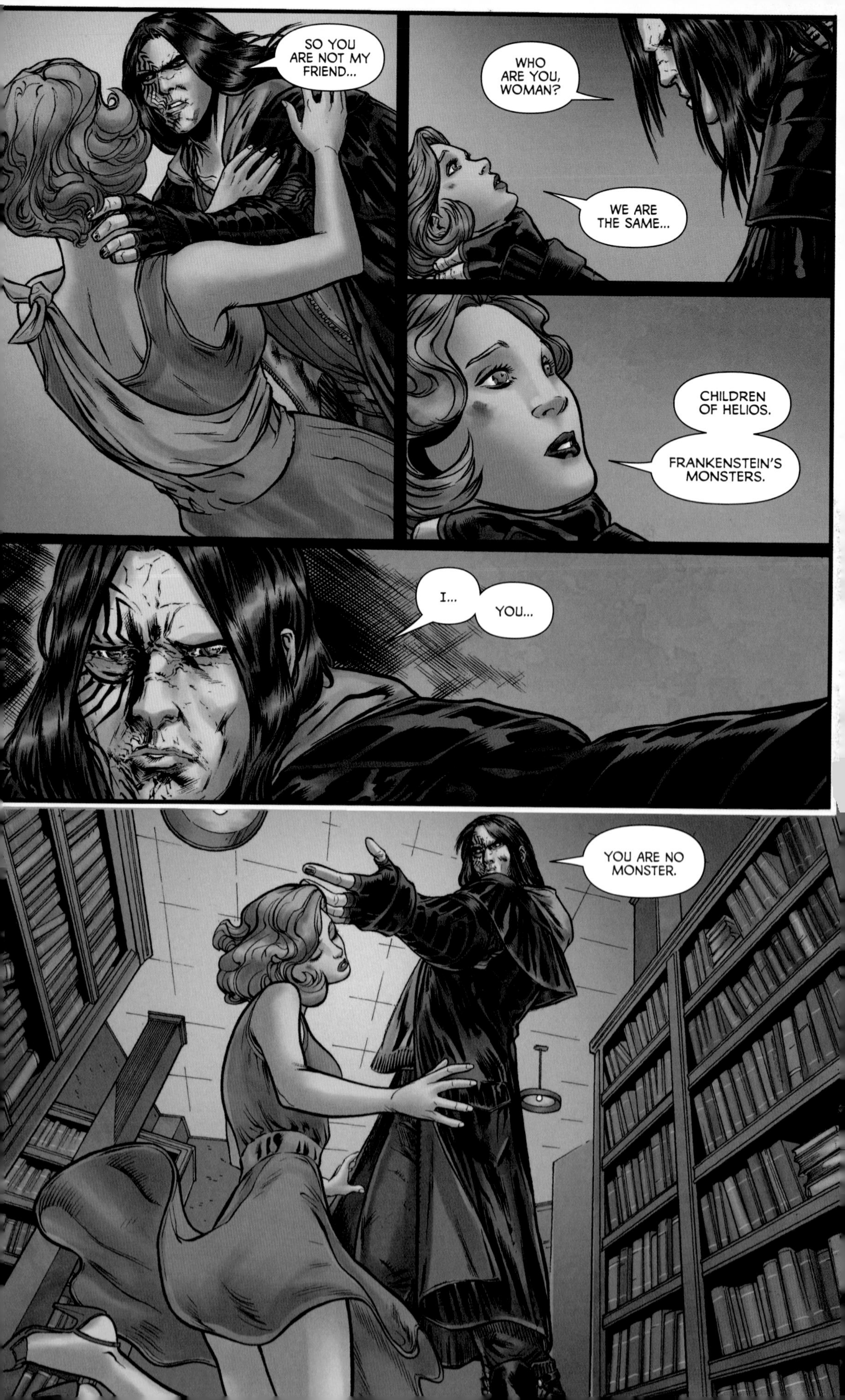

SO YOU ARE NOT MY FRIEND...
WHO ARE YOU, WOMAN?
WE ARE THE SAME...
CHILDREN OF HELIOS.
FRANKENSTEIN'S MONSTERS.
I...
YOU...
YOU ARE NO MONSTER.

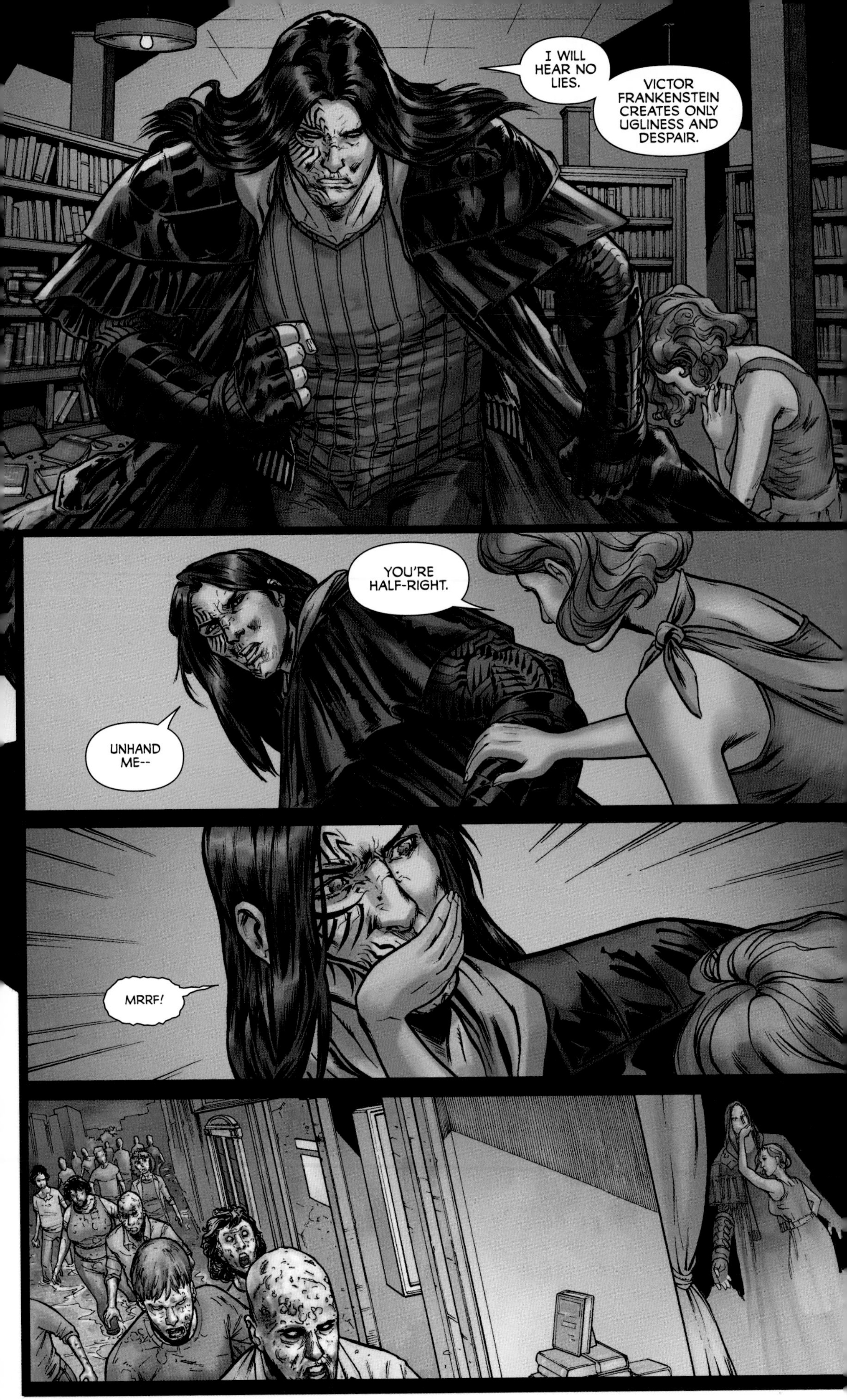
I WILL HEAR NO LIES.
VICTOR FRANKENSTEIN CREATES ONLY UGLINESS AND DESPAIR.
YOU'RE HALF-RIGHT.
UNHAND ME--
MRRF!

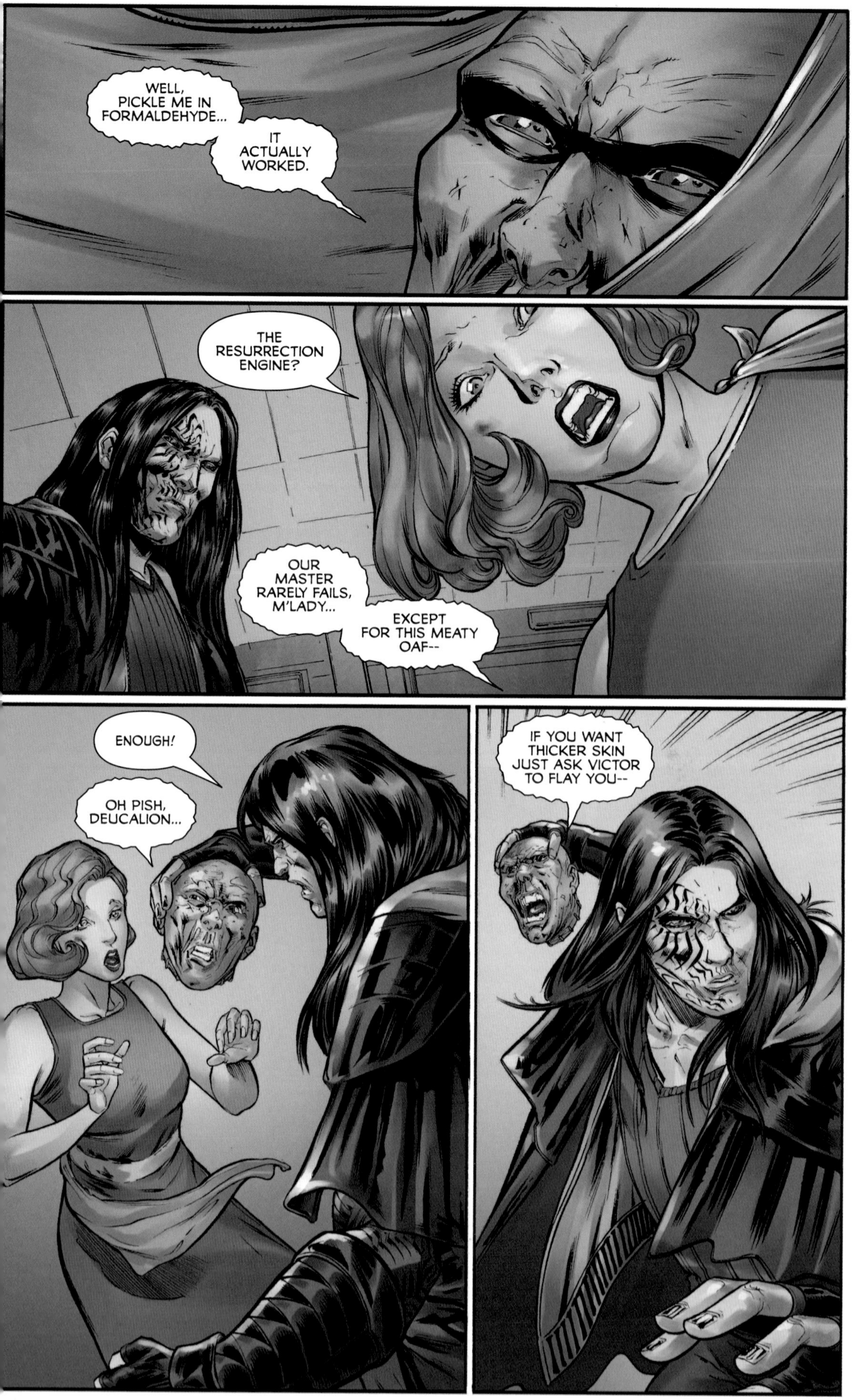
WELL, PICKLE ME IN FORMALDEHYDE...
IT ACTUALLY WORKED.
THE RESURRECTION ENGINE?
OUR MASTER RARELY FAILS, M'LADY...
EXCEPT FOR THIS MEATY OAF--
ENOUGH!
OH PISH, DEUCALION...
IF YOU WANT THICKER SKIN JUST ASK VICTOR TO FLAY YOU--

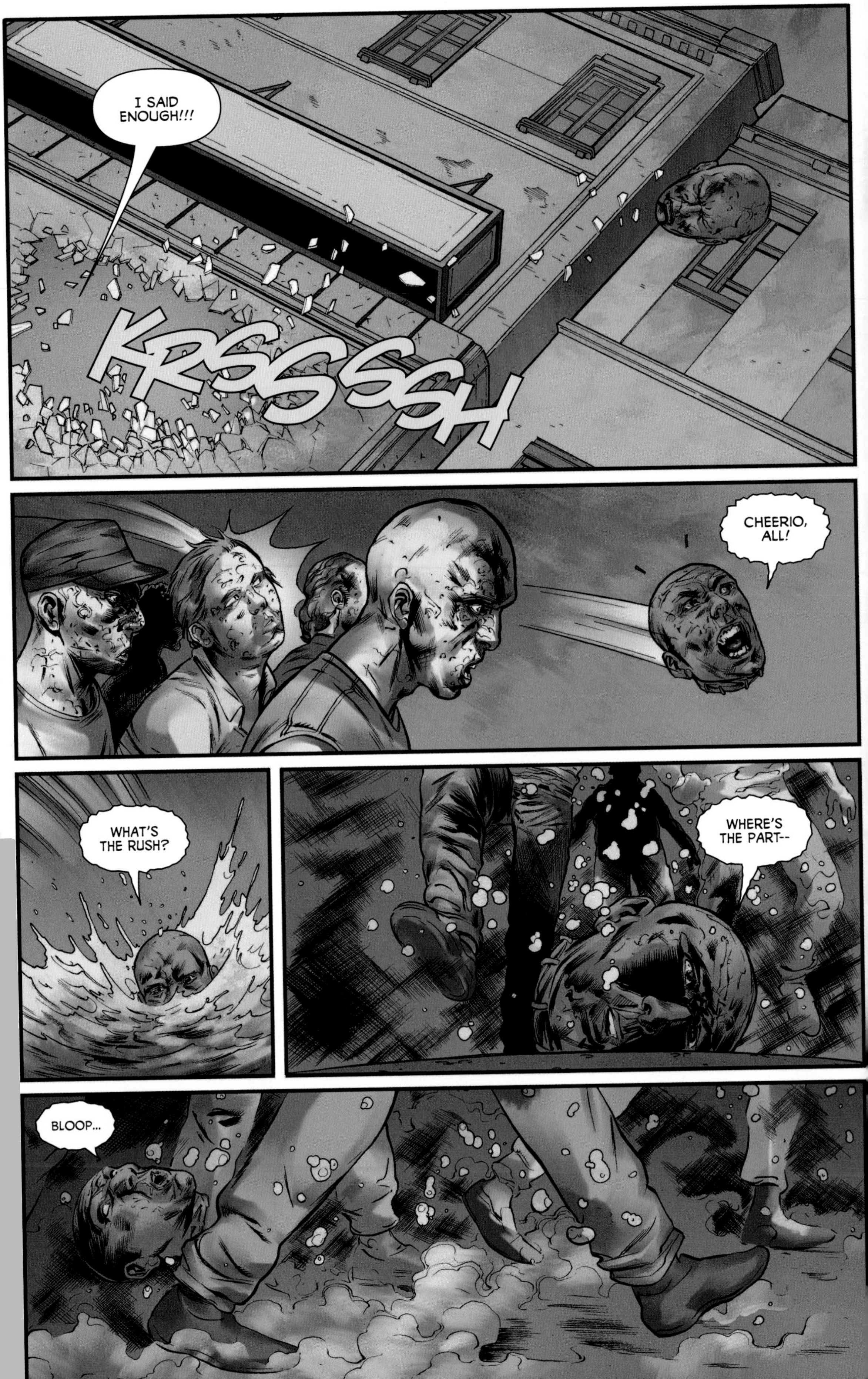
I SAID ENOUGH!!!
KRSSSSH
CHEERIO, ALL!
WHAT'S THE RUSH?
WHERE'S THE PART--
BLOOP...

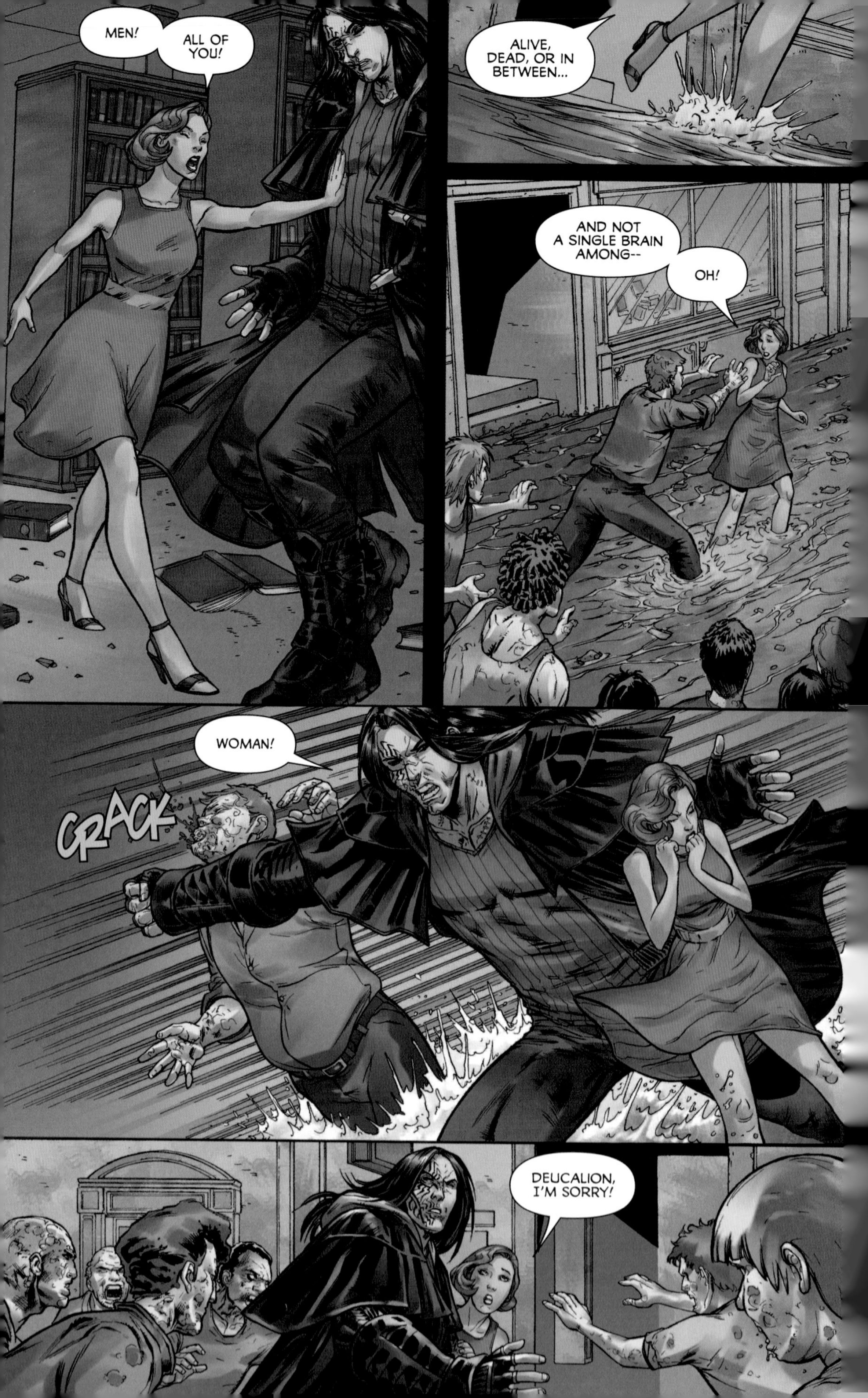

MEN!
ALL OF YOU!
ALIVE, DEAD, OR IN BETWEEN...
AND NOT A SINGLE BRAIN AMONG--
OH!
WOMAN!
CRACK
DEUCALION, I'M SORRY!

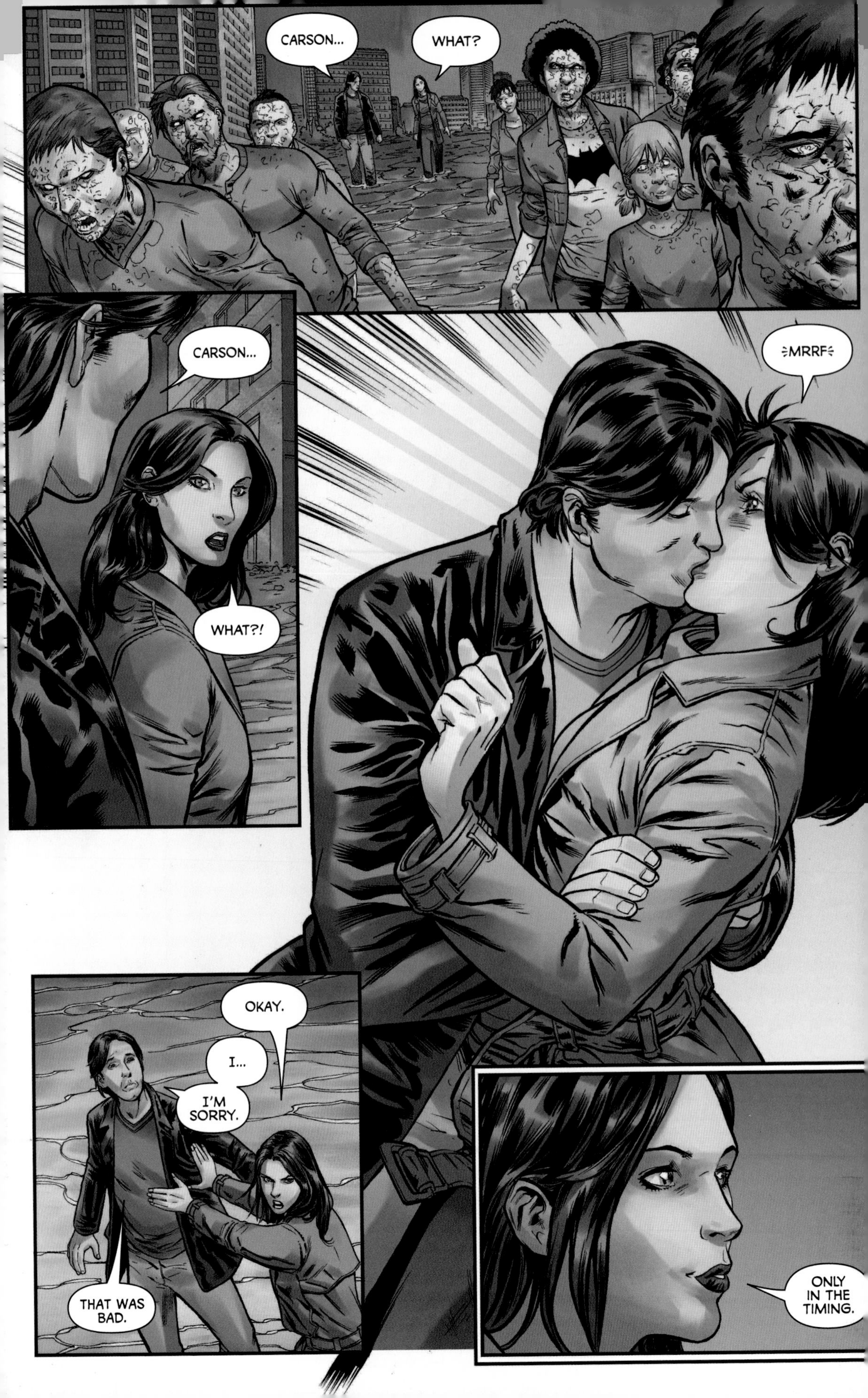
CARSON...
WHAT?
CARSON...
WHAT?!
≑MRRF≑
OKAY.
I...
I'M SORRY.
THAT WAS BAD.
ONLY IN THE TIMING.

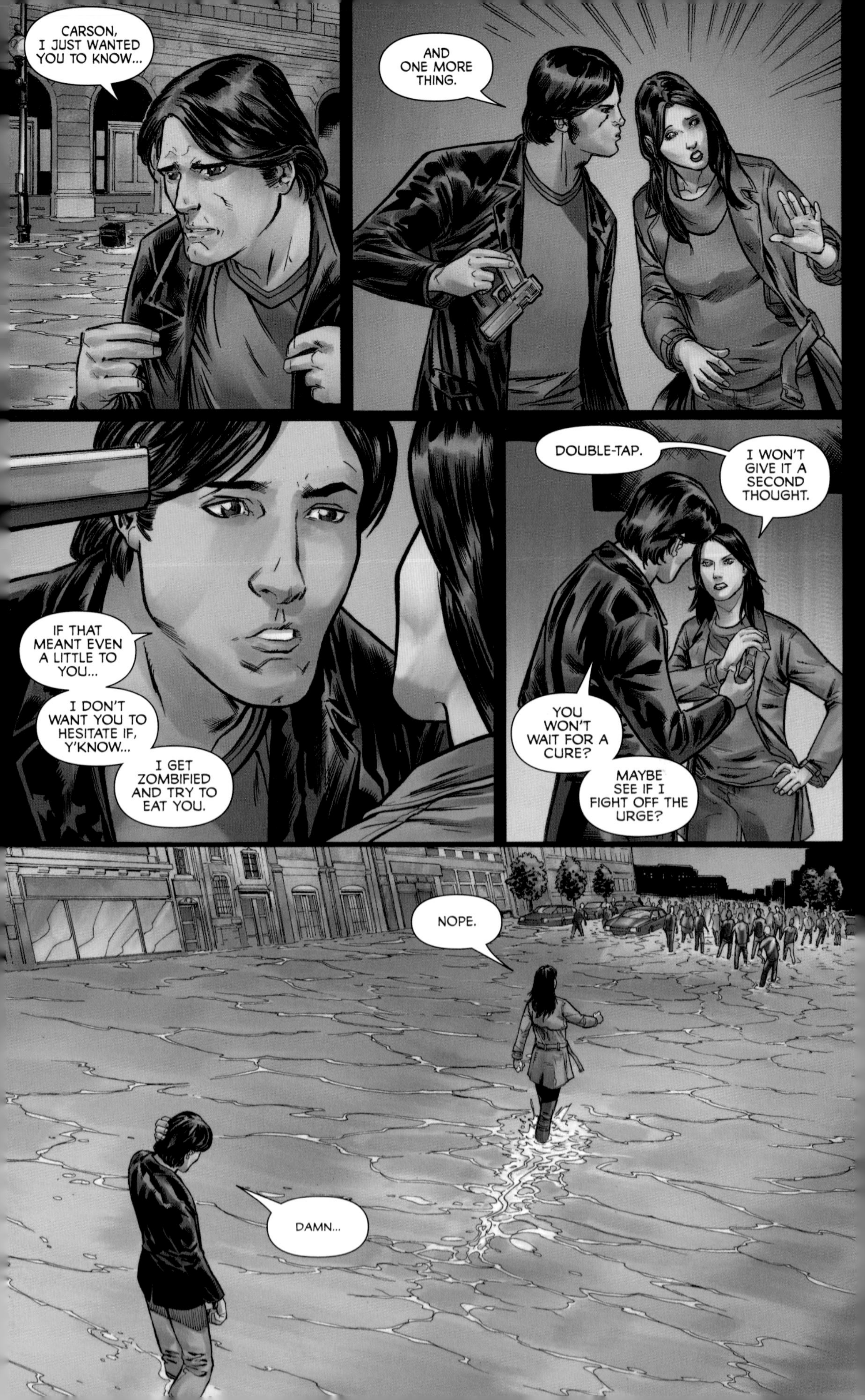
CARSON, I JUST WANTED YOU TO KNOW...
AND ONE MORE THING.
IF THAT MEANT EVEN A LITTLE TO YOU...
I DON'T WANT YOU TO HESITATE IF, Y'KNOW...
I GET ZOMBIFIED AND TRY TO EAT YOU.
DOUBLE-TAP.
I WON'T GIVE IT A SECOND THOUGHT.
YOU WON'T WAIT FOR A CURE?
MAYBE SEE IF I FIGHT OFF THE URGE?
NOPE.
DAMN...

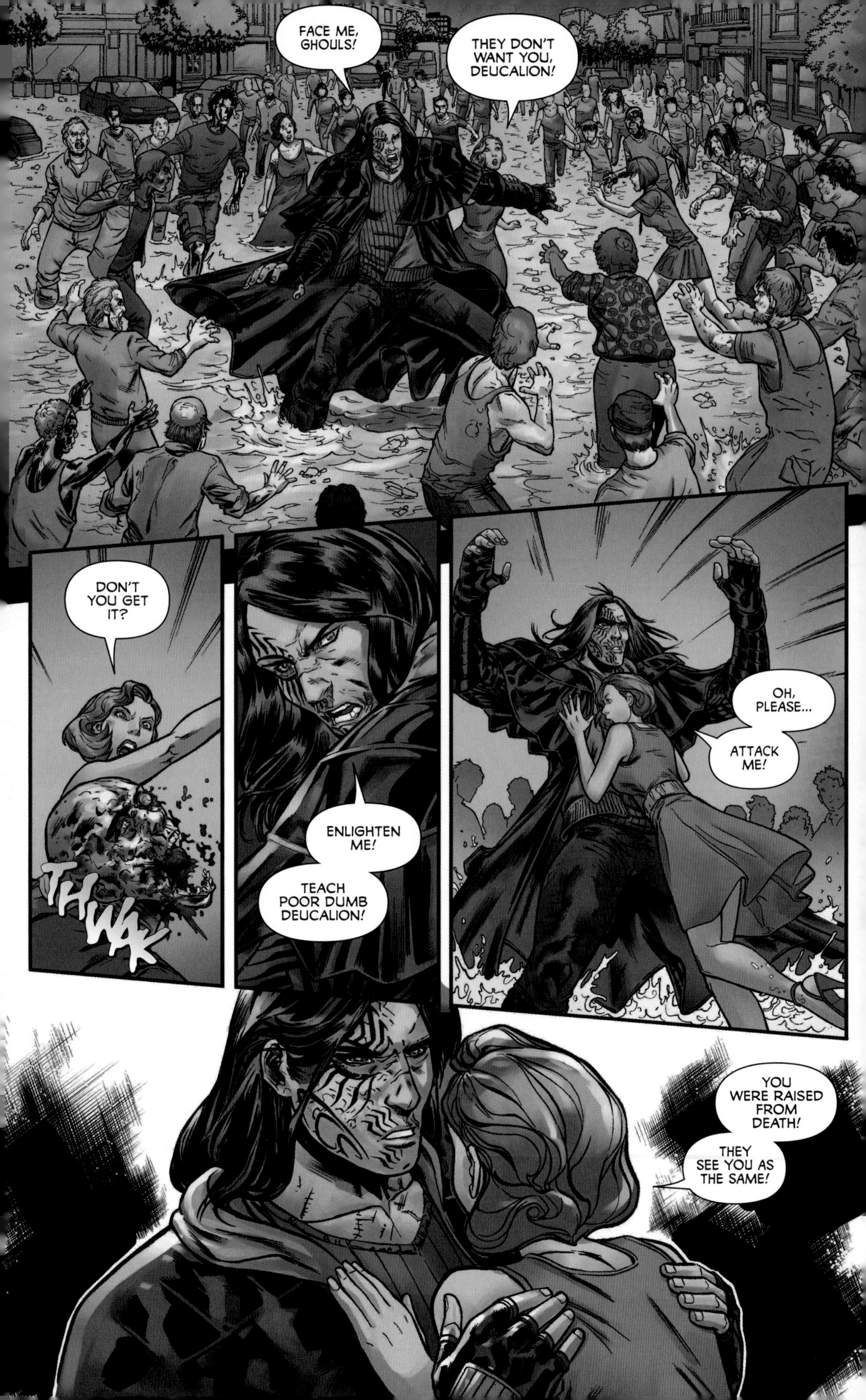
FACE ME, GHOULS!
THEY DON'T WANT YOU, DEUCALION!
DON'T YOU GET IT?
THWAK
ENLIGHTEN ME!
TEACH POOR DUMB DEUCALION!
OH, PLEASE...
ATTACK ME!
YOU WERE RAISED FROM DEATH!
THEY SEE YOU AS THE SAME!

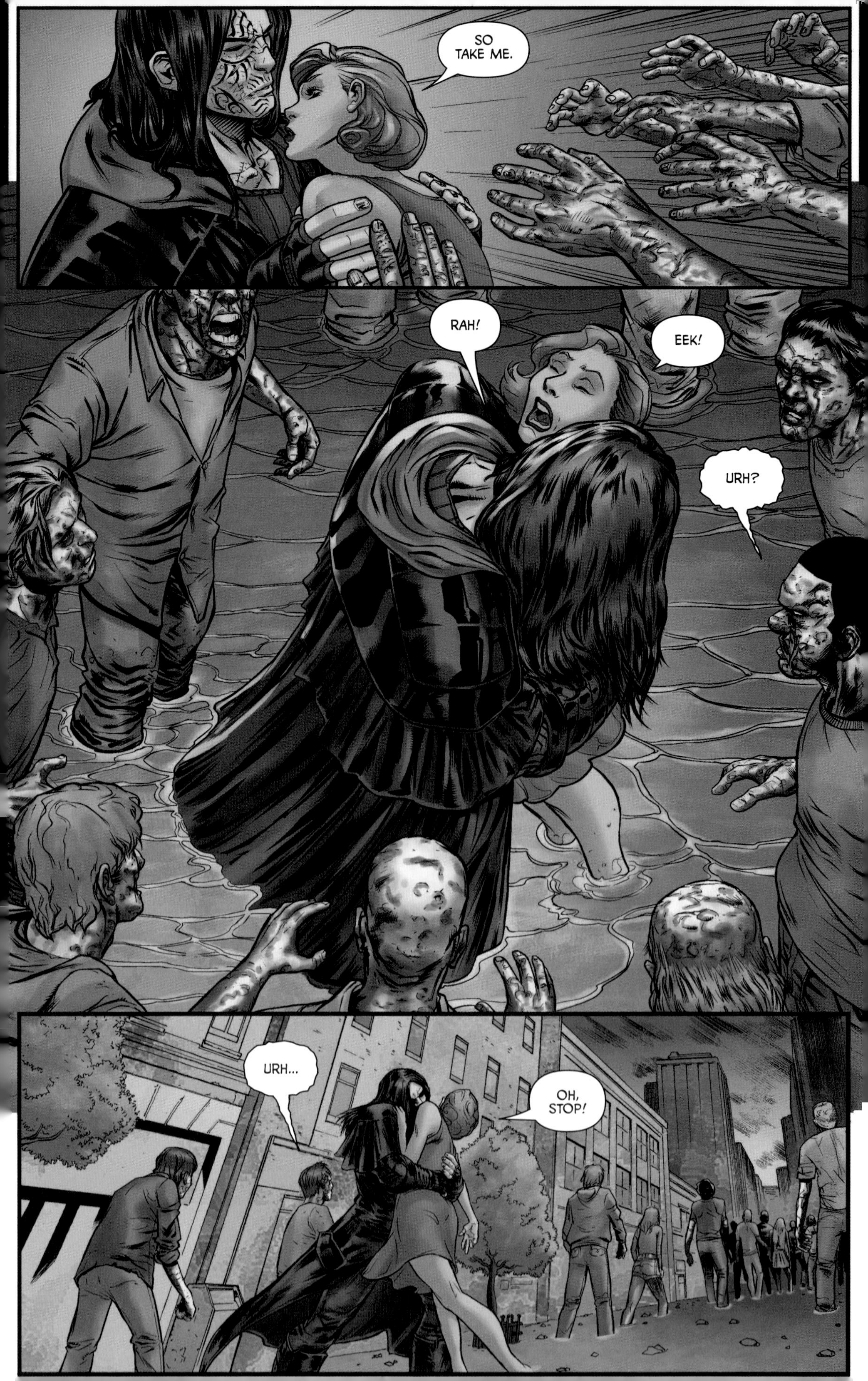
SO TAKE ME.
RAH!
EEK!
URH?
URH...
OH, STOP!

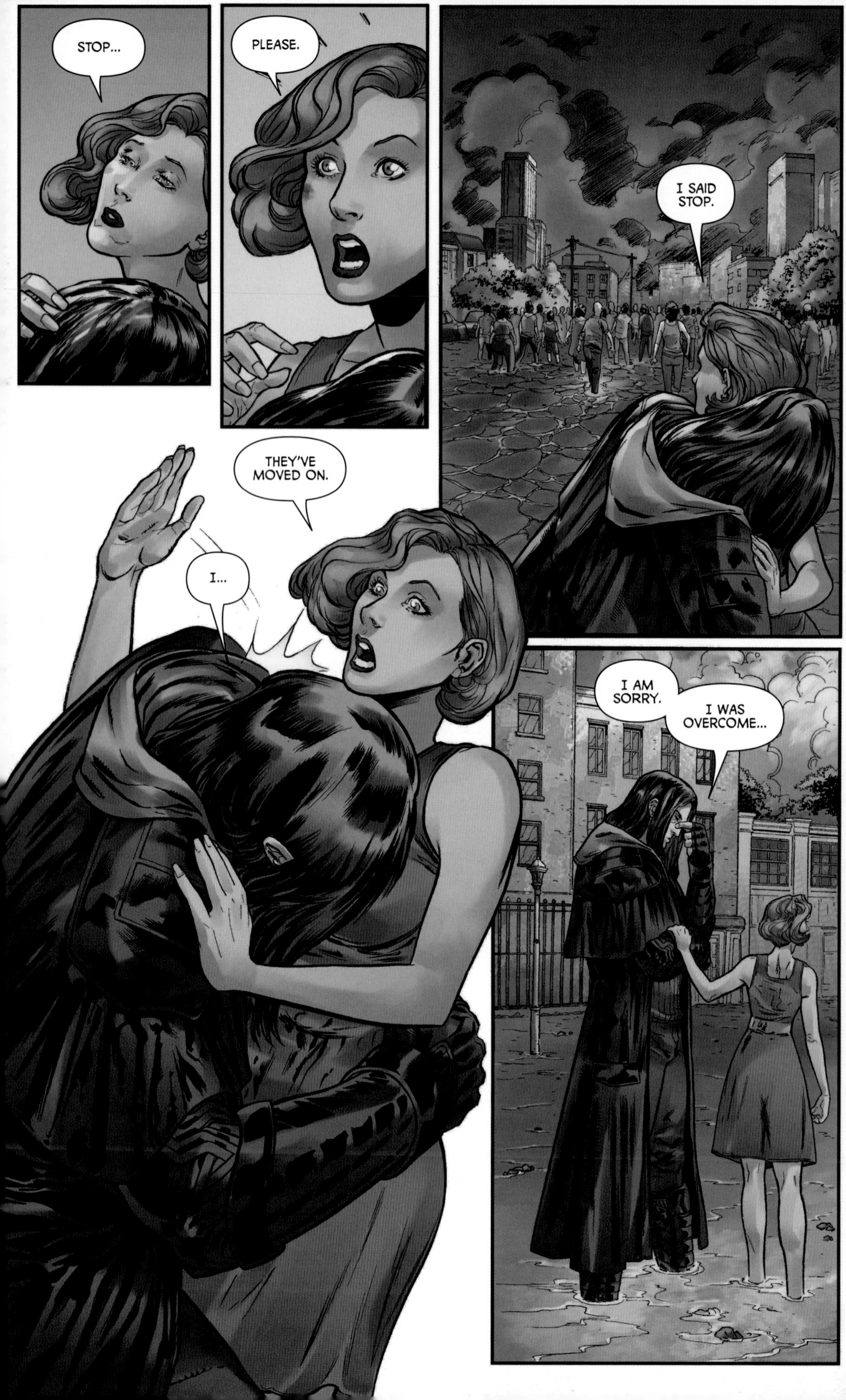
STOP...
PLEASE.
I SAID STOP.
THEY'VE MOVED ON.
I...
I AM SORRY.
I WAS OVERCOME...

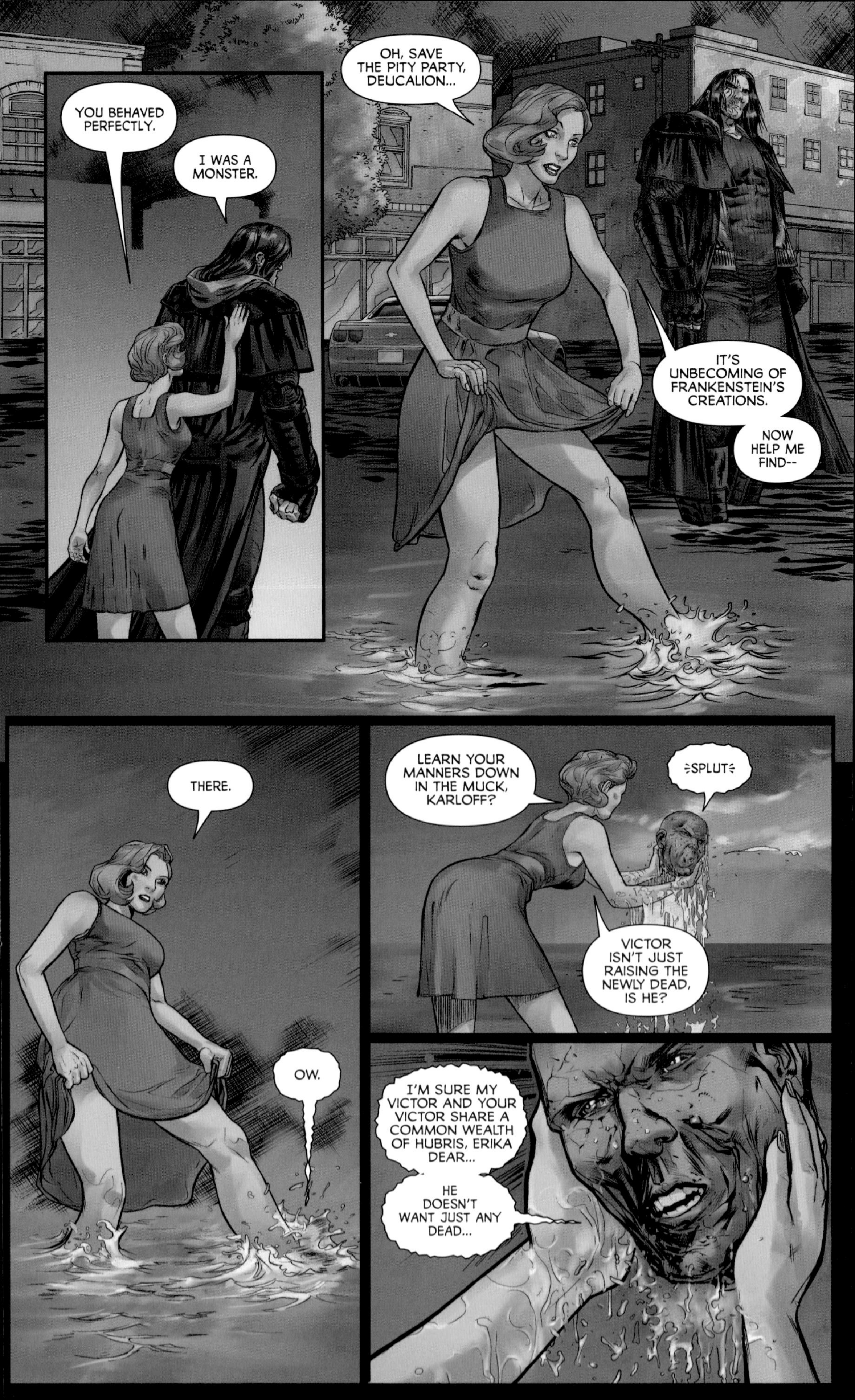
YOU BEHAVED PERFECTLY.
I WAS A MONSTER.
OH, SAVE THE PITY PARTY, DEUCALION...
IT'S UNBECOMING OF FRANKENSTEIN'S CREATIONS.
NOW HELP ME FIND--
THERE.
OW.
LEARN YOUR MANNERS DOWN IN THE MUCK, KARLOFF?
SPLUT
VICTOR ISN'T JUST RAISING THE NEWLY DEAD, IS HE?
I'M SURE MY VICTOR AND YOUR VICTOR SHARE A COMMON WEALTH OF HUBRIS, ERIKA DEAR...
HE DOESN'T WANT JUST ANY DEAD...

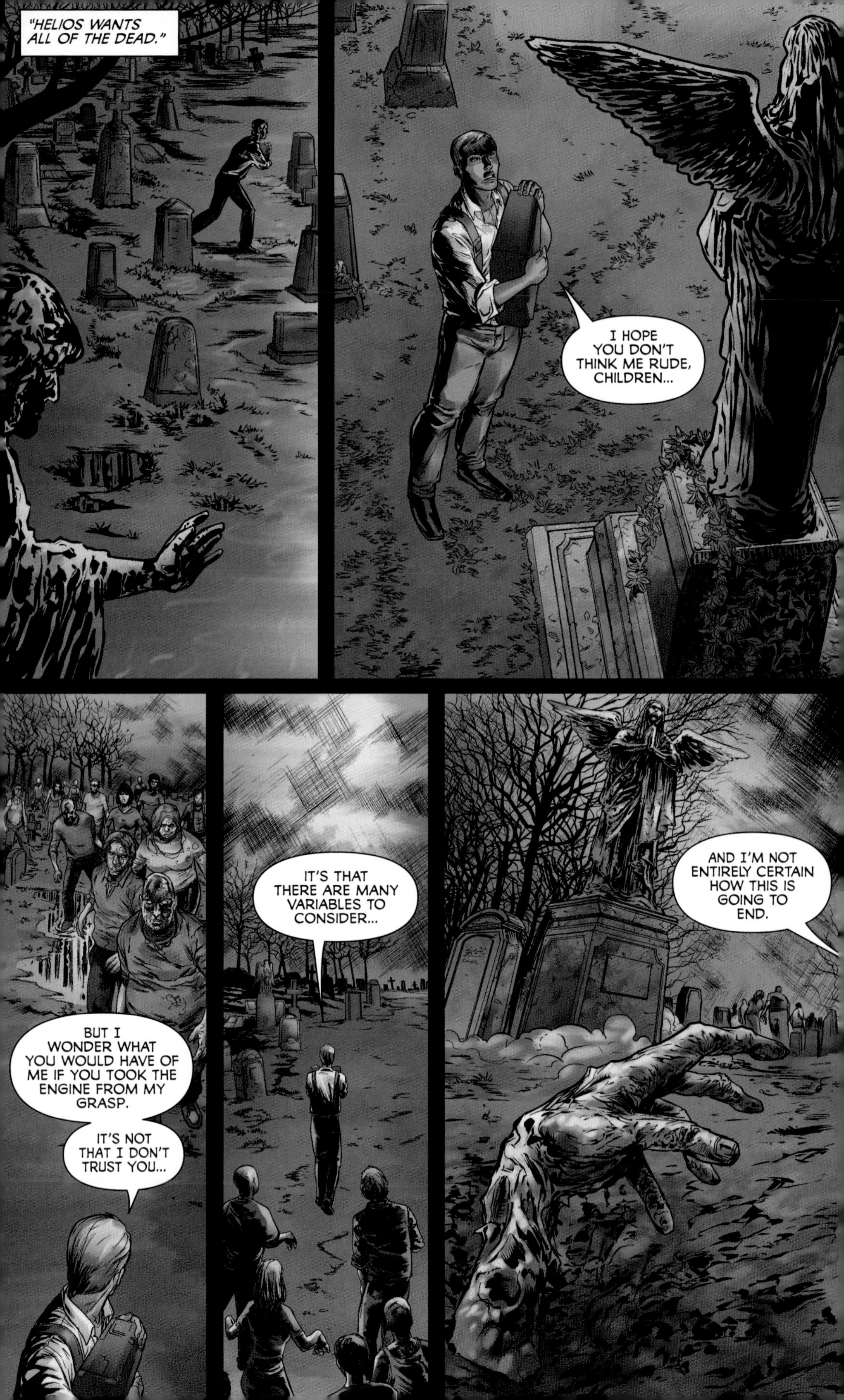
"HELIOS WANTS ALL OF THE DEAD."
I HOPE YOU DON'T THINK ME RUDE, CHILDREN...
BUT I WONDER WHAT YOU WOULD HAVE OF ME IF YOU TOOK THE ENGINE FROM MY GRASP.
IT'S NOT THAT I DON'T TRUST YOU...
IT'S THAT THERE ARE MANY VARIABLES TO CONSIDER...
AND I'M NOT ENTIRELY CERTAIN HOW THIS IS GOING TO END.

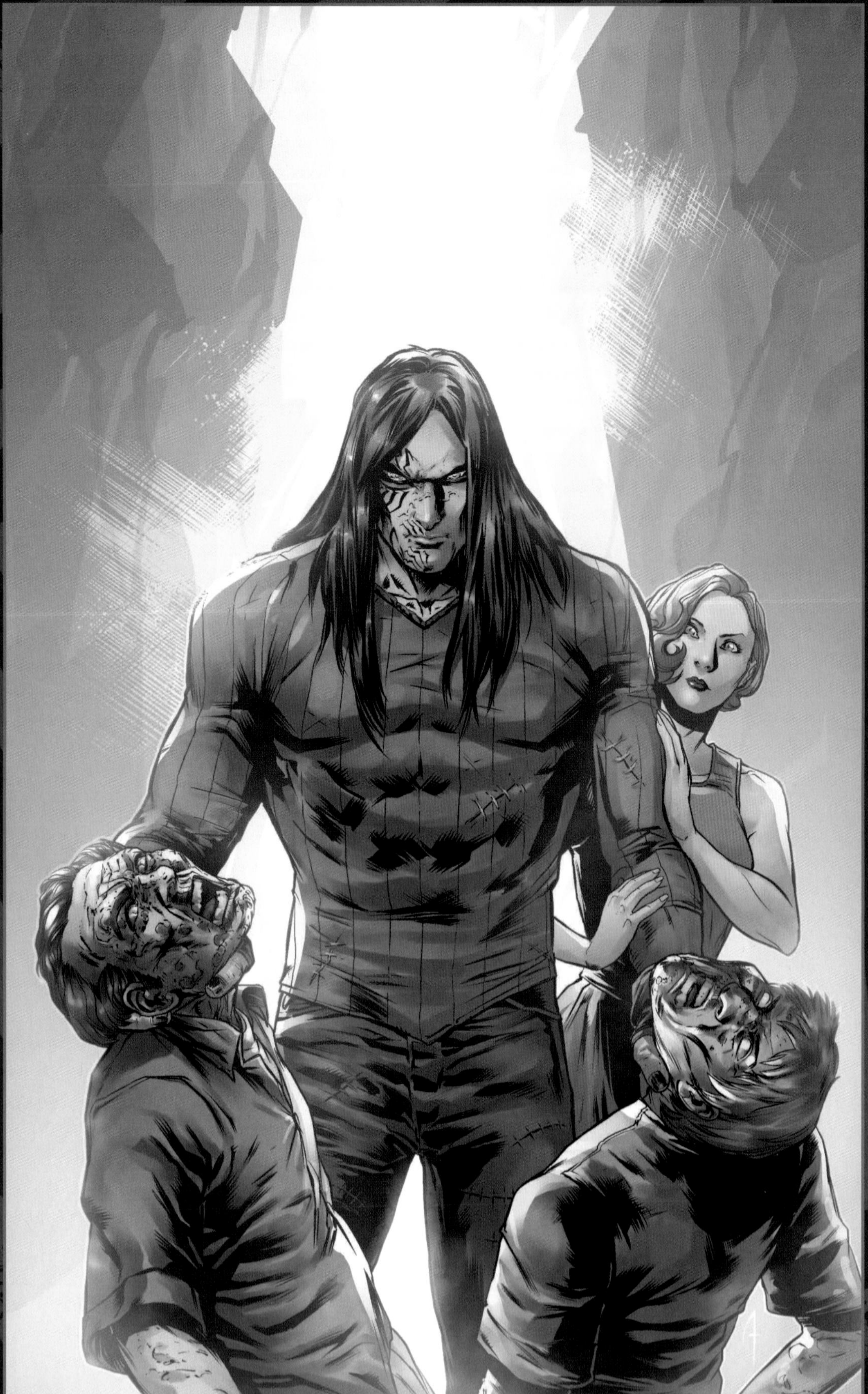

ISSUE FIVE COVER
ART BY ANDRES PONCE COLORS BY MOHAN

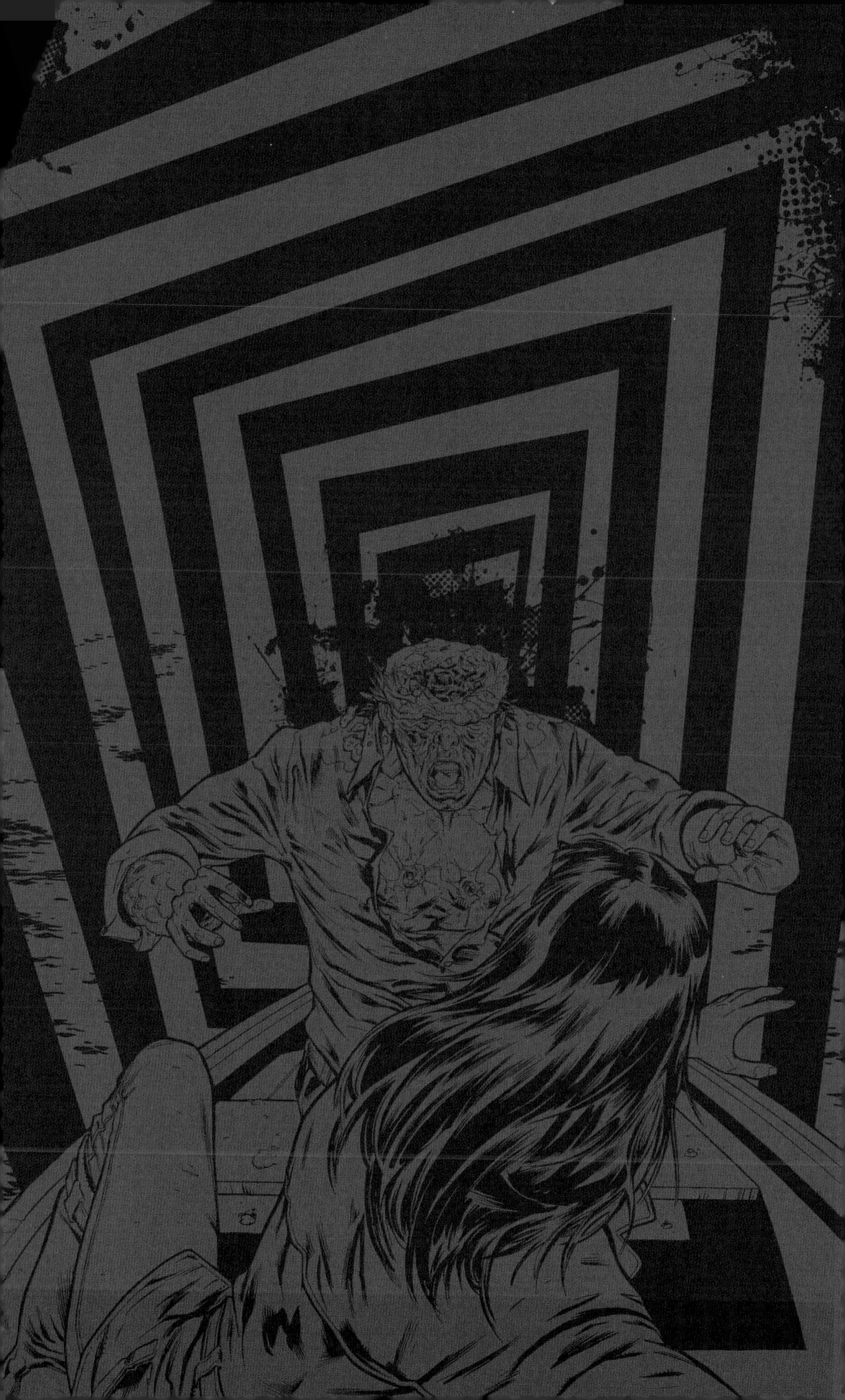

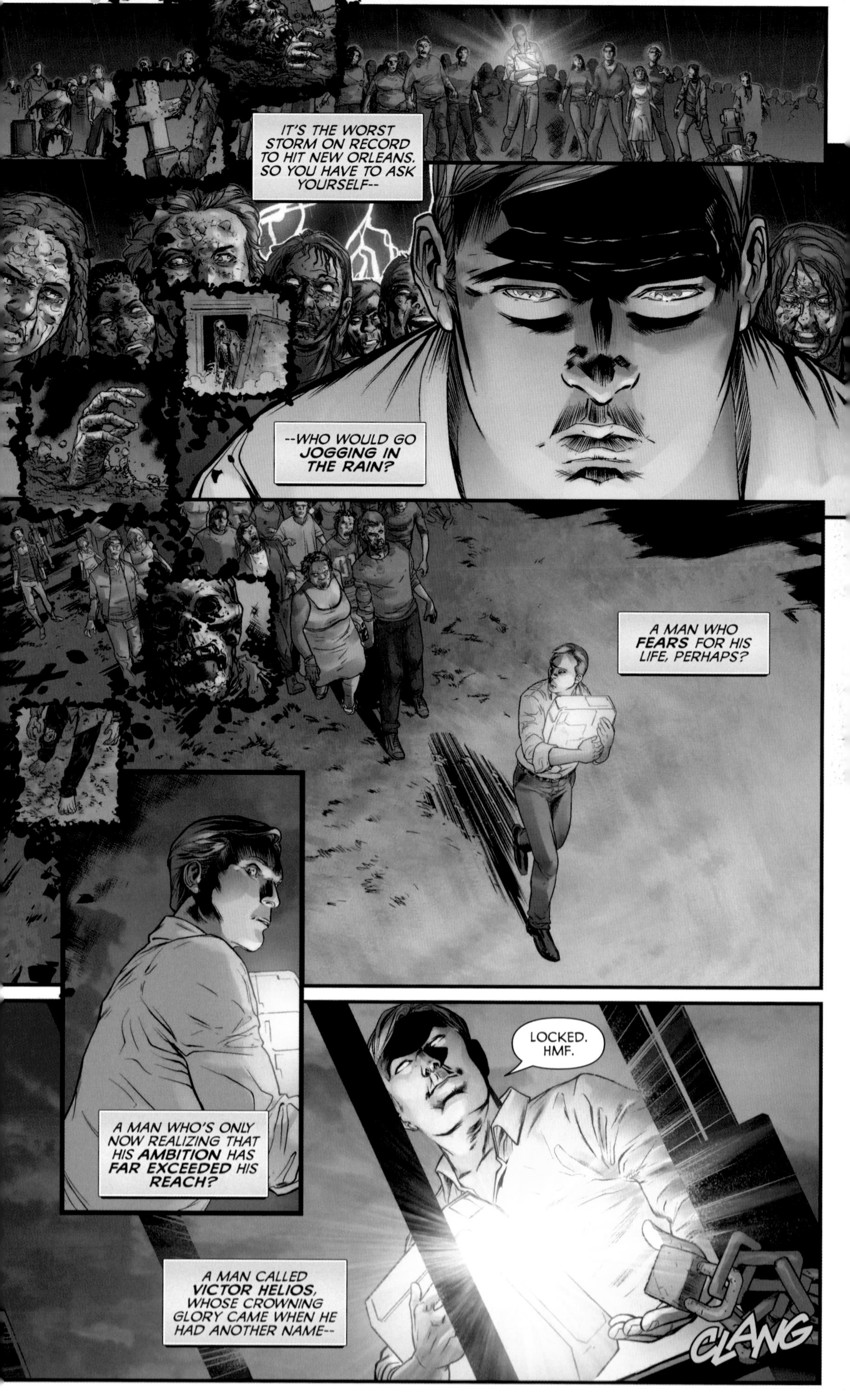
IT'S THE WORST STORM ON RECORD TO HIT NEW ORLEANS. SO YOU HAVE TO ASK YOURSELF--
--WHO WOULD GO JOGGING IN THE RAIN?
A MAN WHO FEARS FOR HIS LIFE, PERHAPS?
A MAN WHO'S ONLY NOW REALIZING THAT HIS AMBITION HAS FAR EXCEEDED HIS REACH?
A MAN CALLED VICTOR HELIOS, WHOSE CROWNING GLORY CAME WHEN HE HAD ANOTHER NAME--
LOCKED. HMF.
CLANG

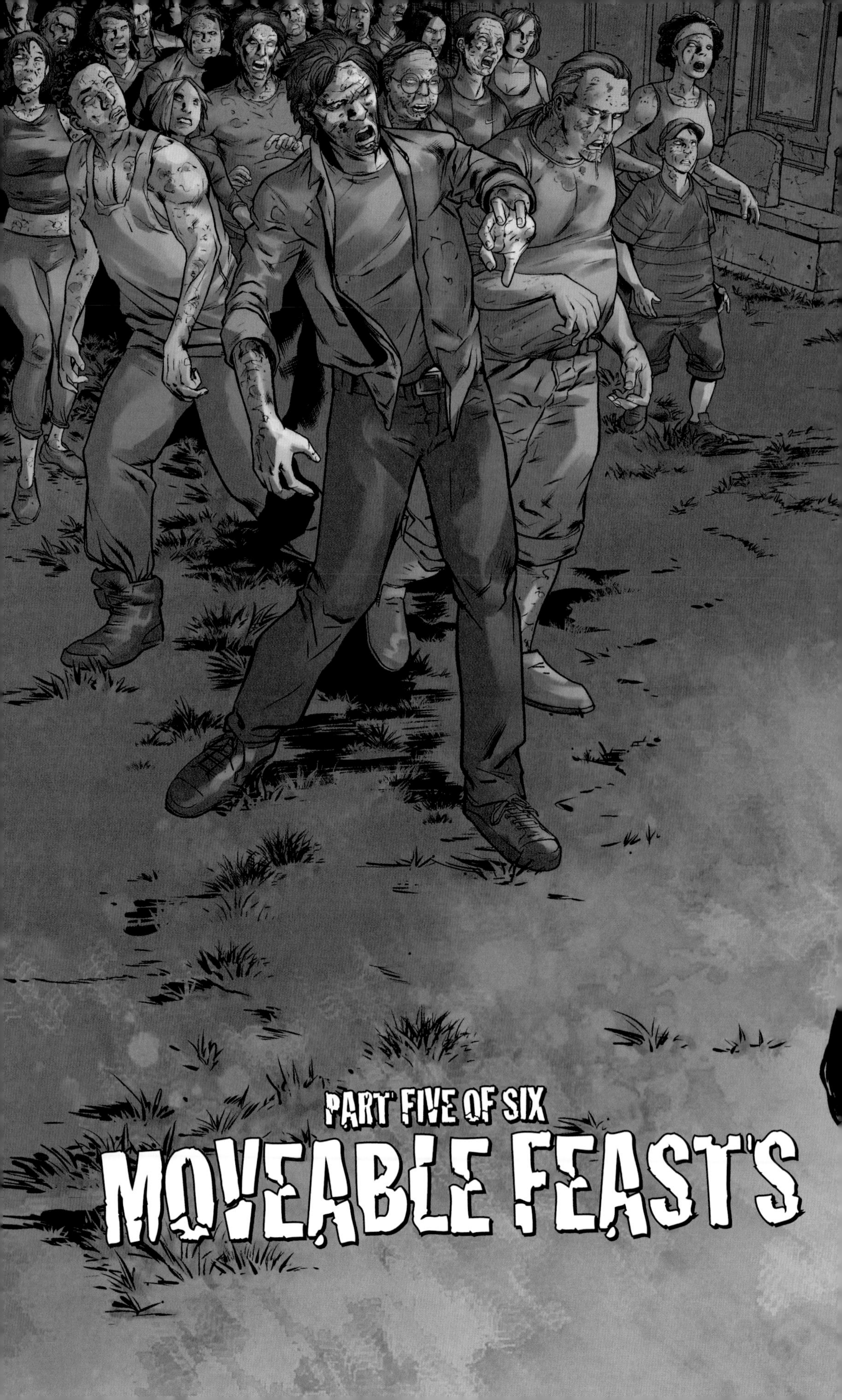
PART FIVE OF SIX
MOVEABLE FEASTS

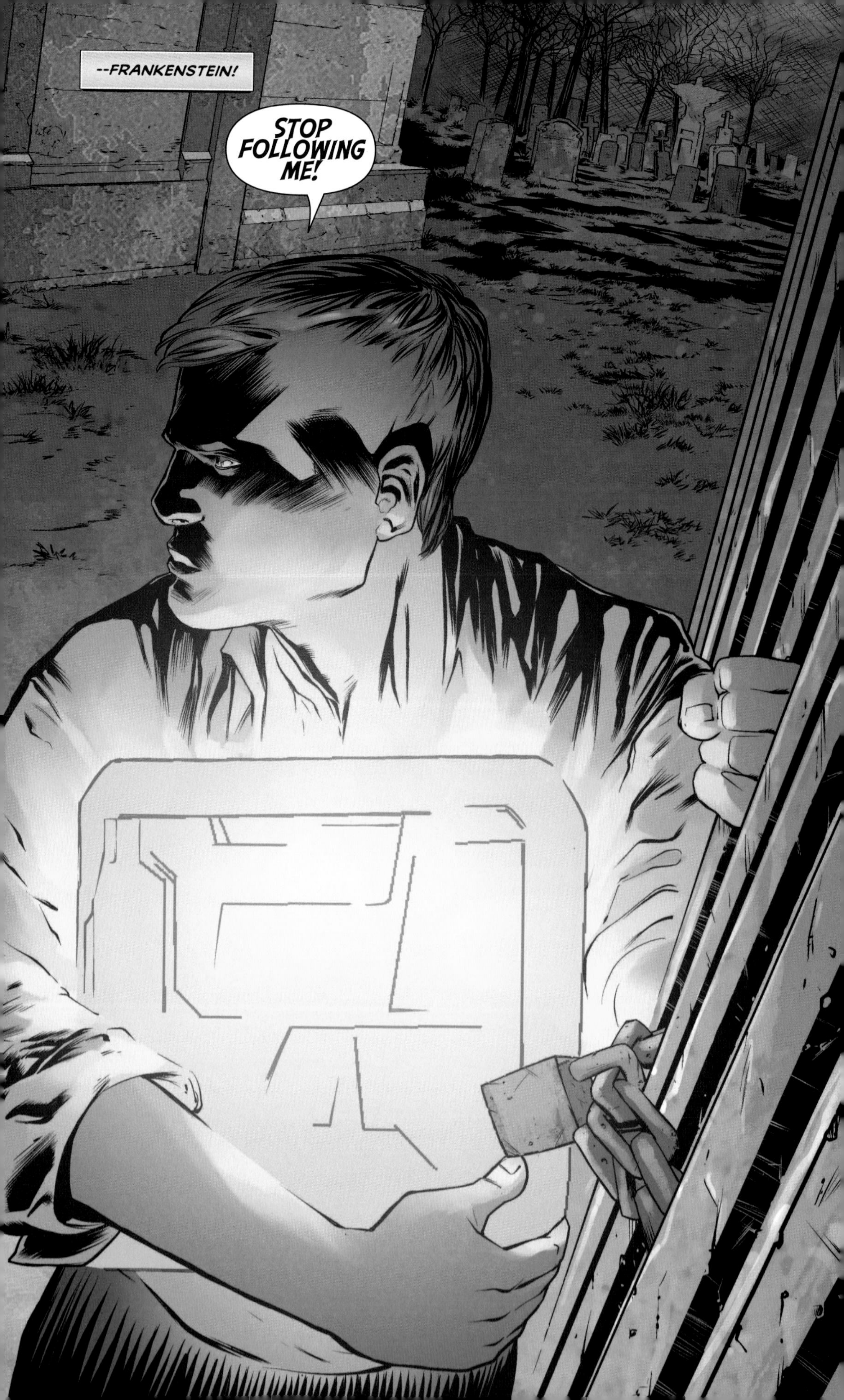
--FRANKENSTEIN!
STOP FOLLOWING ME!

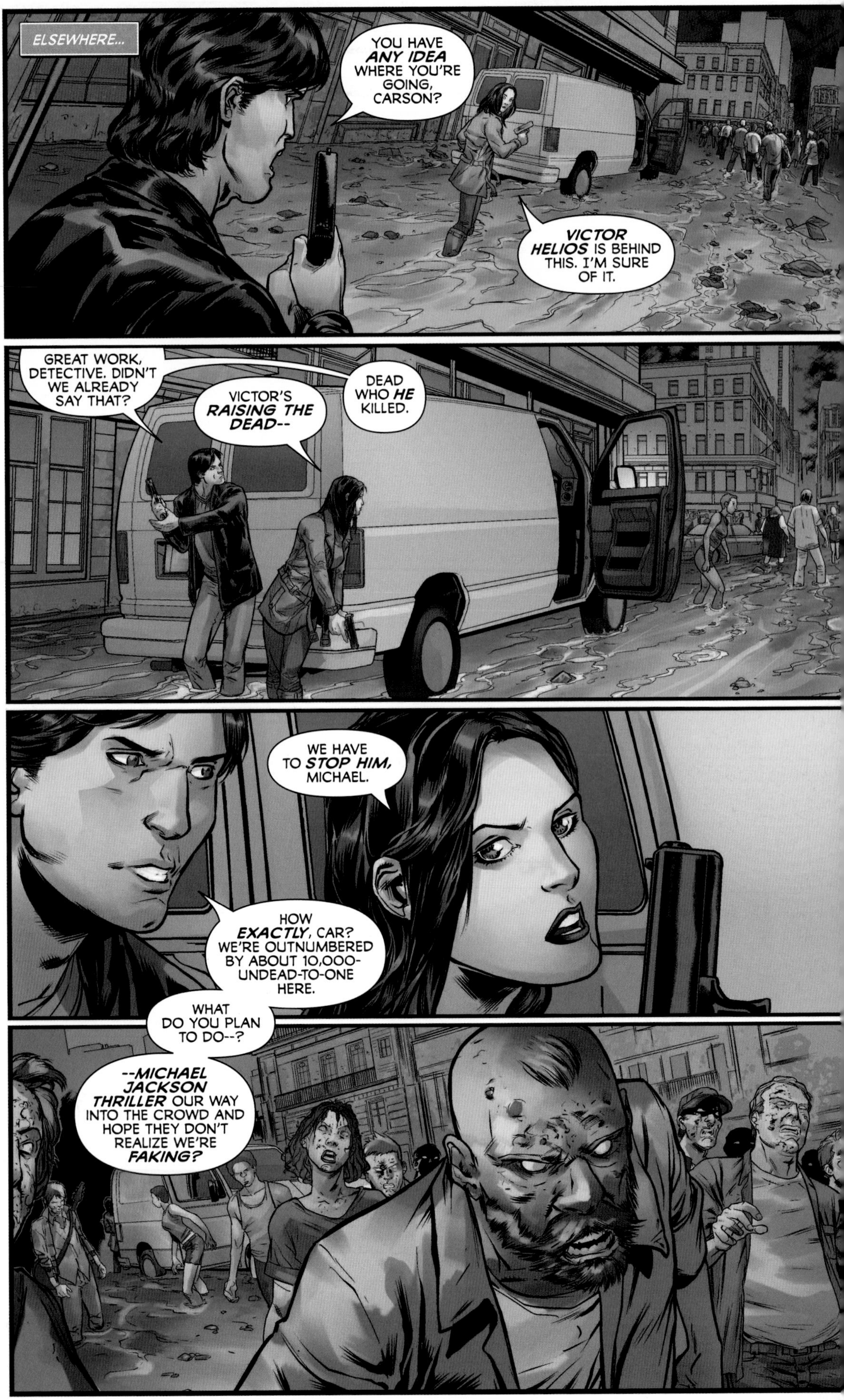

ELSEWHERE...
YOU HAVE ANY IDEA WHERE YOU'RE GOING, CARSON?
VICTOR HELIOS IS BEHIND THIS. I'M SURE OF IT.
GREAT WORK, DETECTIVE. DIDN'T WE ALREADY SAY THAT?
VICTOR'S RAISING THE DEAD--
DEAD WHO HE KILLED.
WE HAVE TO STOP HIM, MICHAEL.
HOW EXACTLY, CAR? WE'RE OUTNUMBERED BY ABOUT 10,000-UNDEAD-TO-ONE HERE.
WHAT DO YOU PLAN TO DO--?
--MICHAEL JACKSON THRILLER OUR WAY INTO THE CROWD AND HOPE THEY DON'T REALIZE WE'RE FAKING?

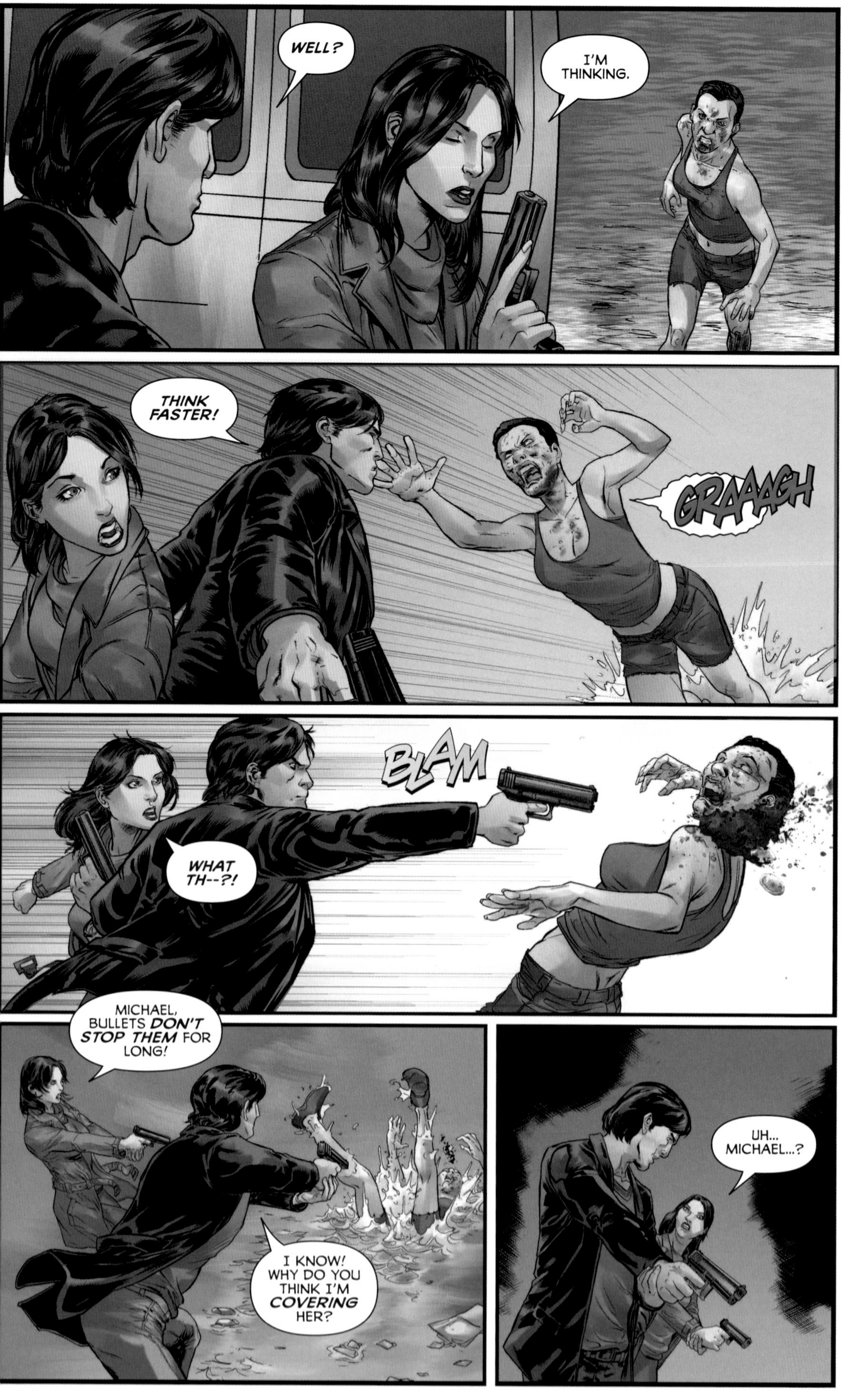
WELL?
I'M THINKING.
THINK FASTER!
GRAAAGH
BLAM
WHAT TH--?!
MICHAEL, BULLETS DON'T STOP THEM FOR LONG!
I KNOW! WHY DO YOU THINK I'M COVERING HER?
UH... MICHAEL...?

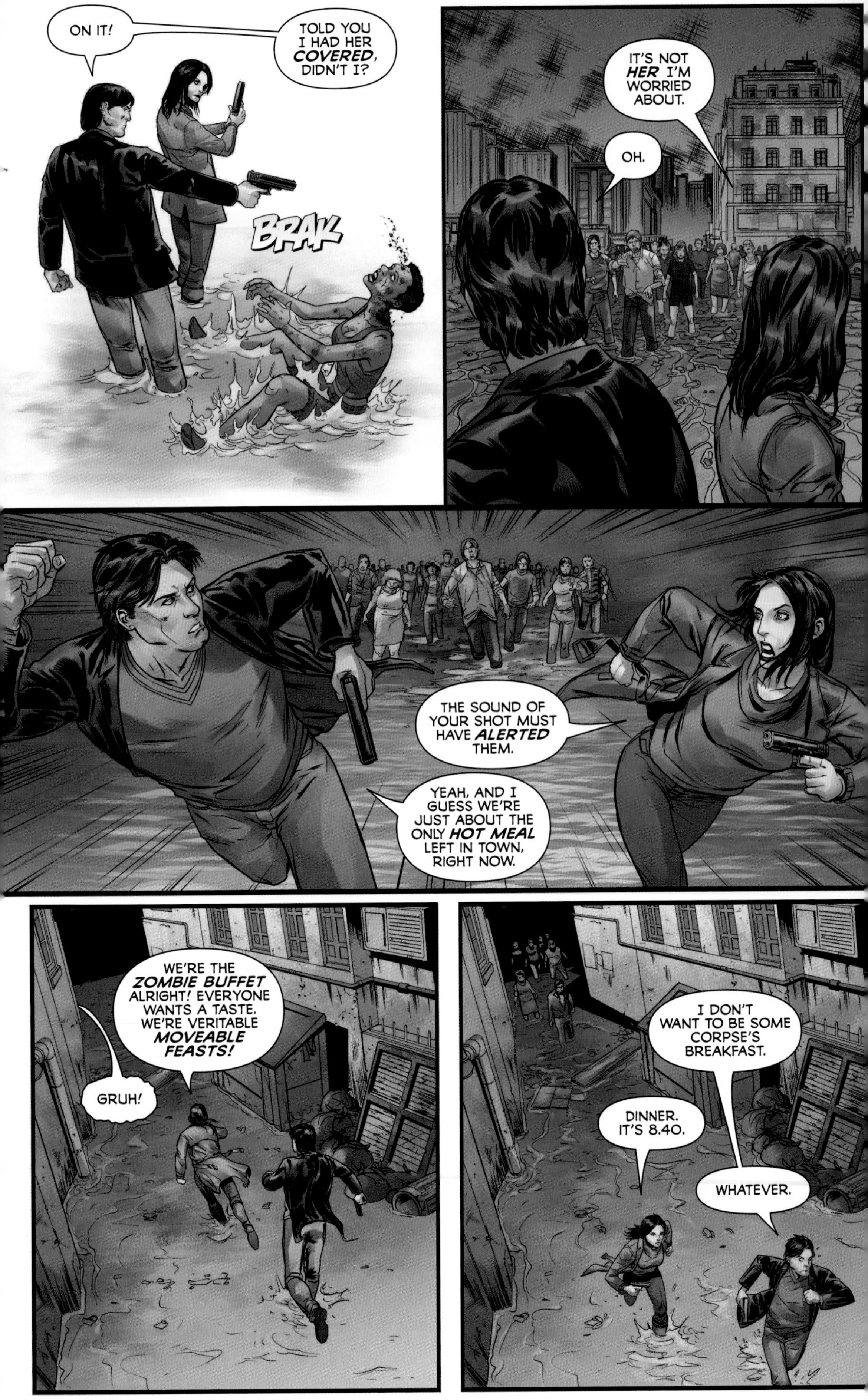
ON IT!
TOLD YOU I HAD HER COVERED, DIDN'T I?
BRAK
IT'S NOT HER I'M WORRIED ABOUT.
OH.
THE SOUND OF YOUR SHOT MUST HAVE ALERTED THEM.
YEAH, AND I GUESS WE'RE JUST ABOUT THE ONLY HOT MEAL LEFT IN TOWN, RIGHT NOW.
WE'RE THE ZOMBIE BUFFET ALRIGHT! EVERYONE WANTS A TASTE. WE'RE VERITABLE MOVEABLE FEASTS!
GRUH!
I DON'T WANT TO BE SOME CORPSE'S BREAKFAST.
DINNER. IT'S 8.40.
WHATEVER.

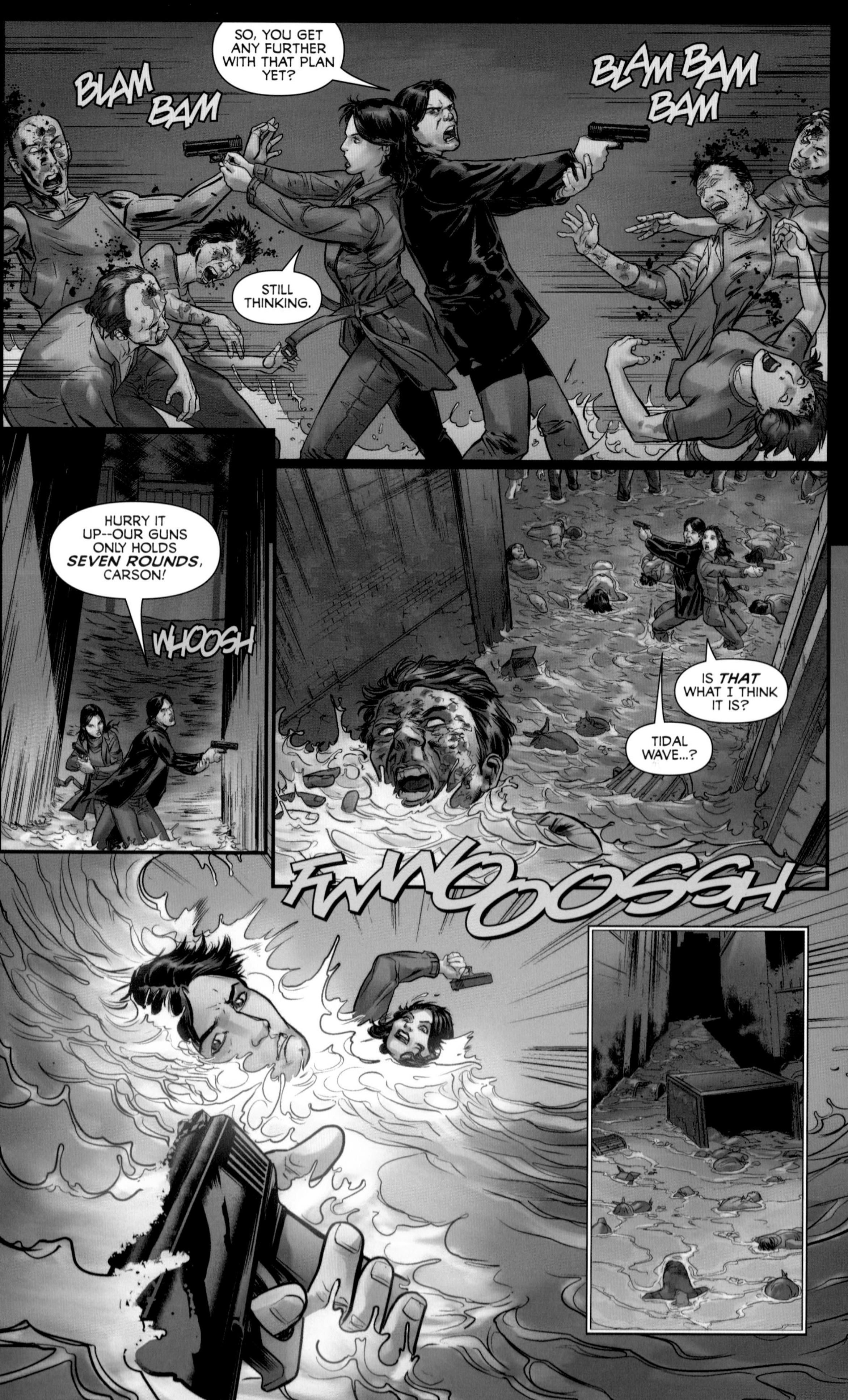
BLAM
BAM
SO, YOU GET ANY FURTHER WITH THAT PLAN YET?
BLAM BAM BAM
STILL THINKING.
HURRY IT UP--OUR GUNS ONLY HOLDS SEVEN ROUNDS, CARSON!
WHOOSH
IS THAT WHAT I THINK IT IS?
TIDAL WAVE...?
FWWOOOSSH

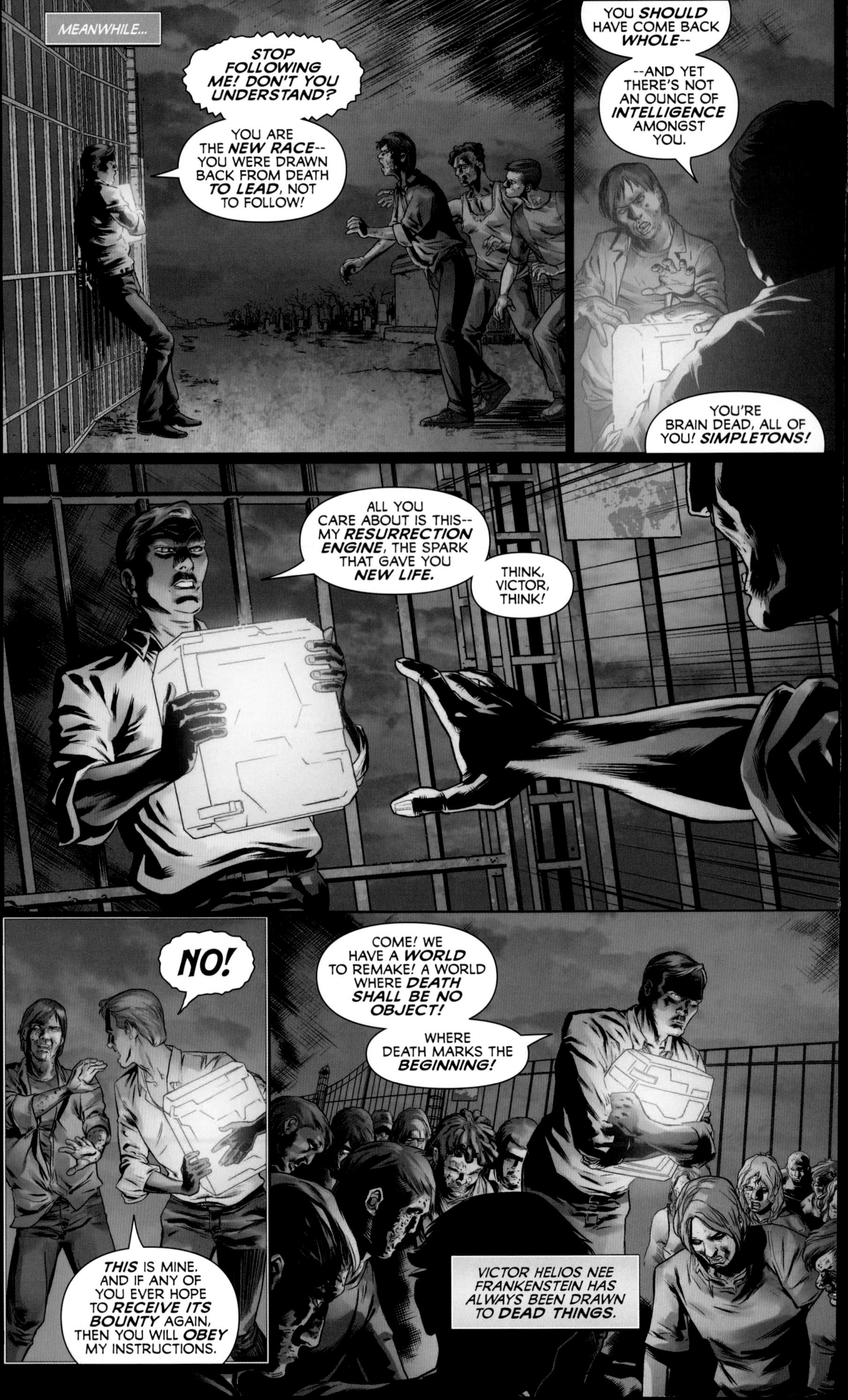

MEANWHILE...
STOP FOLLOWING ME! DON'T YOU UNDERSTAND?
YOU ARE THE NEW RACE-- YOU WERE DRAWN BACK FROM DEATH TO LEAD, NOT TO FOLLOW!
YOU SHOULD HAVE COME BACK WHOLE--
--AND YET THERE'S NOT AN OUNCE OF INTELLIGENCE AMONGST YOU.
YOU'RE BRAIN DEAD, ALL OF YOU! SIMPLETONS!
ALL YOU CARE ABOUT IS THIS-- MY RESURRECTION ENGINE, THE SPARK THAT GAVE YOU NEW LIFE.
THINK, VICTOR, THINK!
NO!
THIS IS MINE. AND IF ANY OF YOU EVER HOPE TO RECEIVE ITS BOUNTY AGAIN, THEN YOU WILL OBEY MY INSTRUCTIONS.
COME! WE HAVE A WORLD TO REMAKE! A WORLD WHERE DEATH SHALL BE NO OBJECT!
WHERE DEATH MARKS THE BEGINNING!
VICTOR HELIOS NEE FRANKENSTEIN HAS ALWAYS BEEN DRAWN TO DEAD THINGS.

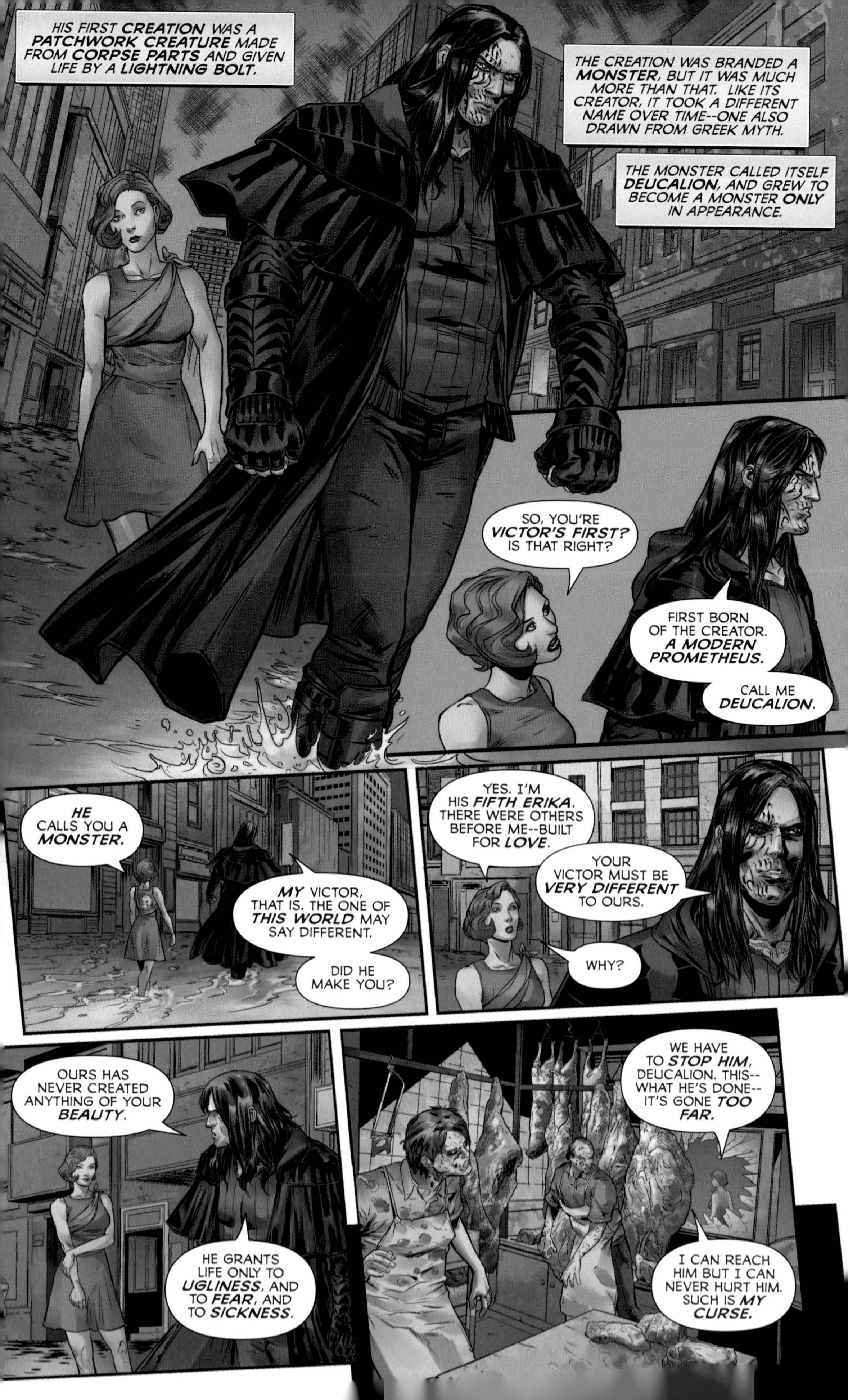
HIS FIRST CREATION WAS A PATCHWORK CREATURE MADE FROM CORPSE PARTS AND GIVEN LIFE BY A LIGHTNING BOLT.
THE CREATION WAS BRANDED A MONSTER, BUT IT WAS MUCH MORE THAN THAT. LIKE ITS CREATOR, IT TOOK A DIFFERENT NAME OVER TIME--ONE ALSO DRAWN FROM GREEK MYTH.
THE MONSTER CALLED ITSELF DEUCALION, AND GREW TO BECOME A MONSTER ONLY IN APPEARANCE.
SO, YOU'RE VICTOR'S FIRST? IS THAT RIGHT?
FIRST BORN OF THE CREATOR. A MODERN PROMETHEUS.
CALL ME DEUCALION.
HE CALLS YOU A MONSTER.
MY VICTOR, THAT IS. THE ONE OF THIS WORLD MAY SAY DIFFERENT.
DID HE MAKE YOU?
YES. I'M HIS FIFTH ERIKA. THERE WERE OTHERS BEFORE ME--BUILT FOR LOVE.
YOUR VICTOR MUST BE VERY DIFFERENT TO OURS.
WHY?
OURS HAS NEVER CREATED ANYTHING OF YOUR BEAUTY.
HE GRANTS LIFE ONLY TO UGLINESS, AND TO FEAR, AND TO SICKNESS.
WE HAVE TO STOP HIM, DEUCALION. THIS-- WHAT HE'S DONE-- IT'S GONE TOO FAR.
I CAN REACH HIM BUT I CAN NEVER HURT HIM. SUCH IS MY CURSE.

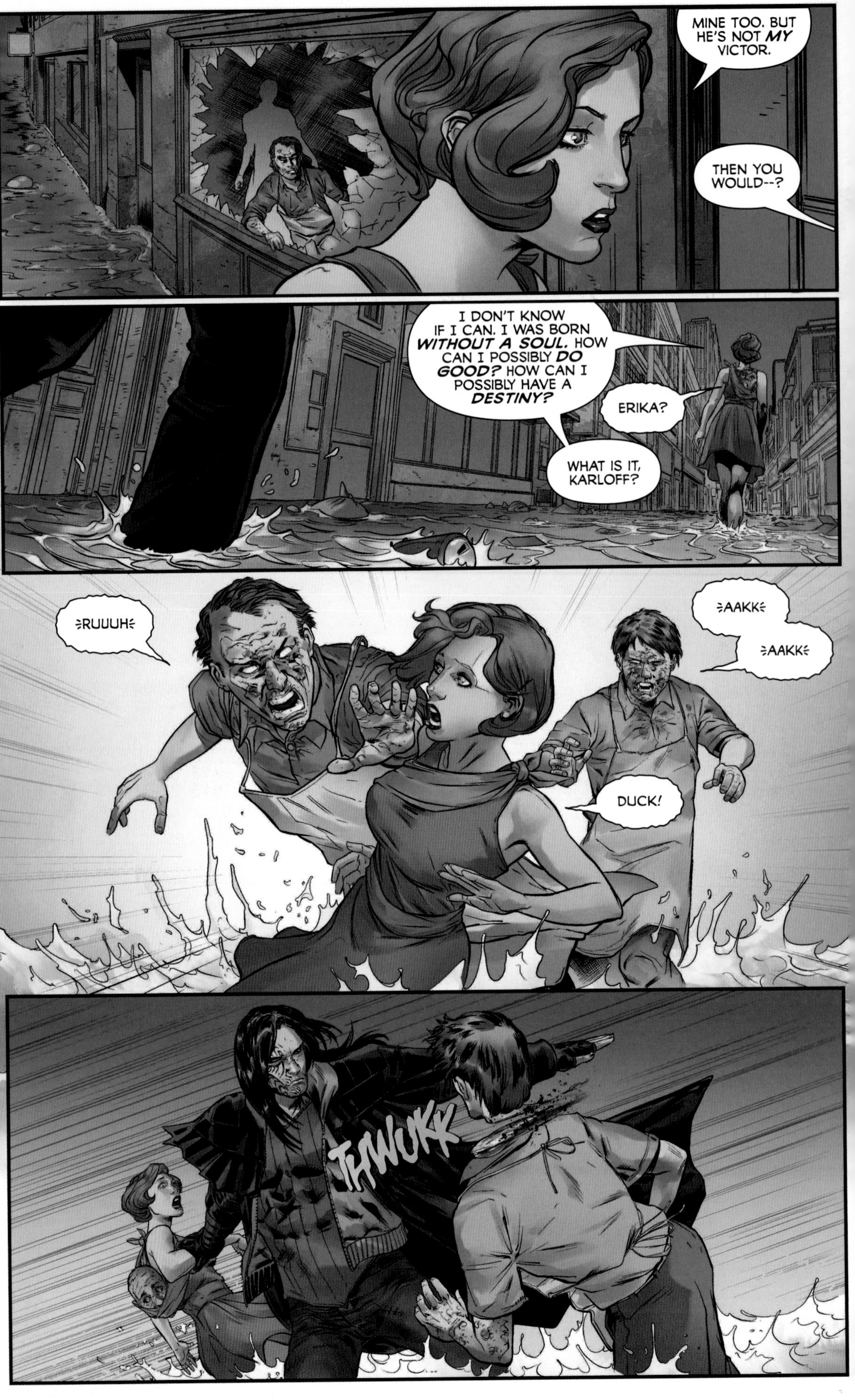
MINE TOO. BUT HE'S NOT *MY* VICTOR.
THEN YOU WOULD--?
I DON'T KNOW IF I CAN. I WAS BORN *WITHOUT A SOUL.* HOW CAN I POSSIBLY *DO GOOD?* HOW CAN I POSSIBLY HAVE A *DESTINY?*
ERIKA?
WHAT IS IT, KARLOFF?
RUUUH
AAKK
AAKK
DUCK!
THWUKK

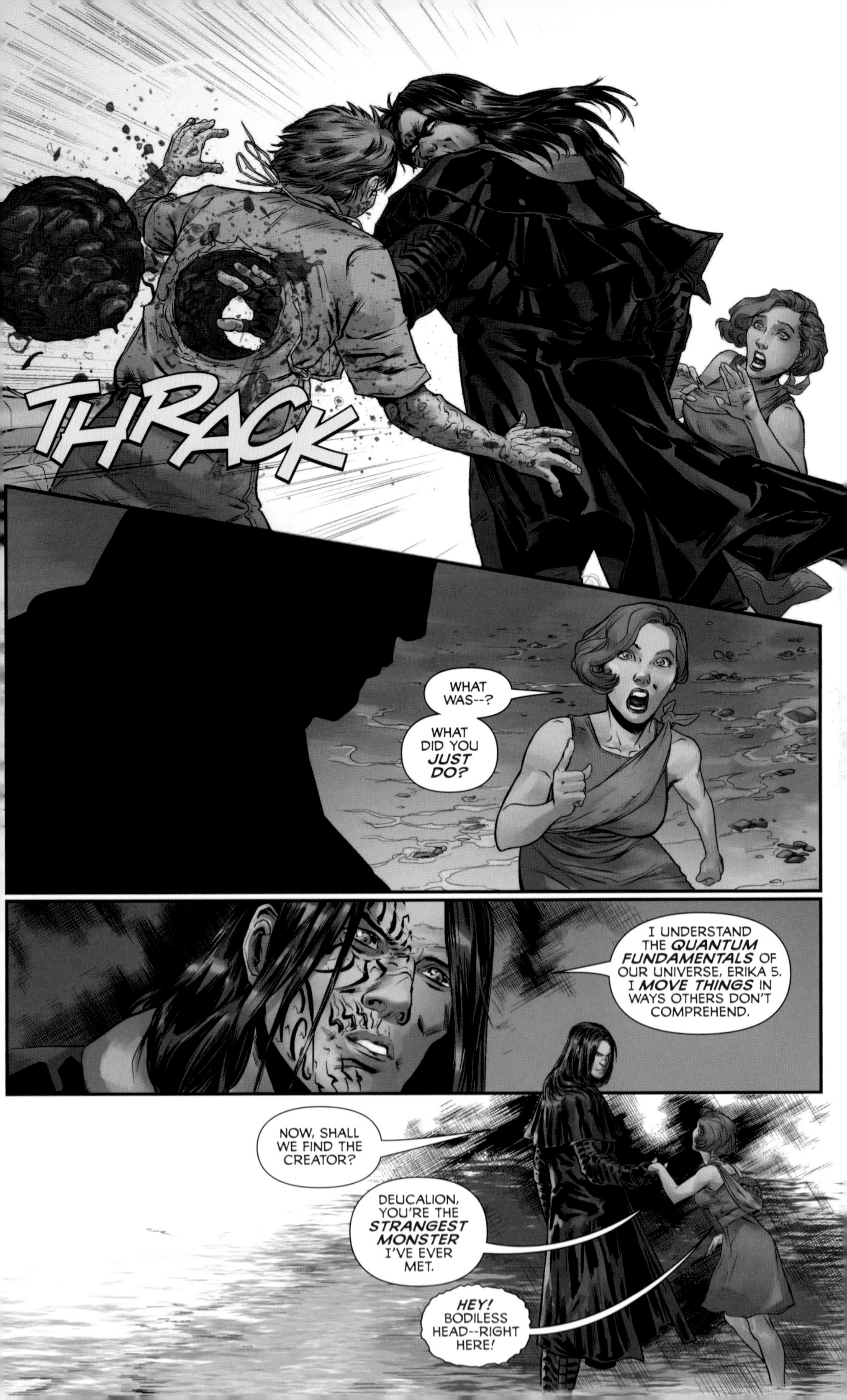
THRACK
WHAT WAS--?
WHAT DID YOU JUST DO?
I UNDERSTAND THE QUANTUM FUNDAMENTALS OF OUR UNIVERSE, ERIKA 5. I MOVE THINGS IN WAYS OTHERS DON'T COMPREHEND.
NOW, SHALL WE FIND THE CREATOR?
DEUCALION, YOU'RE THE STRANGEST MONSTER I'VE EVER MET.
HEY! BODILESS HEAD--RIGHT HERE!

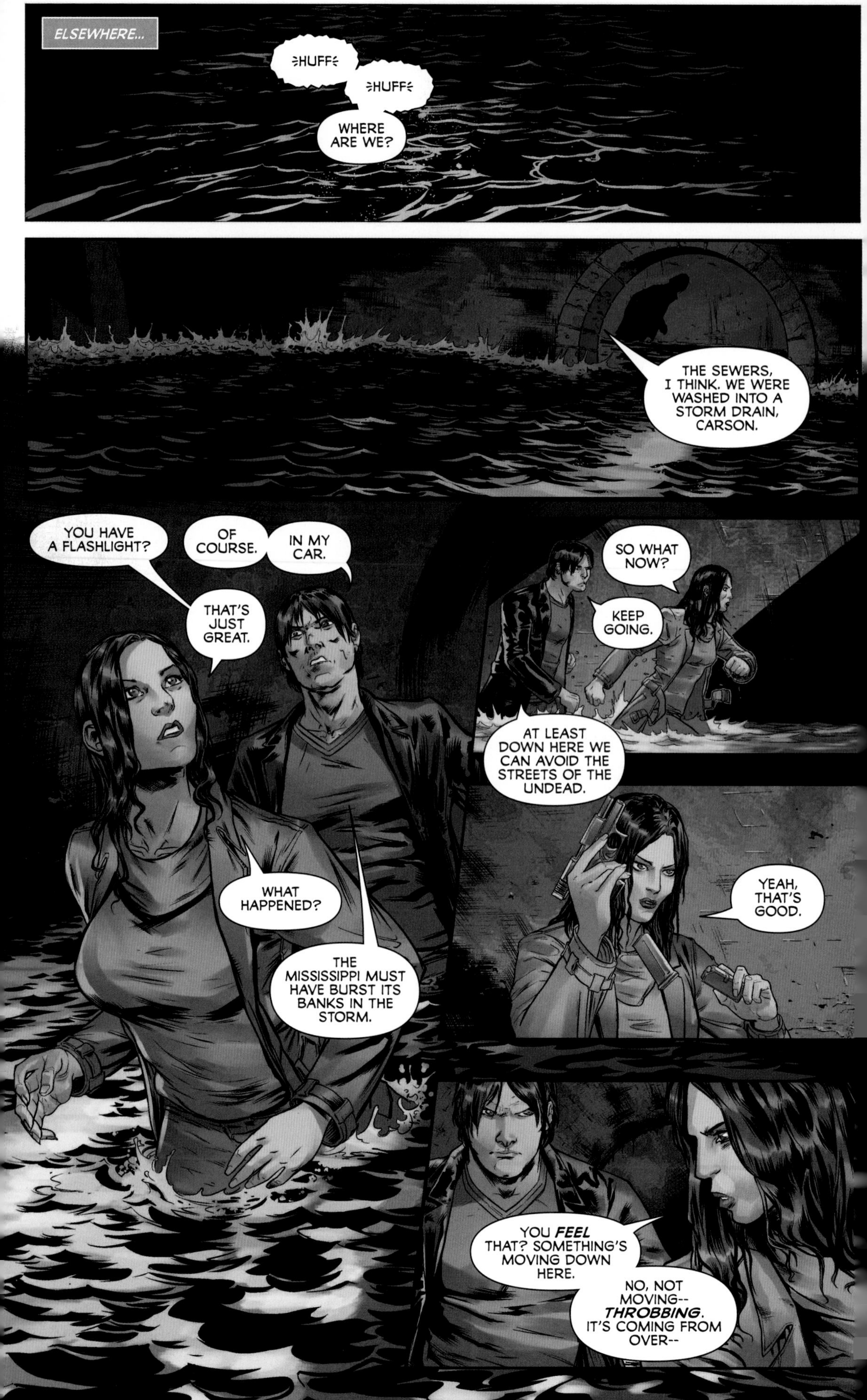
ELSEWHERE...
HUFF
HUFF
WHERE ARE WE?
THE SEWERS, I THINK. WE WERE WASHED INTO A STORM DRAIN, CARSON.
YOU HAVE A FLASHLIGHT?
OF COURSE.
IN MY CAR.
THAT'S JUST GREAT.
WHAT HAPPENED?
THE MISSISSIPPI MUST HAVE BURST ITS BANKS IN THE STORM.
SO WHAT NOW?
KEEP GOING.
AT LEAST DOWN HERE WE CAN AVOID THE STREETS OF THE UNDEAD.
YEAH, THAT'S GOOD.
YOU FEEL THAT? SOMETHING'S MOVING DOWN HERE.
NO, NOT MOVING-- THROBBING. IT'S COMING FROM OVER--

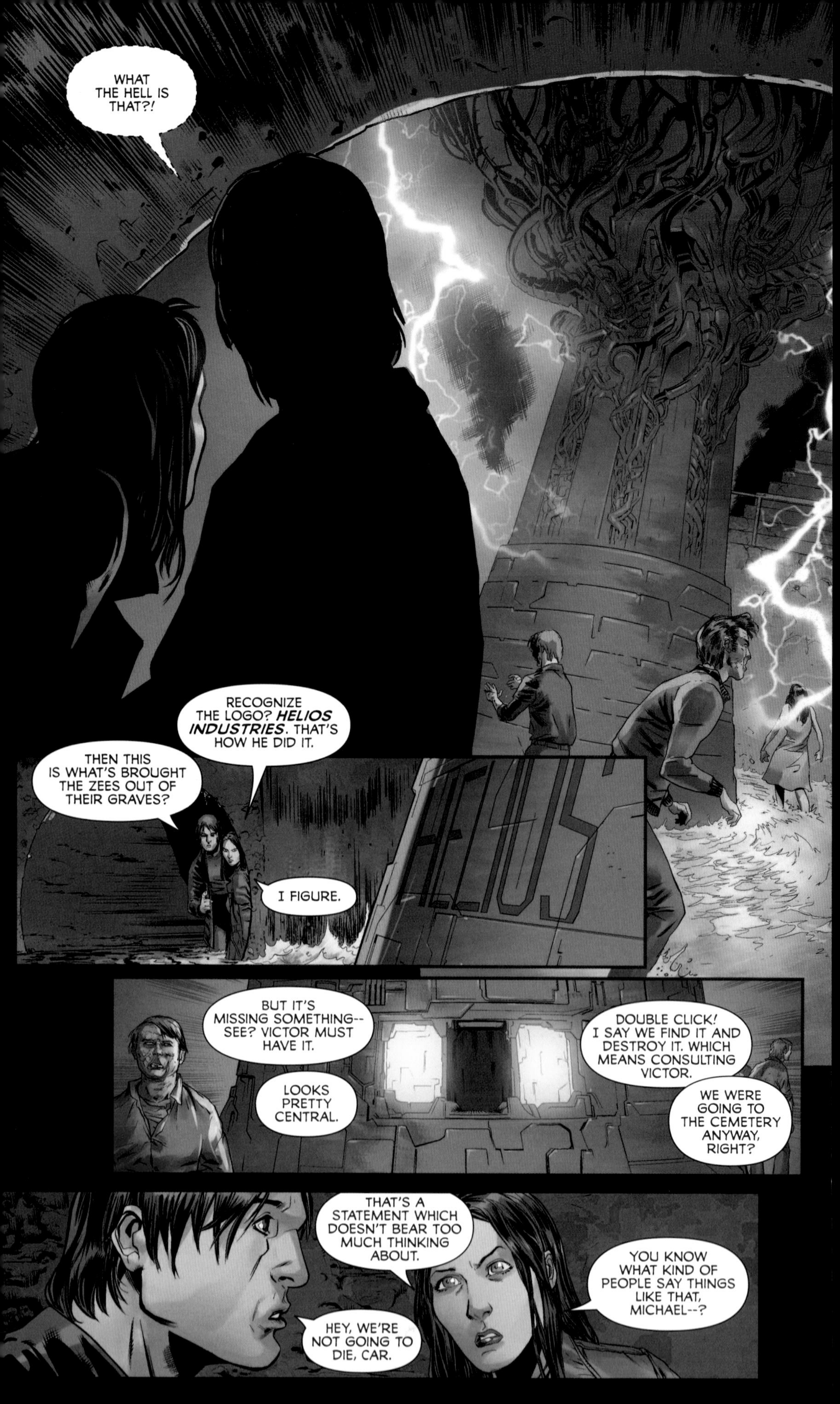
WHAT THE HELL IS THAT?!
RECOGNIZE THE LOGO? ***HELIOS INDUSTRIES***. THAT'S HOW HE DID IT.
THEN THIS IS WHAT'S BROUGHT THE ZEES OUT OF THEIR GRAVES?
I FIGURE.
HELIOS
BUT IT'S MISSING SOMETHING-- SEE? VICTOR MUST HAVE IT.
LOOKS PRETTY CENTRAL.
DOUBLE CLICK! I SAY WE FIND IT AND DESTROY IT. WHICH MEANS CONSULTING VICTOR.
WE WERE GOING TO THE CEMETERY ANYWAY, RIGHT?
THAT'S A STATEMENT WHICH DOESN'T BEAR TOO MUCH THINKING ABOUT.
YOU KNOW WHAT KIND OF PEOPLE SAY THINGS LIKE THAT, MICHAEL--?
HEY, WE'RE NOT GOING TO DIE, CAR.

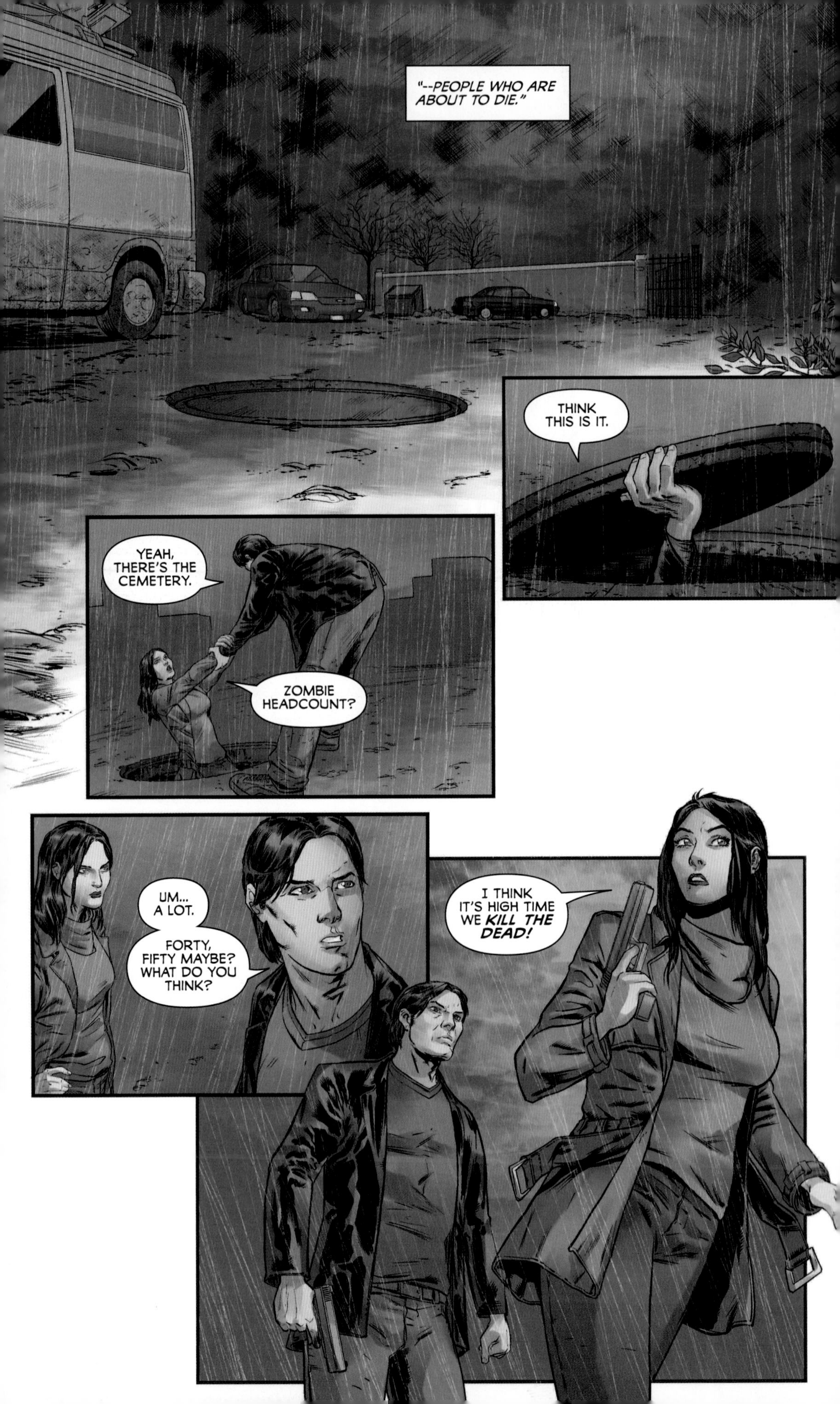
"--PEOPLE WHO ARE ABOUT TO DIE."
THINK THIS IS IT.
YEAH, THERE'S THE CEMETERY.
ZOMBIE HEADCOUNT?
UM... A LOT.
FORTY, FIFTY MAYBE? WHAT DO YOU THINK?
I THINK IT'S HIGH TIME WE *KILL THE DEAD!*

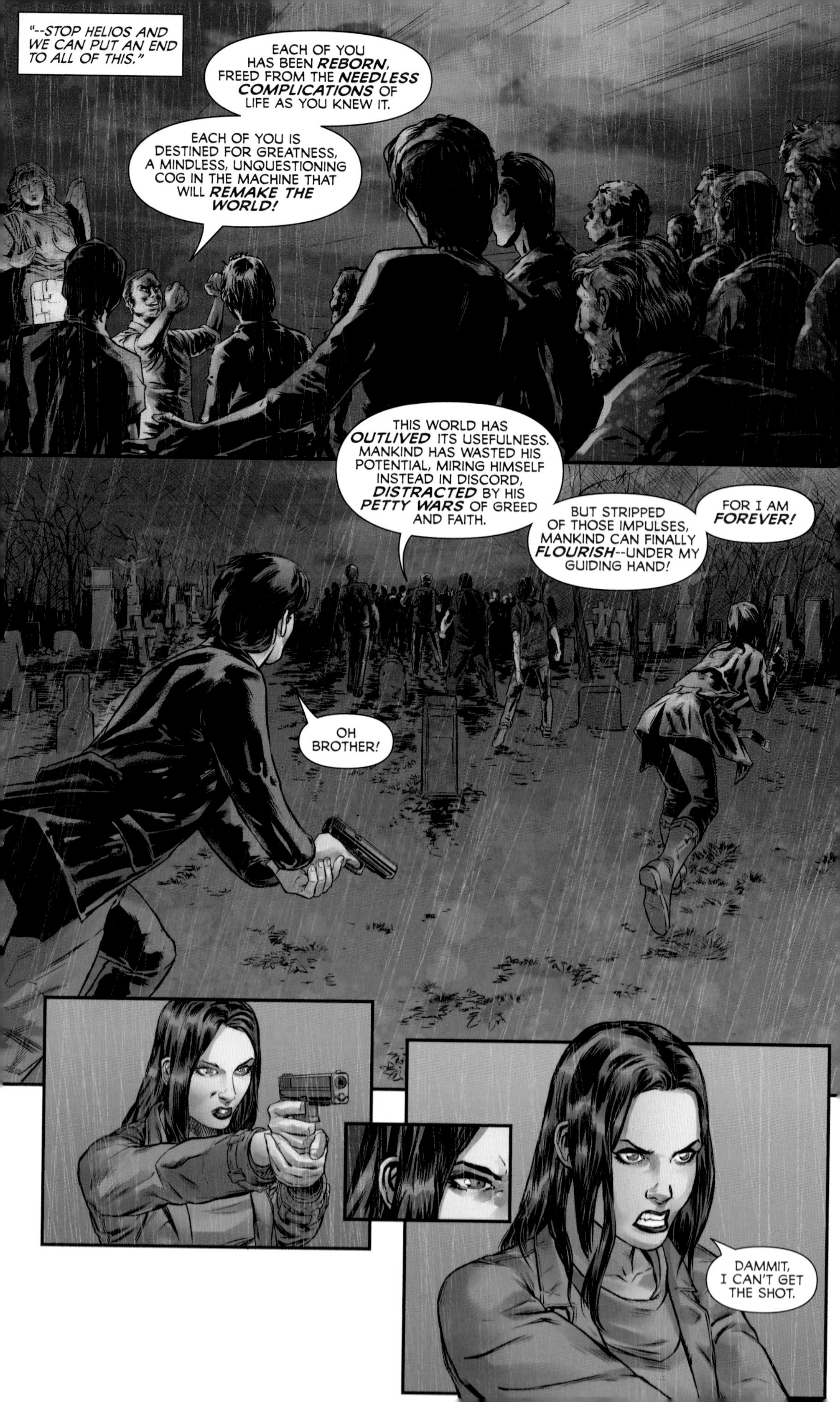
"--STOP HELIOS AND WE CAN PUT AN END TO ALL OF THIS."
EACH OF YOU HAS BEEN REBORN, FREED FROM THE NEEDLESS COMPLICATIONS OF LIFE AS YOU KNEW IT.
EACH OF YOU IS DESTINED FOR GREATNESS, A MINDLESS, UNQUESTIONING COG IN THE MACHINE THAT WILL REMAKE THE WORLD!
THIS WORLD HAS OUTLIVED ITS USEFULNESS. MANKIND HAS WASTED HIS POTENTIAL, MIRING HIMSELF INSTEAD IN DISCORD, DISTRACTED BY HIS PETTY WARS OF GREED AND FAITH.
BUT STRIPPED OF THOSE IMPULSES, MANKIND CAN FINALLY FLOURISH--UNDER MY GUIDING HAND!
FOR I AM FOREVER!
OH BROTHER!
DAMMIT, I CAN'T GET THE SHOT.

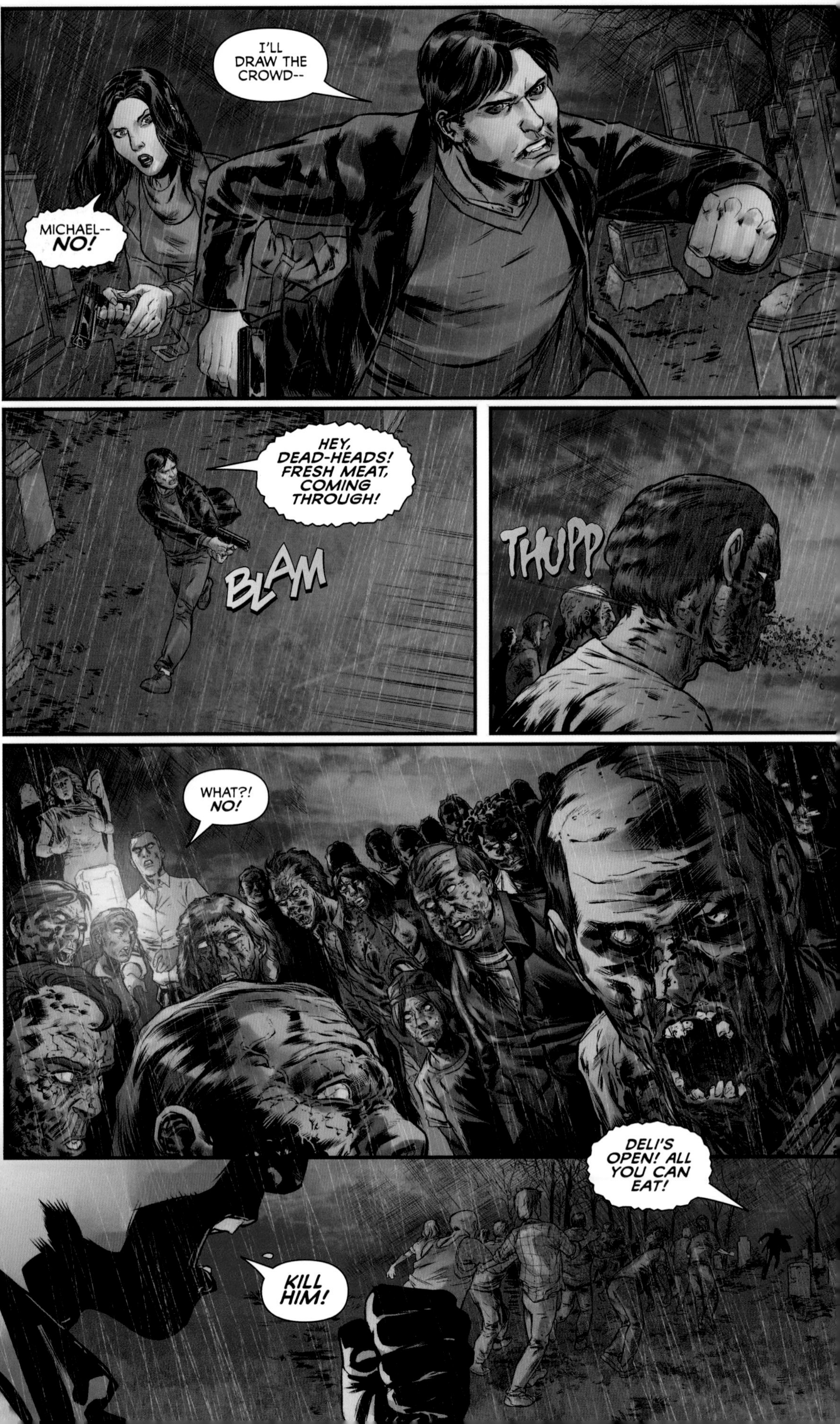
I'LL DRAW THE CROWD--
MICHAEL-- NO!
HEY, DEAD-HEADS! FRESH MEAT, COMING THROUGH!
BLAM
THUPP
WHAT?! NO!
DELI'S OPEN! ALL YOU CAN EAT!
KILL HIM!

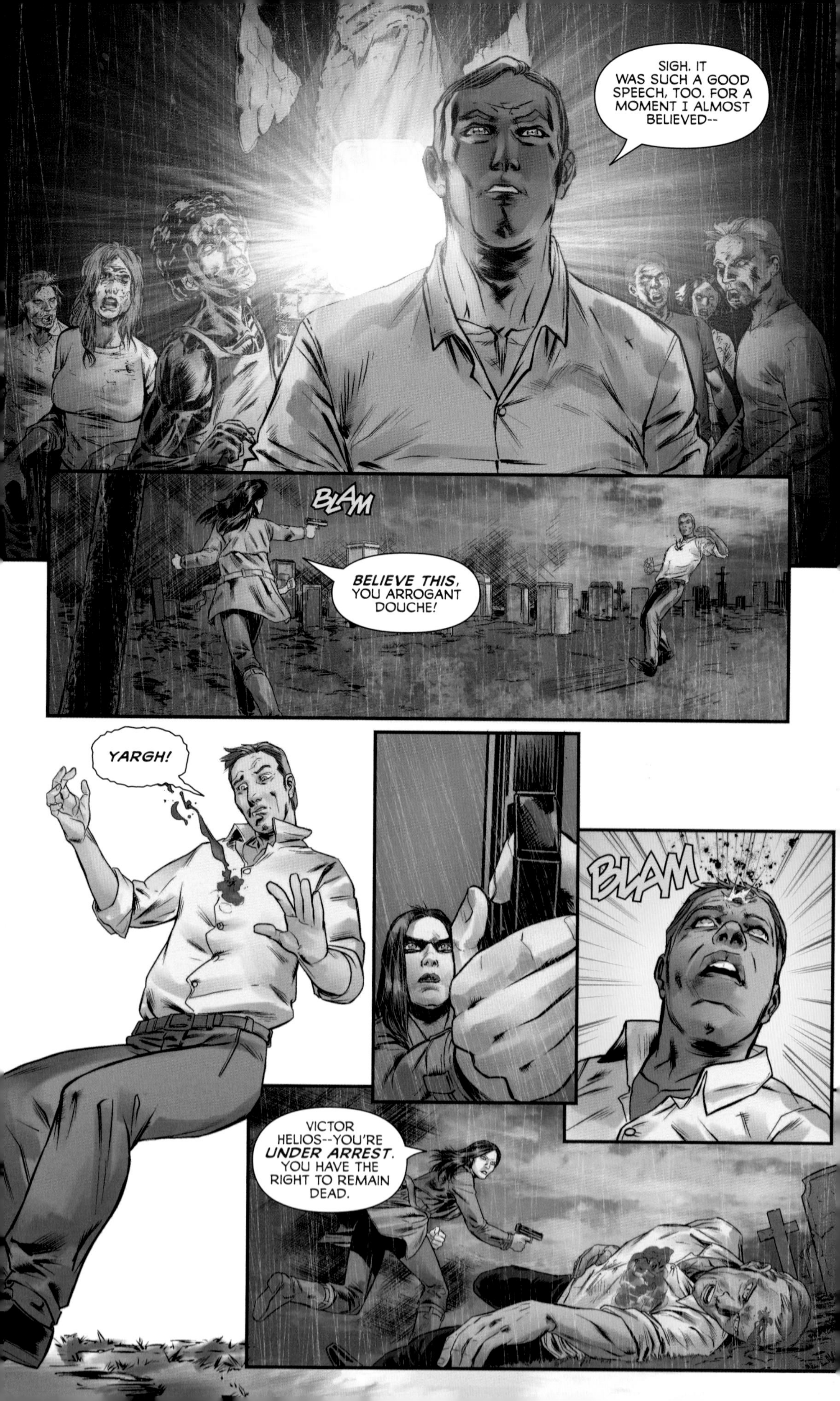
SIGH. IT WAS SUCH A GOOD SPEECH, TOO. FOR A MOMENT I ALMOST BELIEVED--
BLAM
BELIEVE THIS, YOU ARROGANT DOUCHE!
YARGH!
BLAM
VICTOR HELIOS--YOU'RE UNDER ARREST. YOU HAVE THE RIGHT TO REMAIN DEAD.

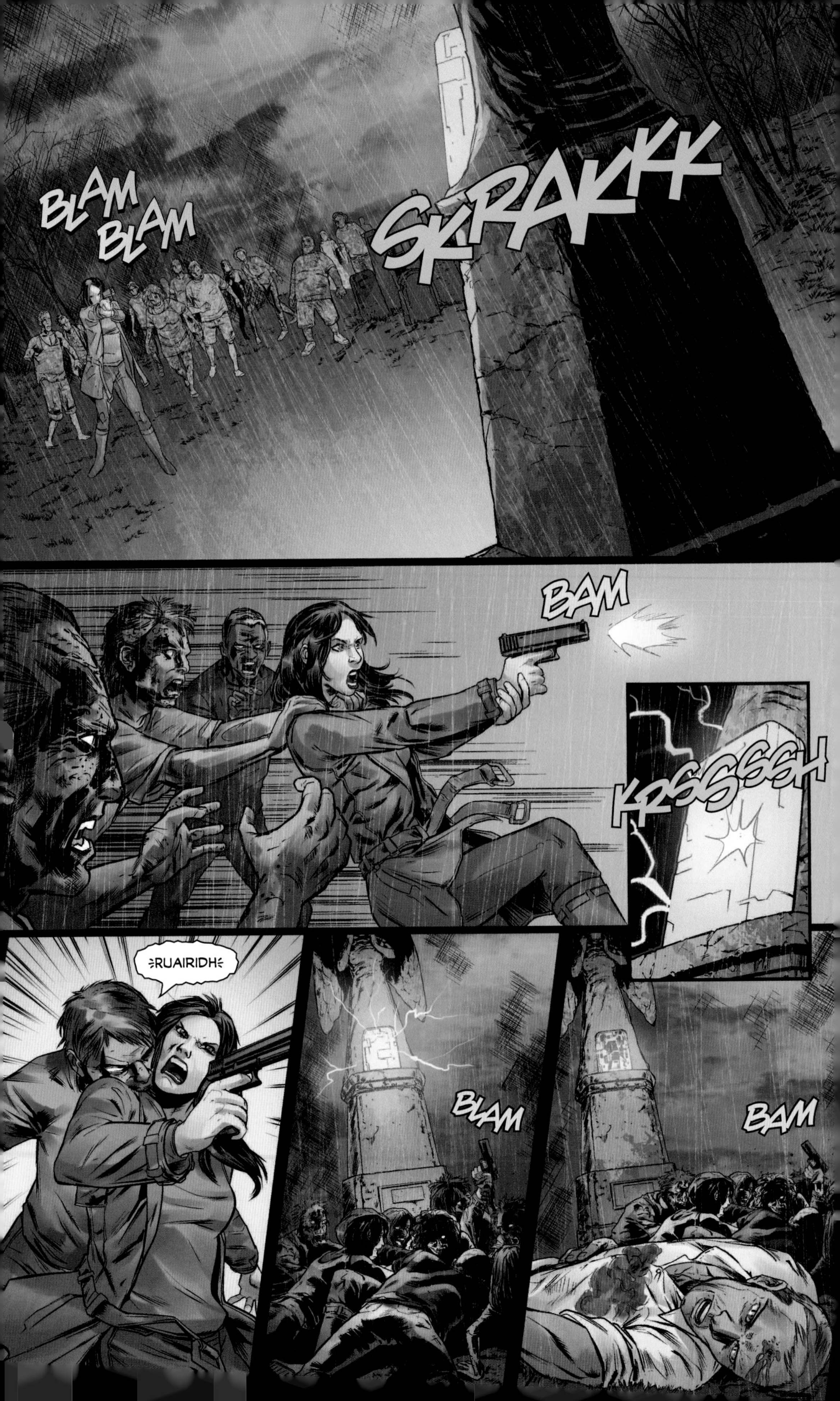
BLAM
BLAM
SKRAKK
BAM
KRSSSSH
RUAIRIDH
BLAM
BAM

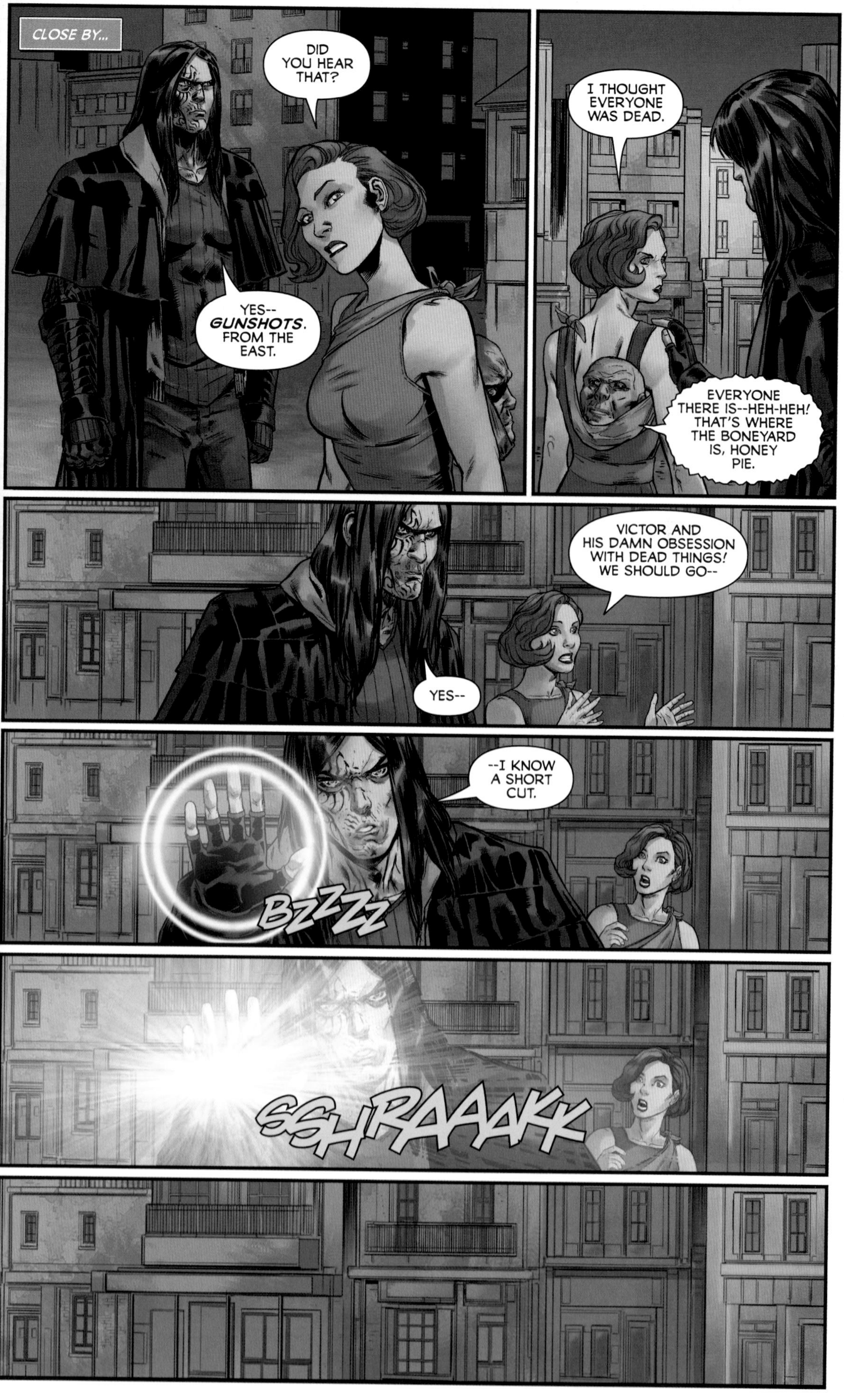
CLOSE BY...
DID YOU HEAR THAT?
YES-- *GUNSHOTS*. FROM THE EAST.
I THOUGHT EVERYONE WAS DEAD.
EVERYONE THERE IS--HEH-HEH! THAT'S WHERE THE BONEYARD IS, HONEY PIE.
VICTOR AND HIS DAMN OBSESSION WITH DEAD THINGS! WE SHOULD GO--
YES--
--I KNOW A SHORT CUT.
BZZZZ
SSHRAAAKK

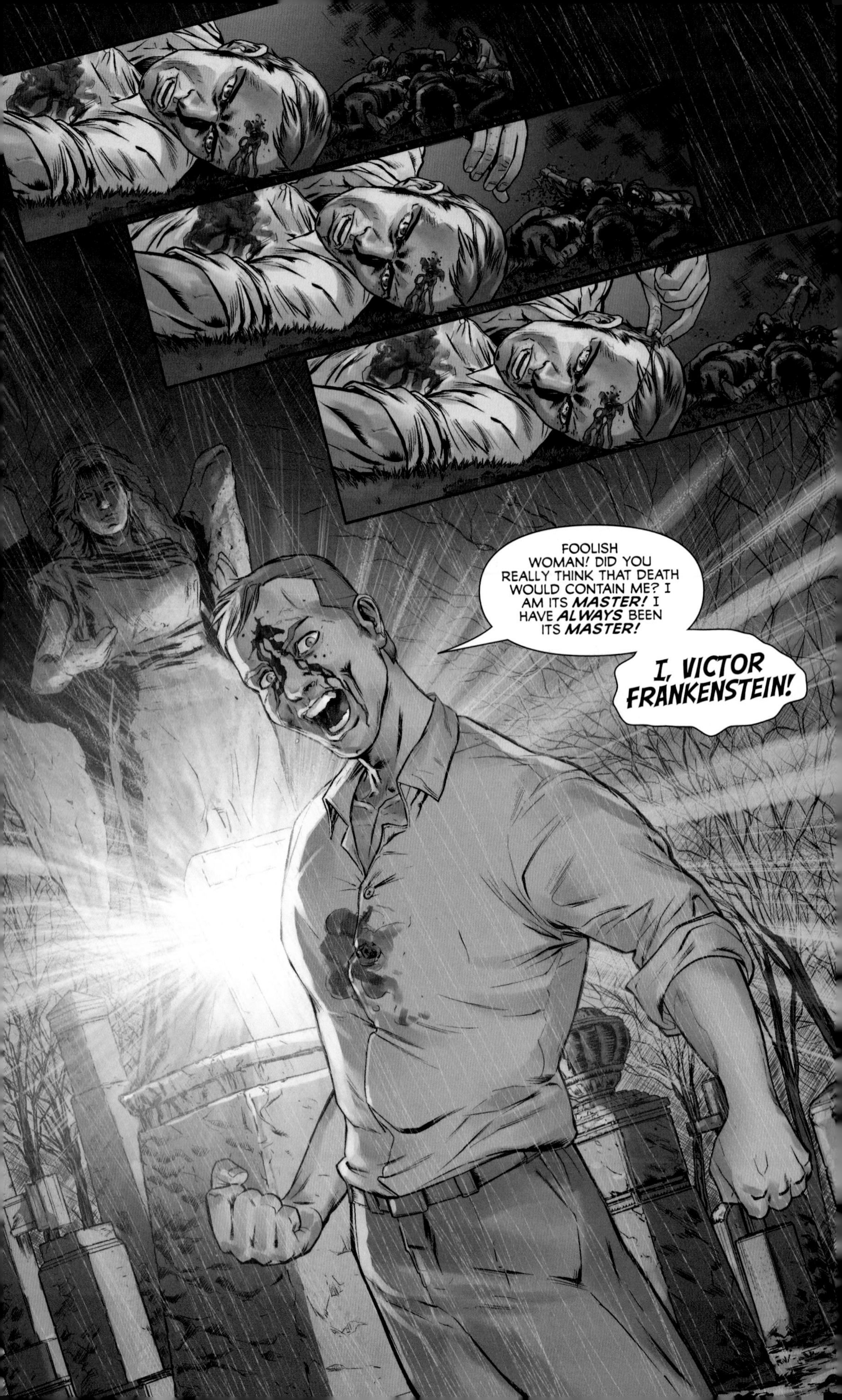
FOOLISH WOMAN! DID YOU REALLY THINK THAT DEATH WOULD CONTAIN ME? I AM ITS MASTER! I HAVE ALWAYS BEEN ITS MASTER!
I, VICTOR FRANKENSTEIN!

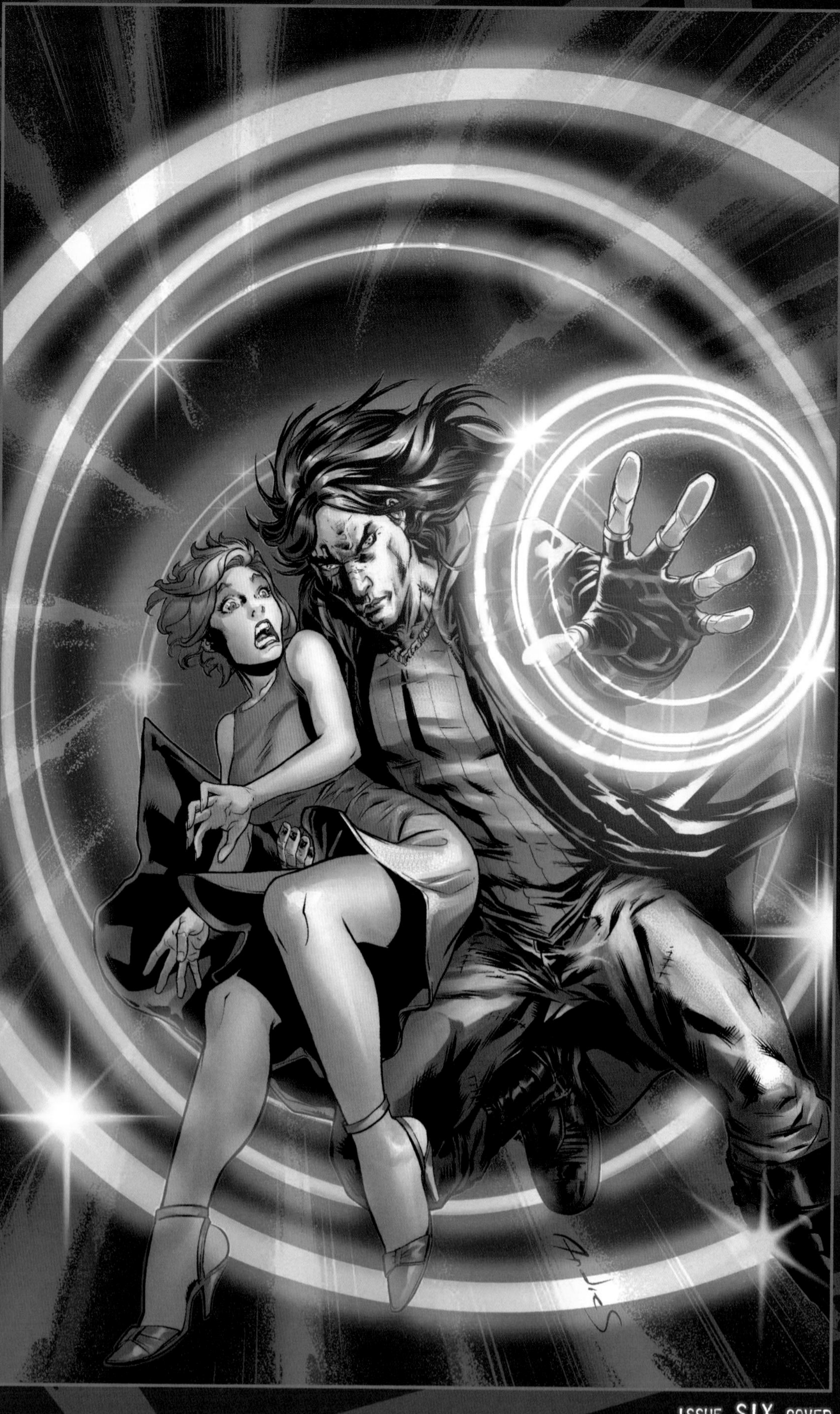

ISSUE SIX COVER
ART BY ANDRES PONCE COLORS BY MOHAN

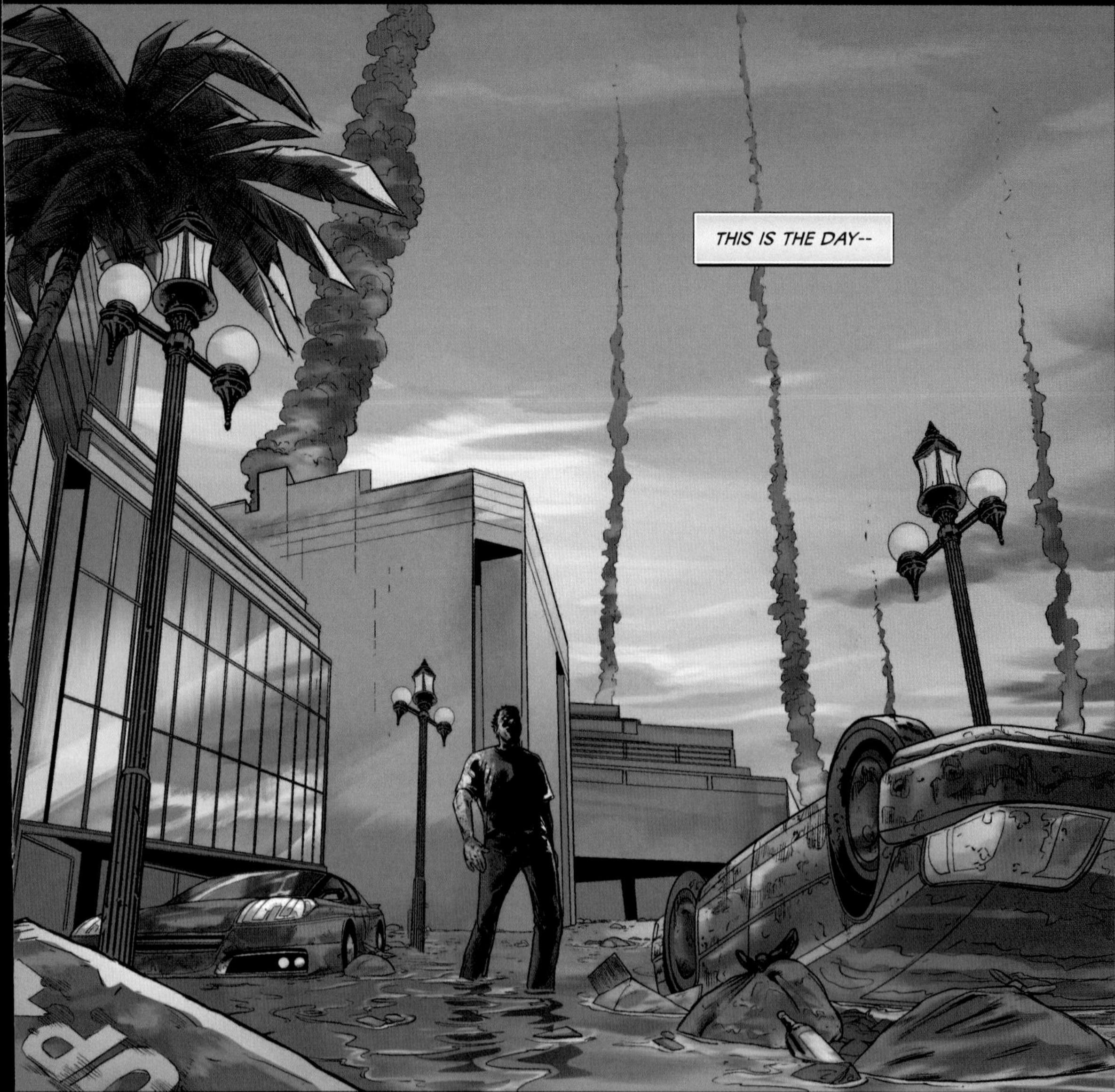
THIS IS THE DAY--

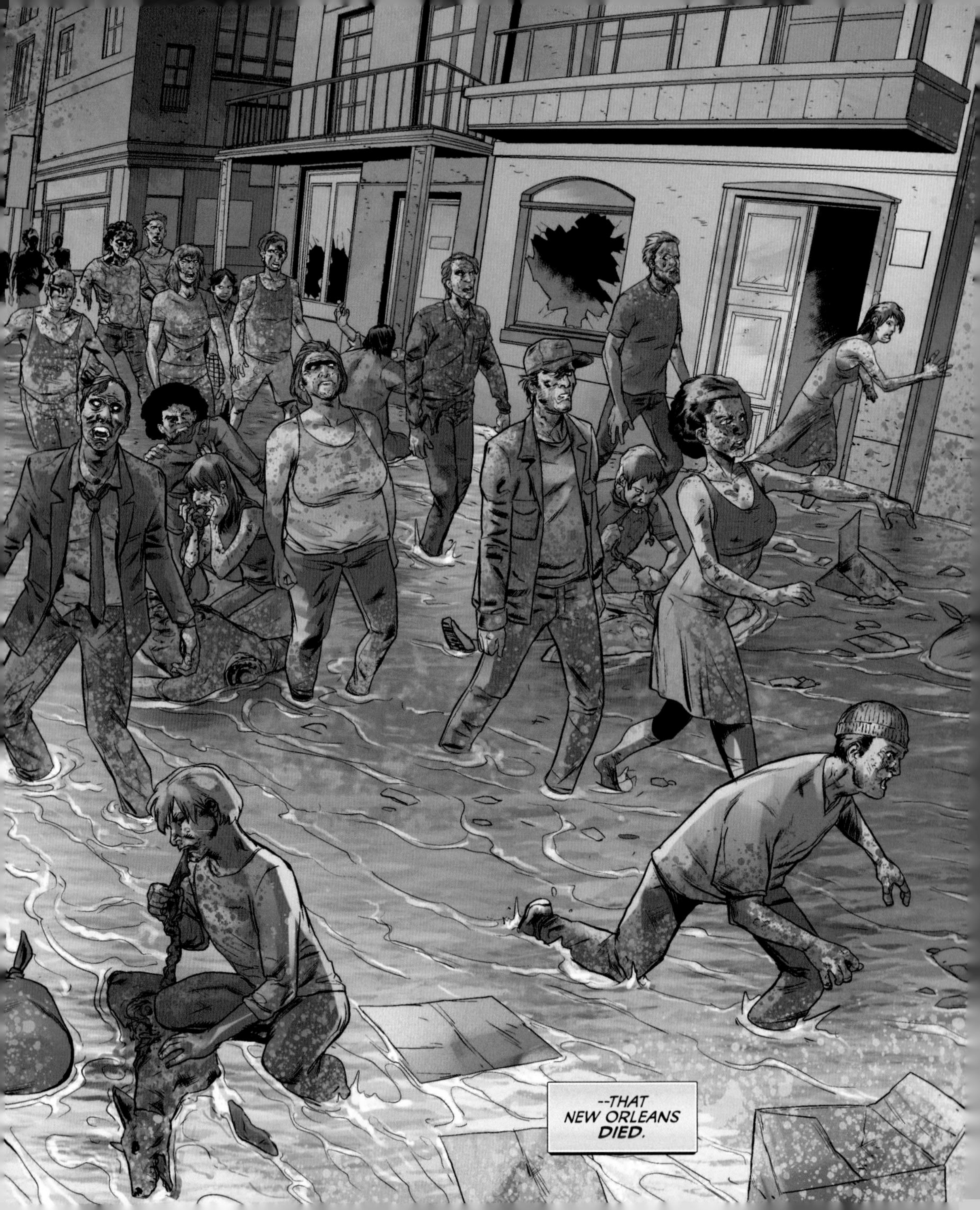
--THAT
NEW ORLEANS
DIED.

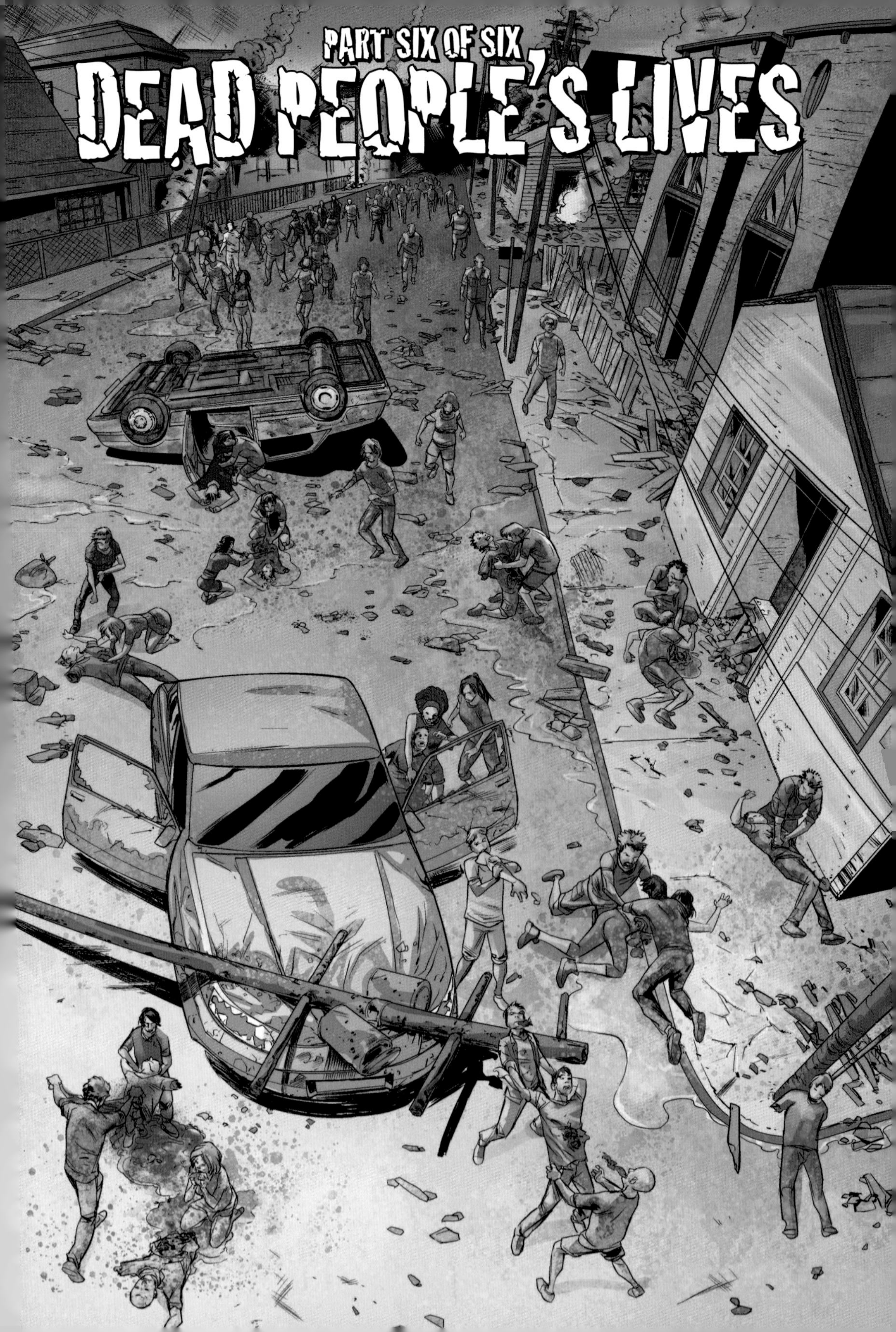
PART SIX OF SIX
DEAD PEOPLE'S LIVES

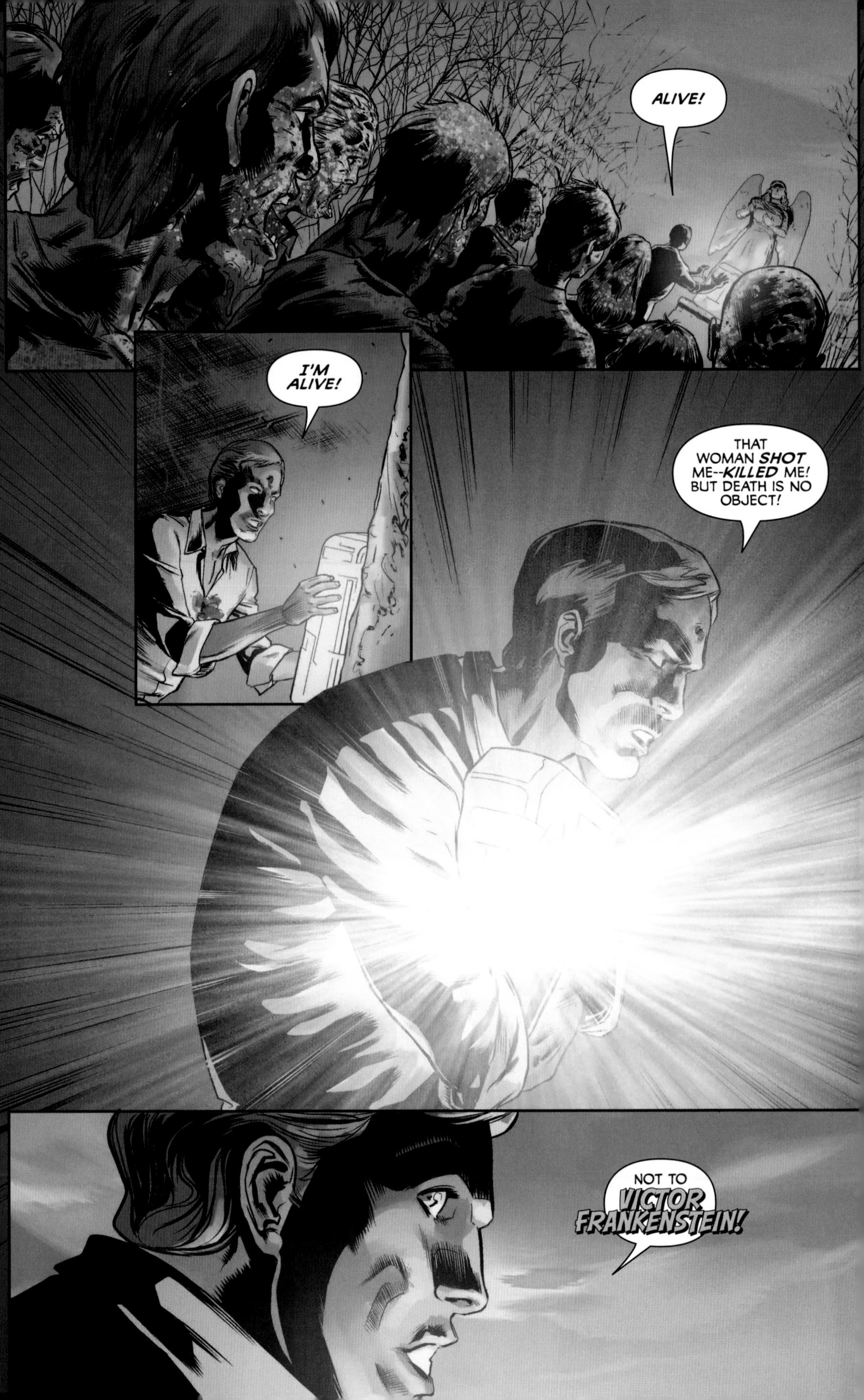
ALIVE!
I'M ALIVE!
THAT WOMAN SHOT ME--KILLED ME! BUT DEATH IS NO OBJECT!
NOT TO VICTOR FRANKENSTEIN!

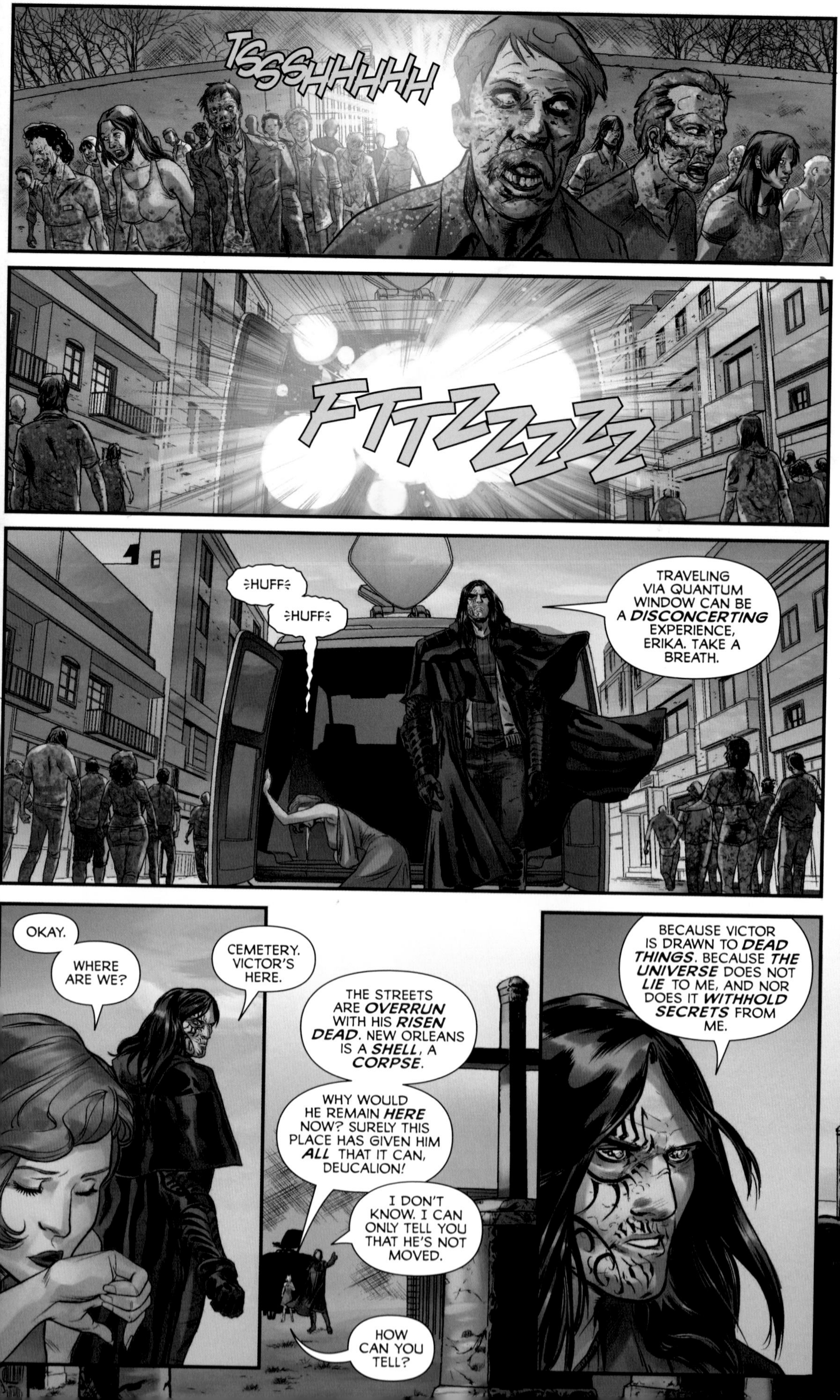
TSSSHHHHH
FTTZZZZZZ
⫶HUFF⫶
⫶HUFF⫶
TRAVELING VIA QUANTUM WINDOW CAN BE A DISCONCERTING EXPERIENCE, ERIKA. TAKE A BREATH.
OKAY.
WHERE ARE WE?
CEMETERY. VICTOR'S HERE.
THE STREETS ARE OVERRUN WITH HIS RISEN DEAD. NEW ORLEANS IS A SHELL, A CORPSE.
WHY WOULD HE REMAIN HERE NOW? SURELY THIS PLACE HAS GIVEN HIM ALL THAT IT CAN, DEUCALION!
I DON'T KNOW. I CAN ONLY TELL YOU THAT HE'S NOT MOVED.
HOW CAN YOU TELL?
BECAUSE VICTOR IS DRAWN TO DEAD THINGS. BECAUSE THE UNIVERSE DOES NOT LIE TO ME, AND NOR DOES IT WITHHOLD SECRETS FROM ME.

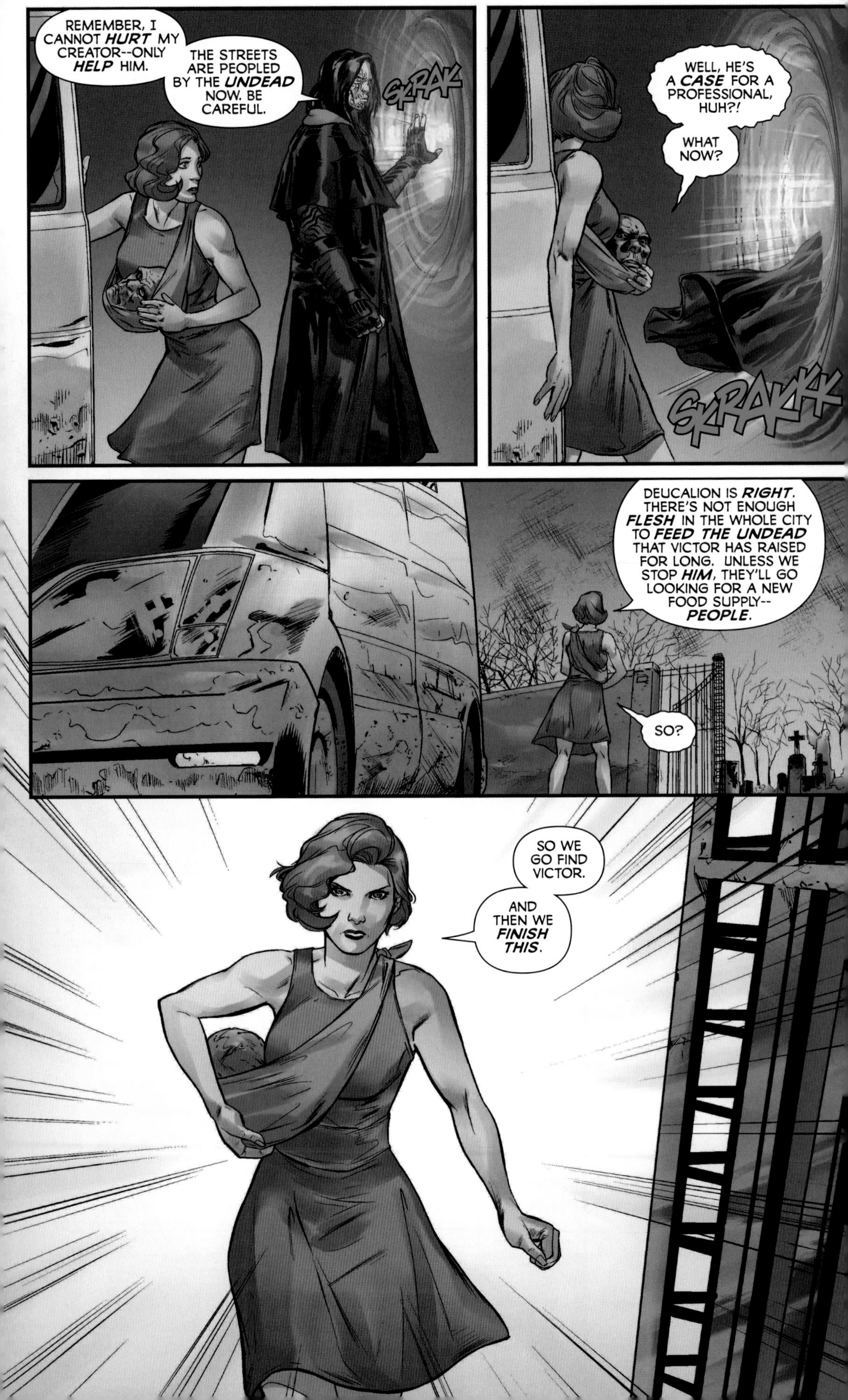
REMEMBER, I CANNOT HURT MY CREATOR--ONLY HELP HIM.
THE STREETS ARE PEOPLED BY THE UNDEAD NOW. BE CAREFUL.
SKRAK
WELL, HE'S A CASE FOR A PROFESSIONAL, HUH?!
WHAT NOW?
SKRAKKK
DEUCALION IS RIGHT. THERE'S NOT ENOUGH FLESH IN THE WHOLE CITY TO FEED THE UNDEAD THAT VICTOR HAS RAISED FOR LONG. UNLESS WE STOP HIM, THEY'LL GO LOOKING FOR A NEW FOOD SUPPLY-- PEOPLE.
SO?
SO WE GO FIND VICTOR.
AND THEN WE FINISH THIS.

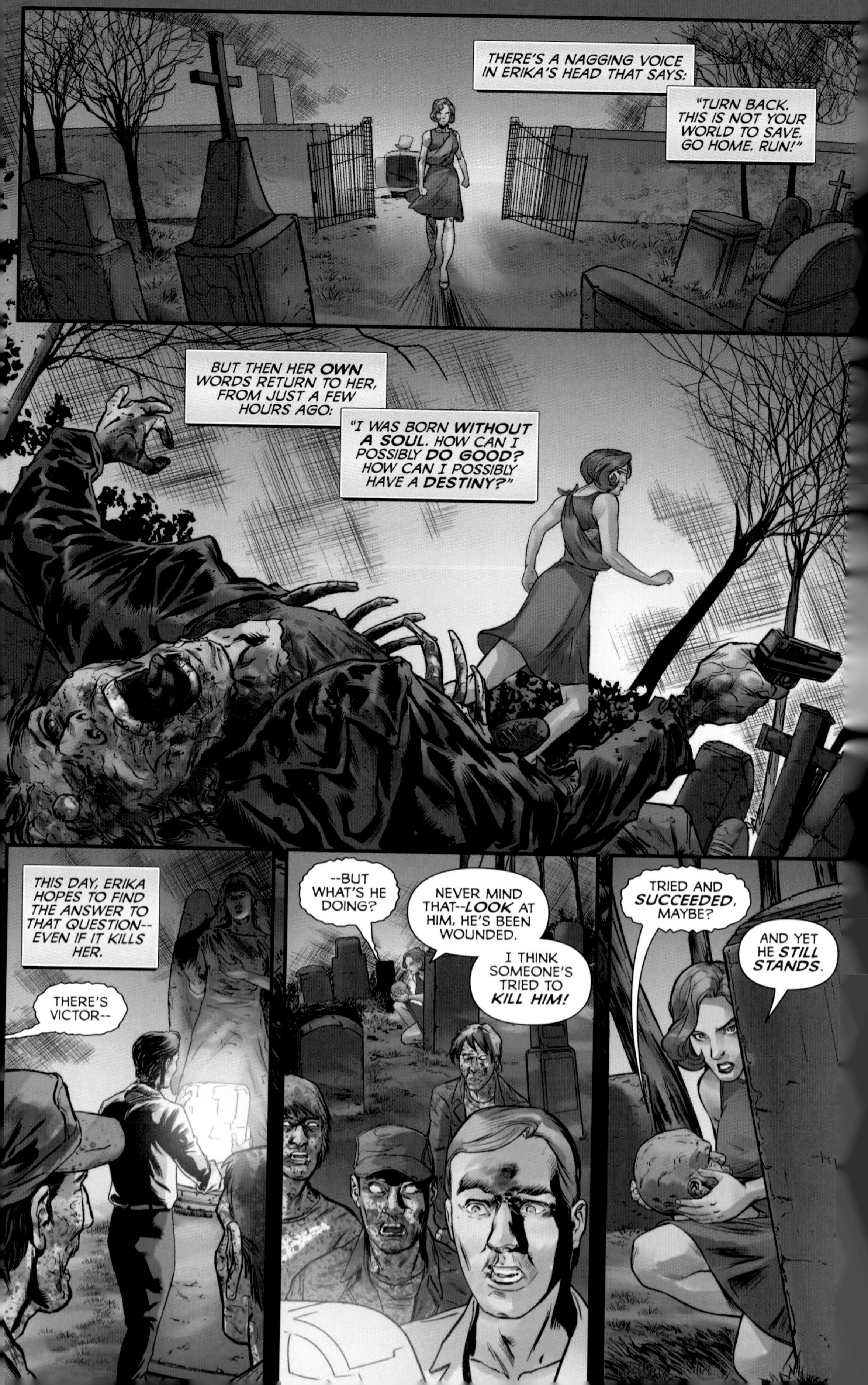
THERE'S A NAGGING VOICE IN ERIKA'S HEAD THAT SAYS:
"TURN BACK. THIS IS NOT YOUR WORLD TO SAVE. GO HOME. RUN!"
BUT THEN HER OWN WORDS RETURN TO HER, FROM JUST A FEW HOURS AGO:
"I WAS BORN WITHOUT A SOUL. HOW CAN I POSSIBLY DO GOOD? HOW CAN I POSSIBLY HAVE A DESTINY?"
THIS DAY, ERIKA HOPES TO FIND THE ANSWER TO THAT QUESTION-- EVEN IF IT KILLS HER.
THERE'S VICTOR--
--BUT WHAT'S HE DOING?
NEVER MIND THAT--LOOK AT HIM, HE'S BEEN WOUNDED.
I THINK SOMEONE'S TRIED TO KILL HIM!
TRIED AND SUCCEEDED, MAYBE?
AND YET HE STILL STANDS.

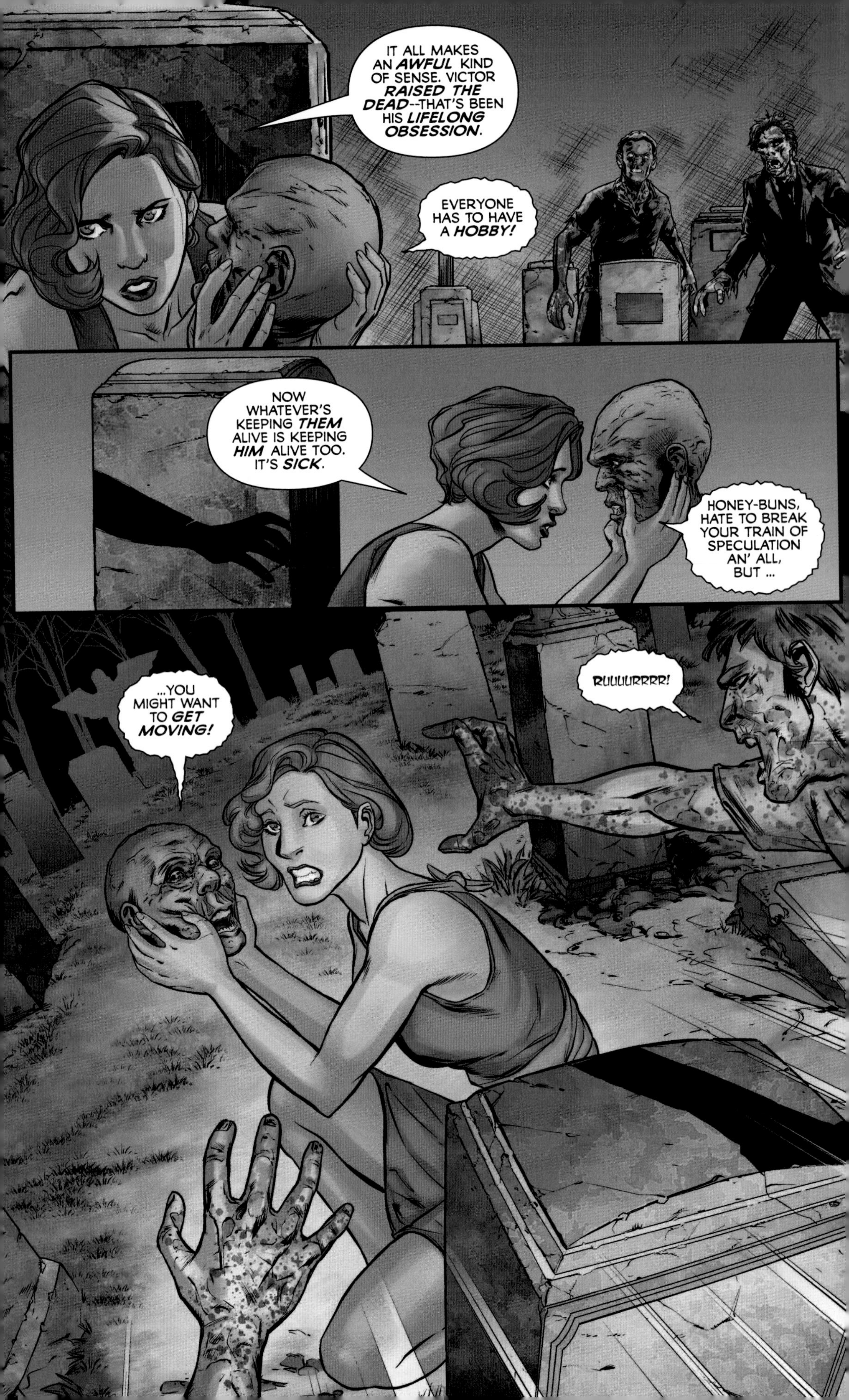
IT ALL MAKES AN AWFUL KIND OF SENSE. VICTOR RAISED THE DEAD--THAT'S BEEN HIS LIFELONG OBSESSION.
EVERYONE HAS TO HAVE A HOBBY!
NOW WHATEVER'S KEEPING THEM ALIVE IS KEEPING HIM ALIVE TOO. IT'S SICK.
HONEY-BUNS, HATE TO BREAK YOUR TRAIN OF SPECULATION AN' ALL, BUT ...
...YOU MIGHT WANT TO GET MOVING!
RUUUURRRR!

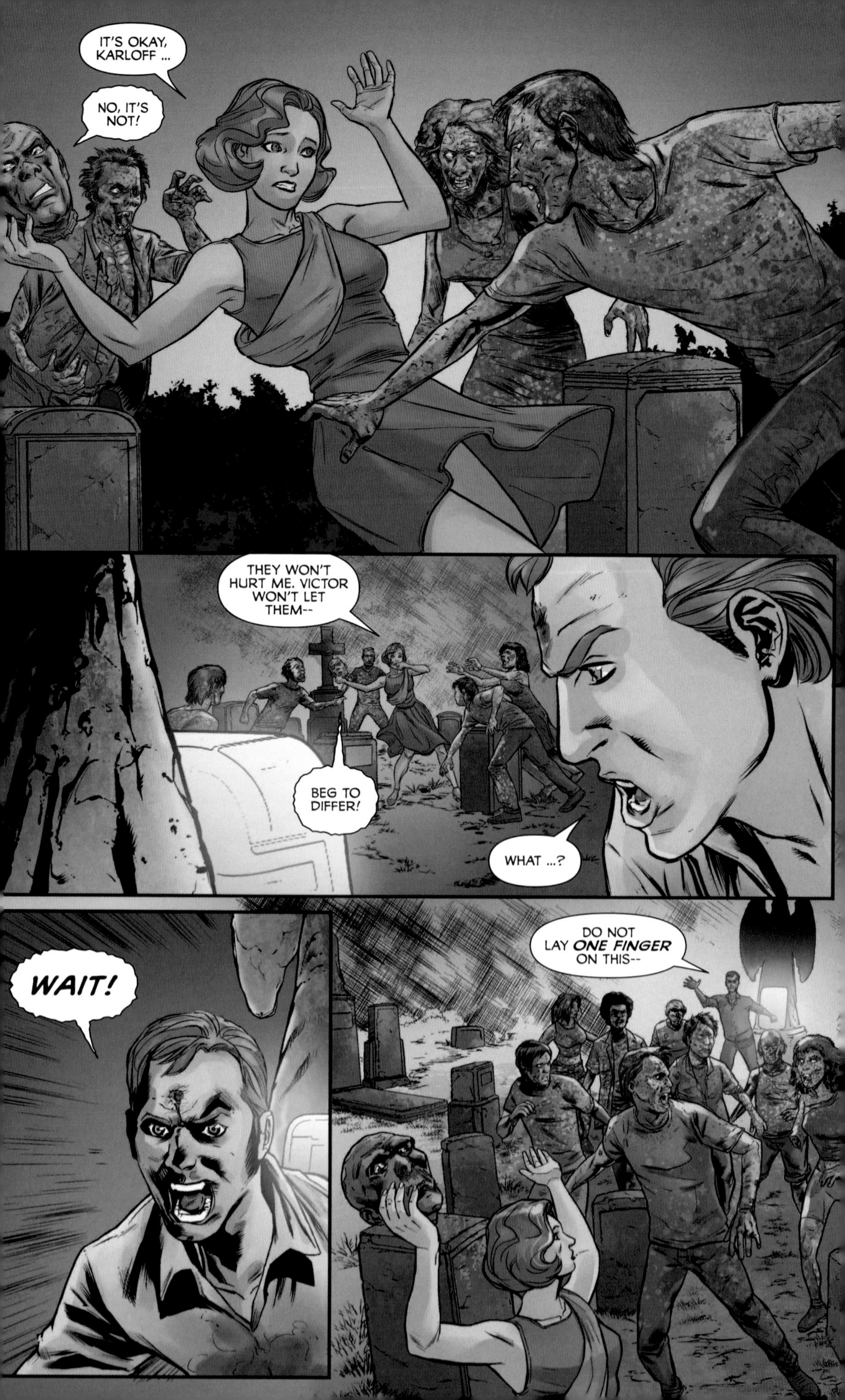
IT'S OKAY, KARLOFF ...
NO, IT'S NOT!
THEY WON'T HURT ME. VICTOR WON'T LET THEM--
BEG TO DIFFER!
WHAT ...?
WAIT!
DO NOT LAY ONE FINGER ON THIS--

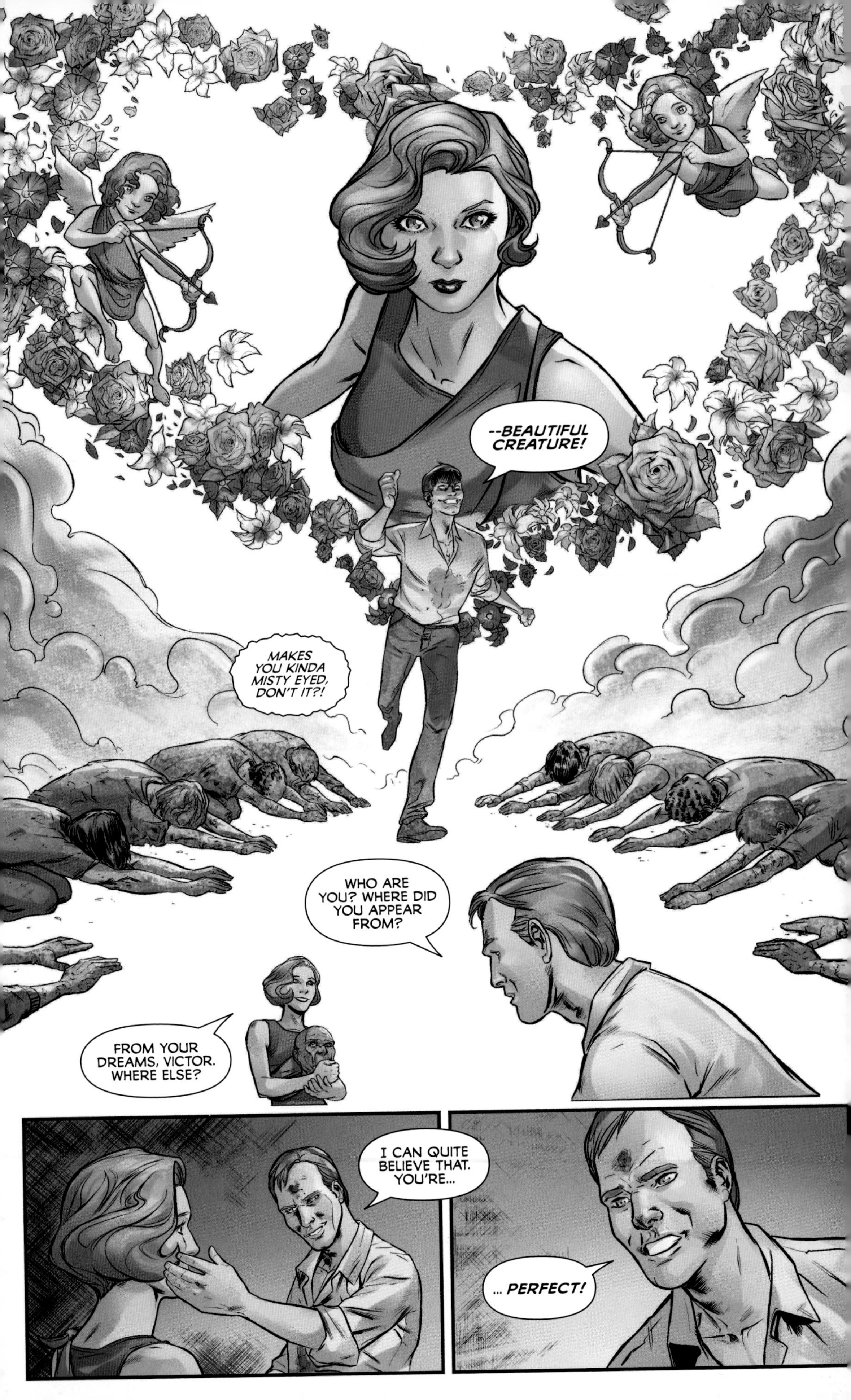
--BEAUTIFUL CREATURE!
MAKES YOU KINDA MISTY EYED, DON'T IT?!
WHO ARE YOU? WHERE DID YOU APPEAR FROM?
FROM YOUR DREAMS, VICTOR. WHERE ELSE?
I CAN QUITE BELIEVE THAT. YOU'RE...
... PERFECT!

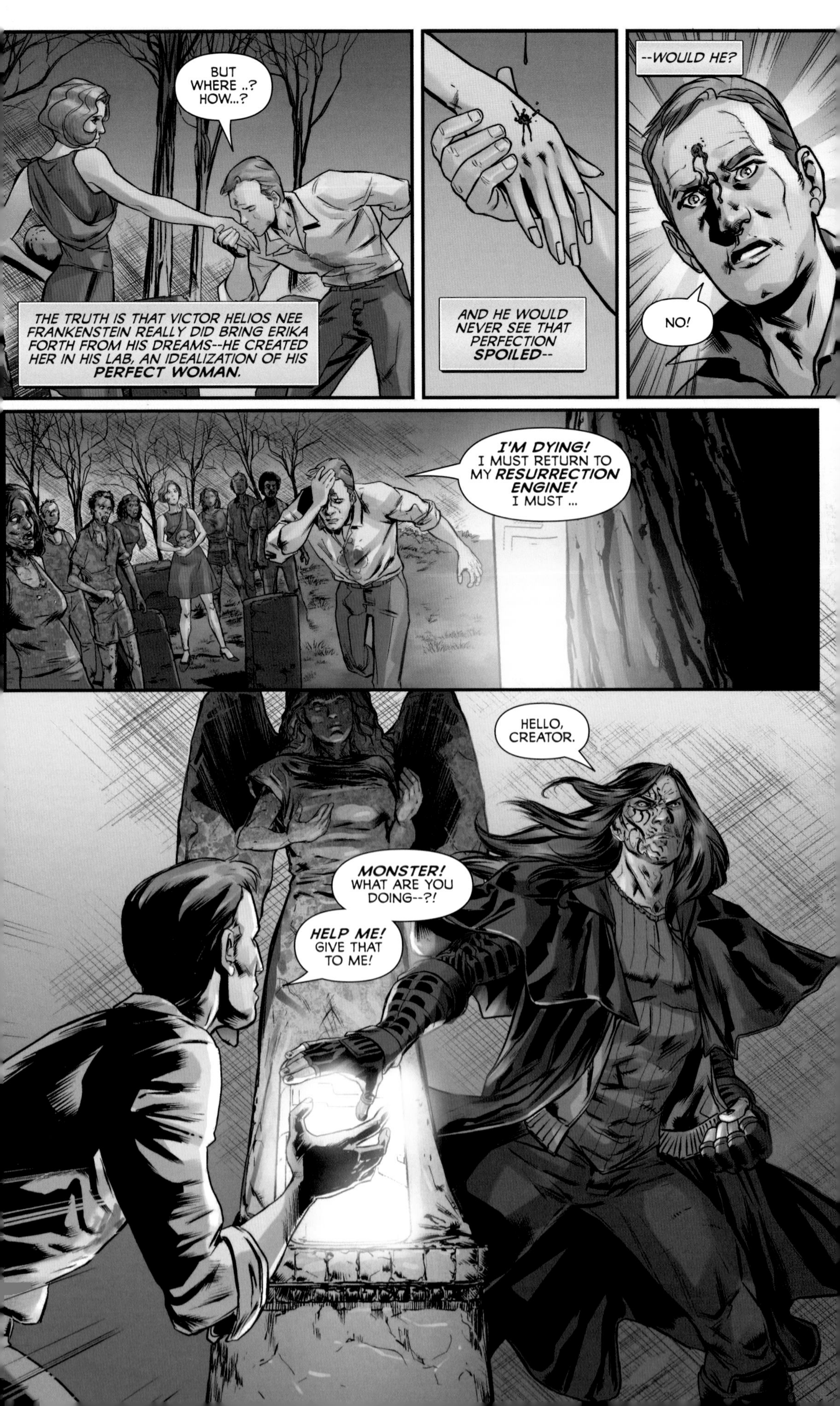

BUT WHERE ..? HOW...?
THE TRUTH IS THAT VICTOR HELIOS NEE FRANKENSTEIN REALLY DID BRING ERIKA FORTH FROM HIS DREAMS--HE CREATED HER IN HIS LAB, AN IDEALIZATION OF HIS PERFECT WOMAN.
AND HE WOULD NEVER SEE THAT PERFECTION SPOILED--
--WOULD HE?
NO!
I'M DYING! I MUST RETURN TO MY RESURRECTION ENGINE! I MUST ...
HELLO, CREATOR.
MONSTER! WHAT ARE YOU DOING--?!
HELP ME! GIVE THAT TO ME!

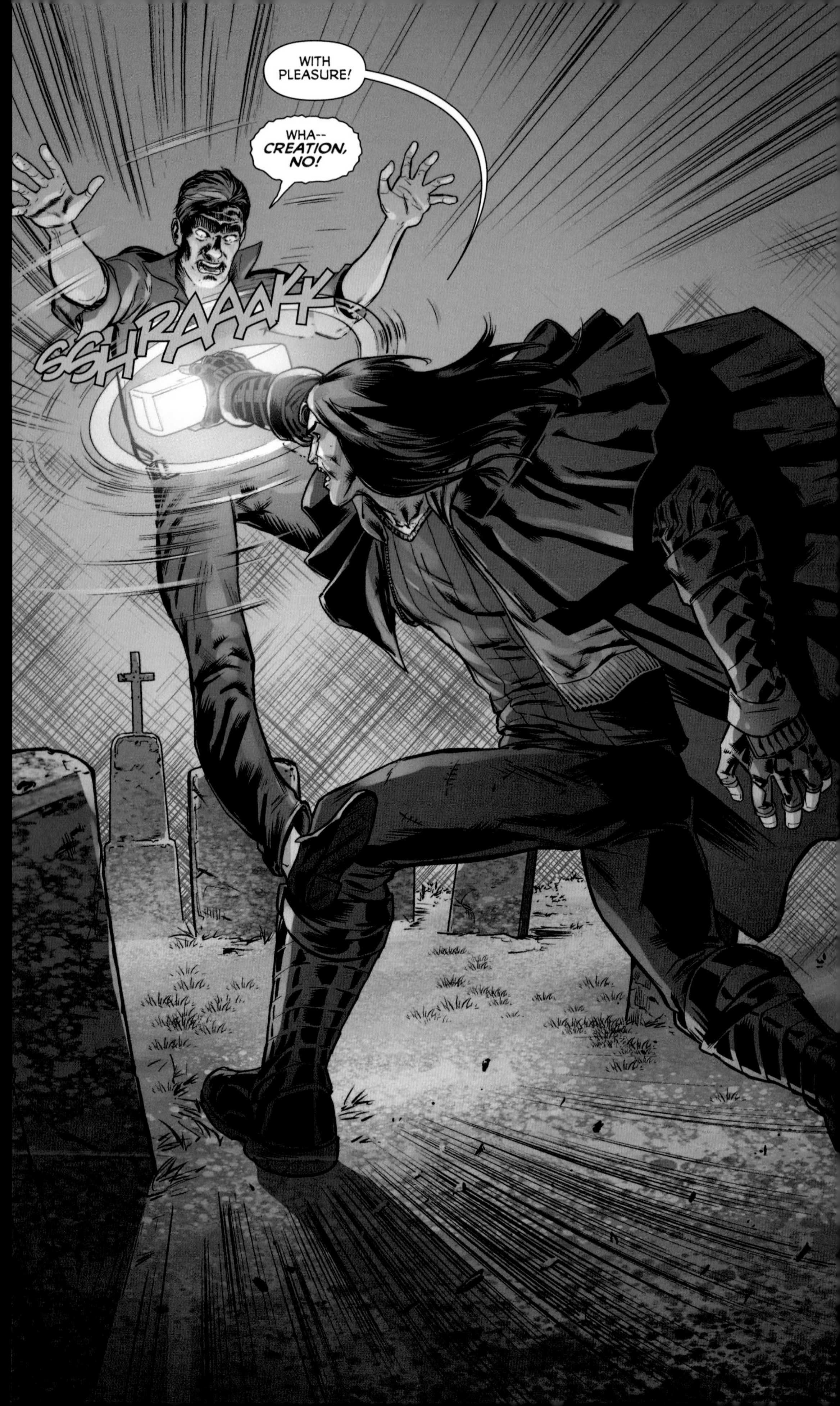

WHA-- *CREATION, NO!*
WITH PLEASURE!
SSHRAAAKK

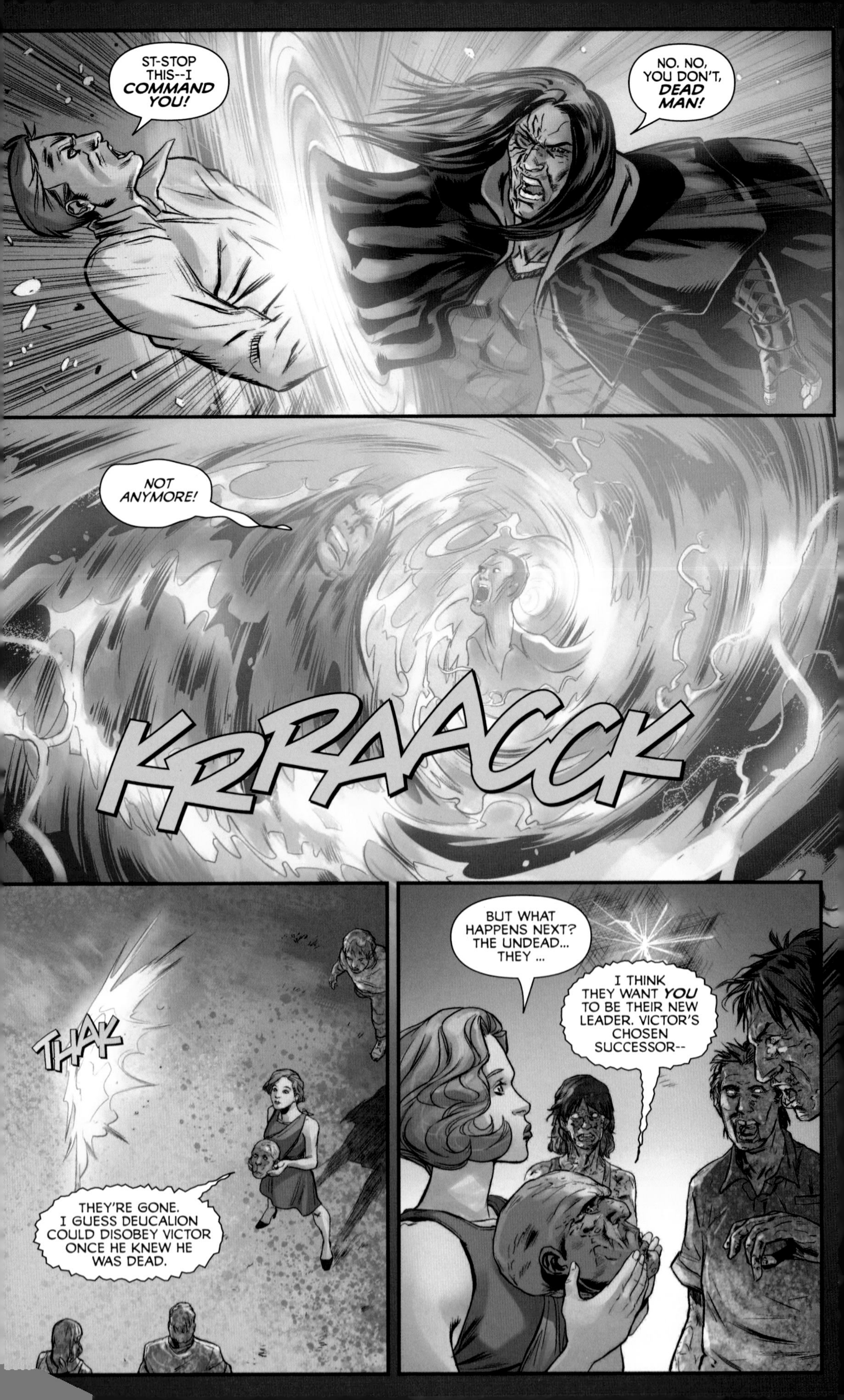
ST-STOP THIS--I COMMAND YOU!
NO. NO, YOU DON'T, DEAD MAN!
NOT ANYMORE!
KRRAACCK
THAK
THEY'RE GONE. I GUESS DEUCALION COULD DISOBEY VICTOR ONCE HE KNEW HE WAS DEAD.
BUT WHAT HAPPENS NEXT? THE UNDEAD... THEY ...
I THINK THEY WANT YOU TO BE THEIR NEW LEADER. VICTOR'S CHOSEN SUCCESSOR--

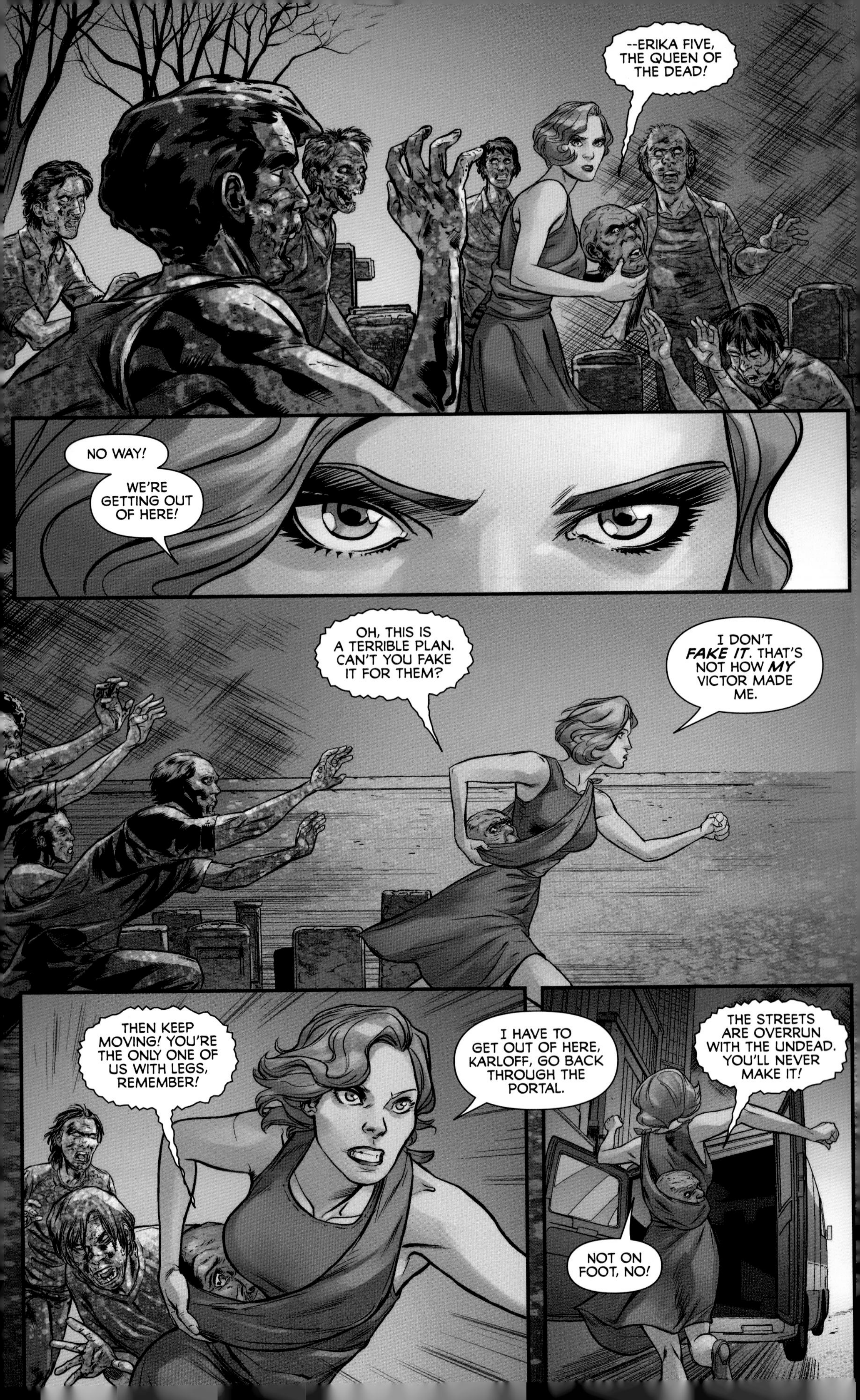
--ERIKA FIVE, THE QUEEN OF THE DEAD!
NO WAY!
WE'RE GETTING OUT OF HERE!
OH, THIS IS A TERRIBLE PLAN. CAN'T YOU FAKE IT FOR THEM?
I DON'T *FAKE IT*. THAT'S NOT HOW *MY* VICTOR MADE ME.
THEN KEEP MOVING! YOU'RE THE ONLY ONE OF US WITH LEGS, REMEMBER!
I HAVE TO GET OUT OF HERE, KARLOFF, GO BACK THROUGH THE PORTAL.
THE STREETS ARE OVERRUN WITH THE UNDEAD. YOU'LL NEVER MAKE IT!
NOT ON FOOT, NO!

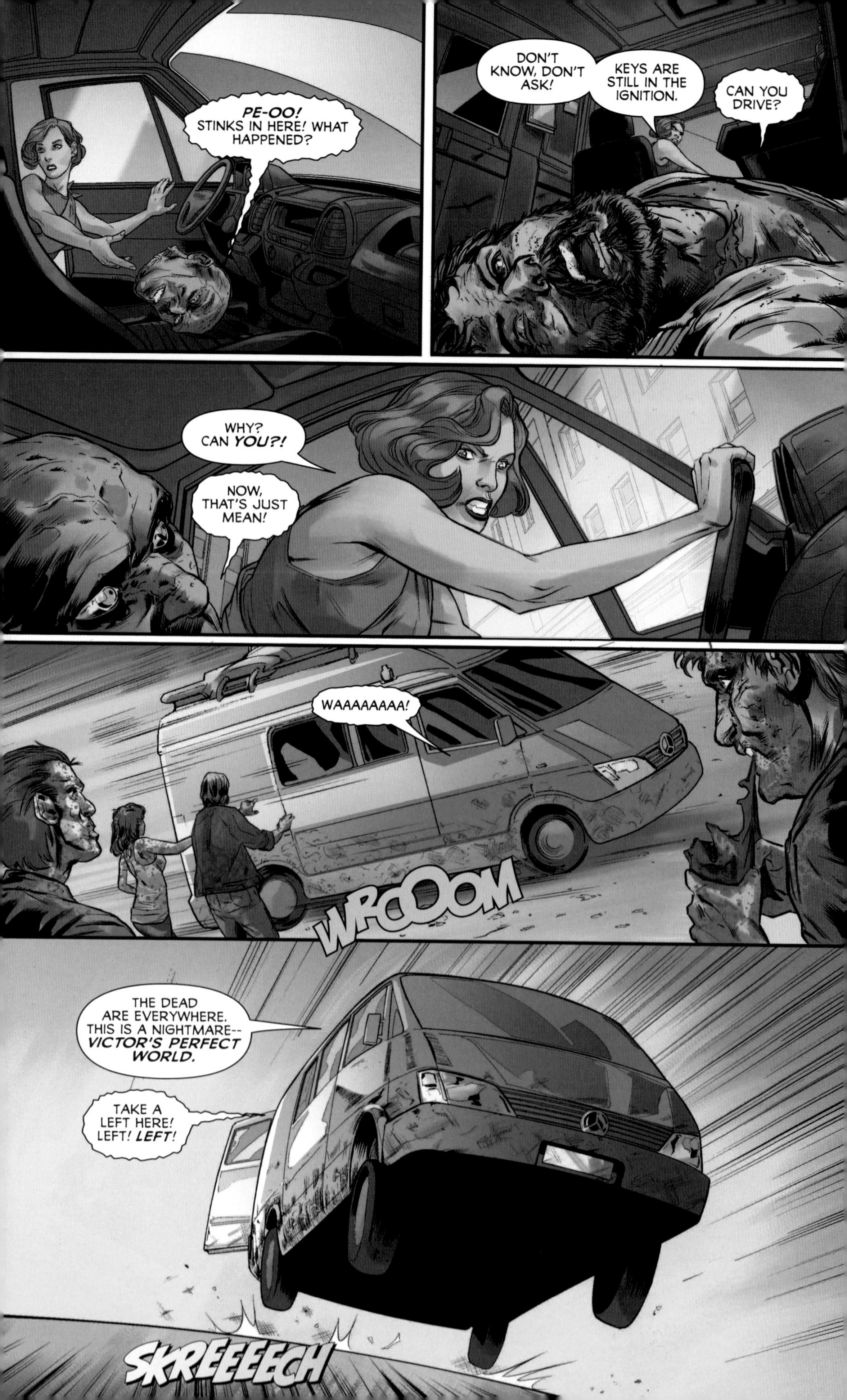
PE-OO! STINKS IN HERE! WHAT HAPPENED?
DON'T KNOW, DON'T ASK!
KEYS ARE STILL IN THE IGNITION.
CAN YOU DRIVE?
WHY? CAN YOU?!
NOW, THAT'S JUST MEAN!
WAAAAAAAA!
WROOOM
THE DEAD ARE EVERYWHERE. THIS IS A NIGHTMARE-- VICTOR'S PERFECT WORLD.
TAKE A LEFT HERE! LEFT! LEFT!
SKREEEECH

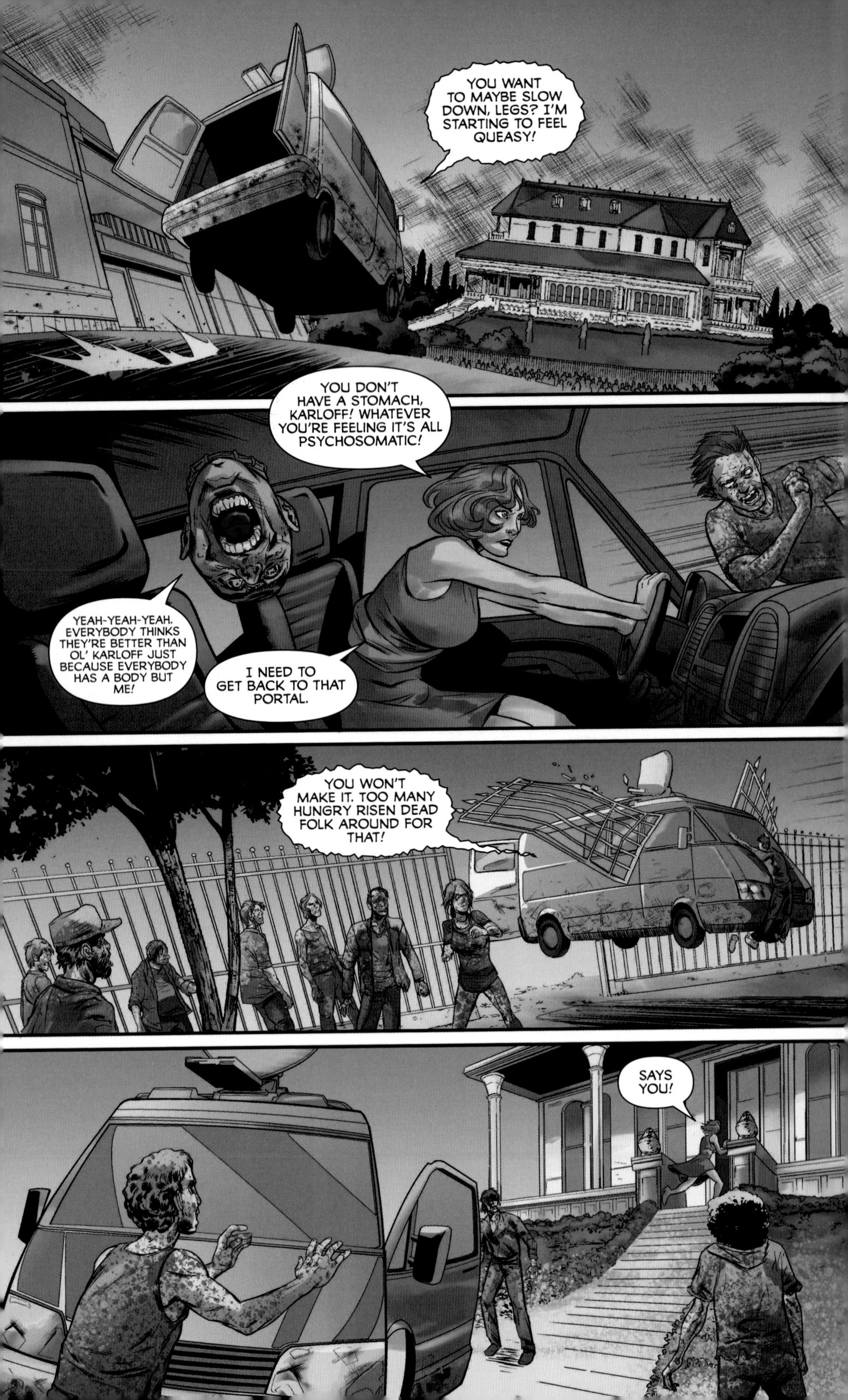
YOU WANT TO MAYBE SLOW DOWN, LEGS? I'M STARTING TO FEEL QUEASY!
YOU DON'T HAVE A STOMACH, KARLOFF! WHATEVER YOU'RE FEELING IT'S ALL PSYCHOSOMATIC!
YEAH-YEAH-YEAH. EVERYBODY THINKS THEY'RE BETTER THAN OL' KARLOFF JUST BECAUSE EVERYBODY HAS A BODY BUT ME!
I NEED TO GET BACK TO THAT PORTAL.
YOU WON'T MAKE IT. TOO MANY HUNGRY RISEN DEAD FOLK AROUND FOR THAT!
SAYS YOU!

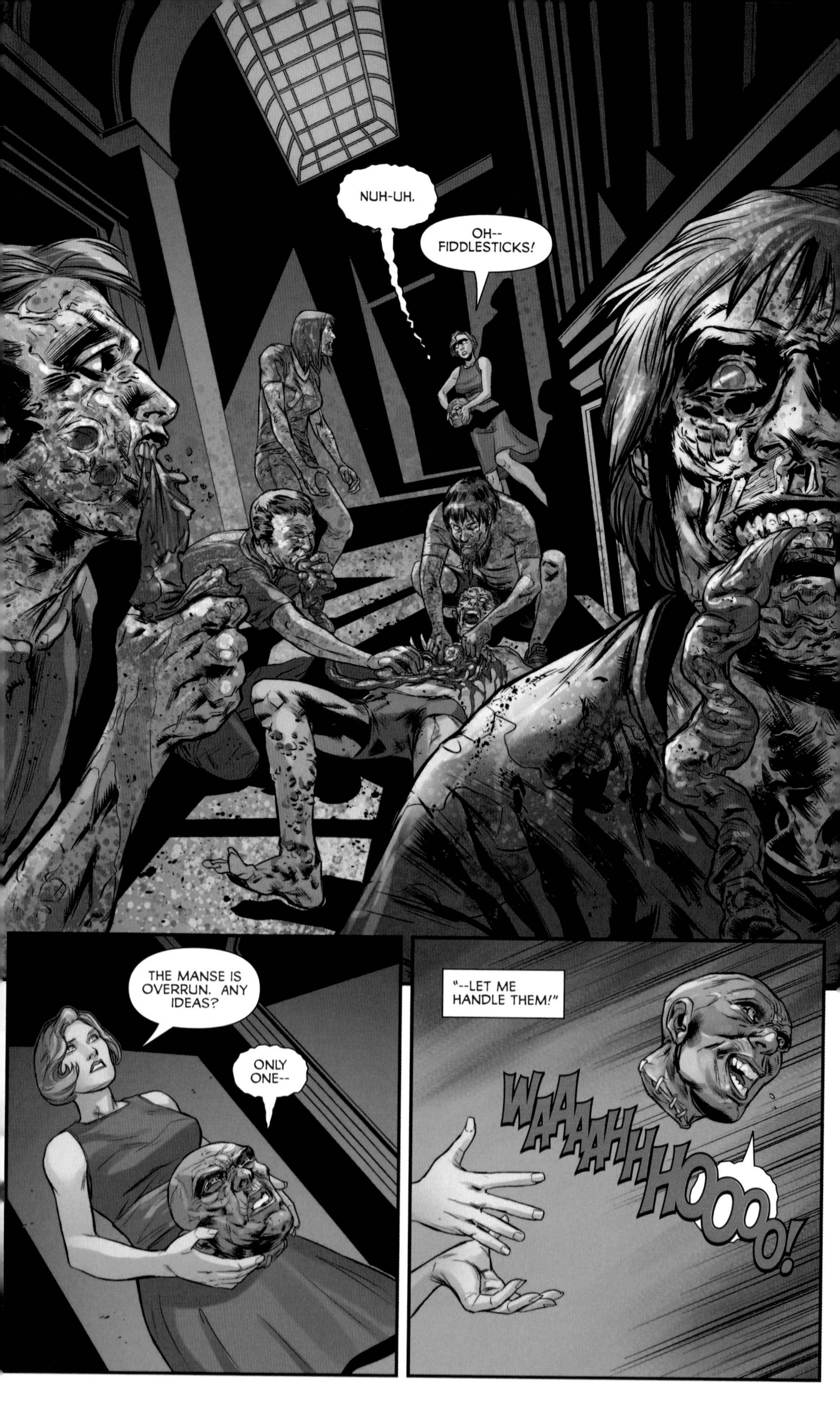
NUH-UH.
OH-- FIDDLESTICKS!
THE MANSE IS OVERRUN. ANY IDEAS?
ONLY ONE--
"--LET ME HANDLE THEM!"
WAAAAHHHOOOO!

"THEY'RE DRAWN TO LIVING THINGS. THEY WON'T BE ABLE TO RESIST EASY PREY LIKE ME."

"IT'LL ONLY GIVE YOU A FEW SECONDS AT MOST, ERIKA--"

CRACK

"--BUT THAT'S ALL I GOT!"

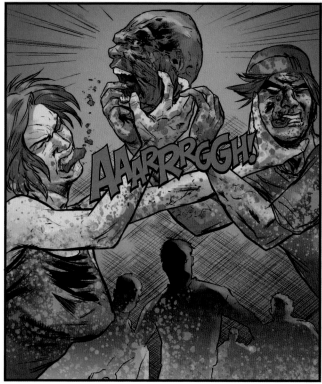

AAARRRGGH!

ARRGHH!

BE BRAVE, KARLOFF. BE--

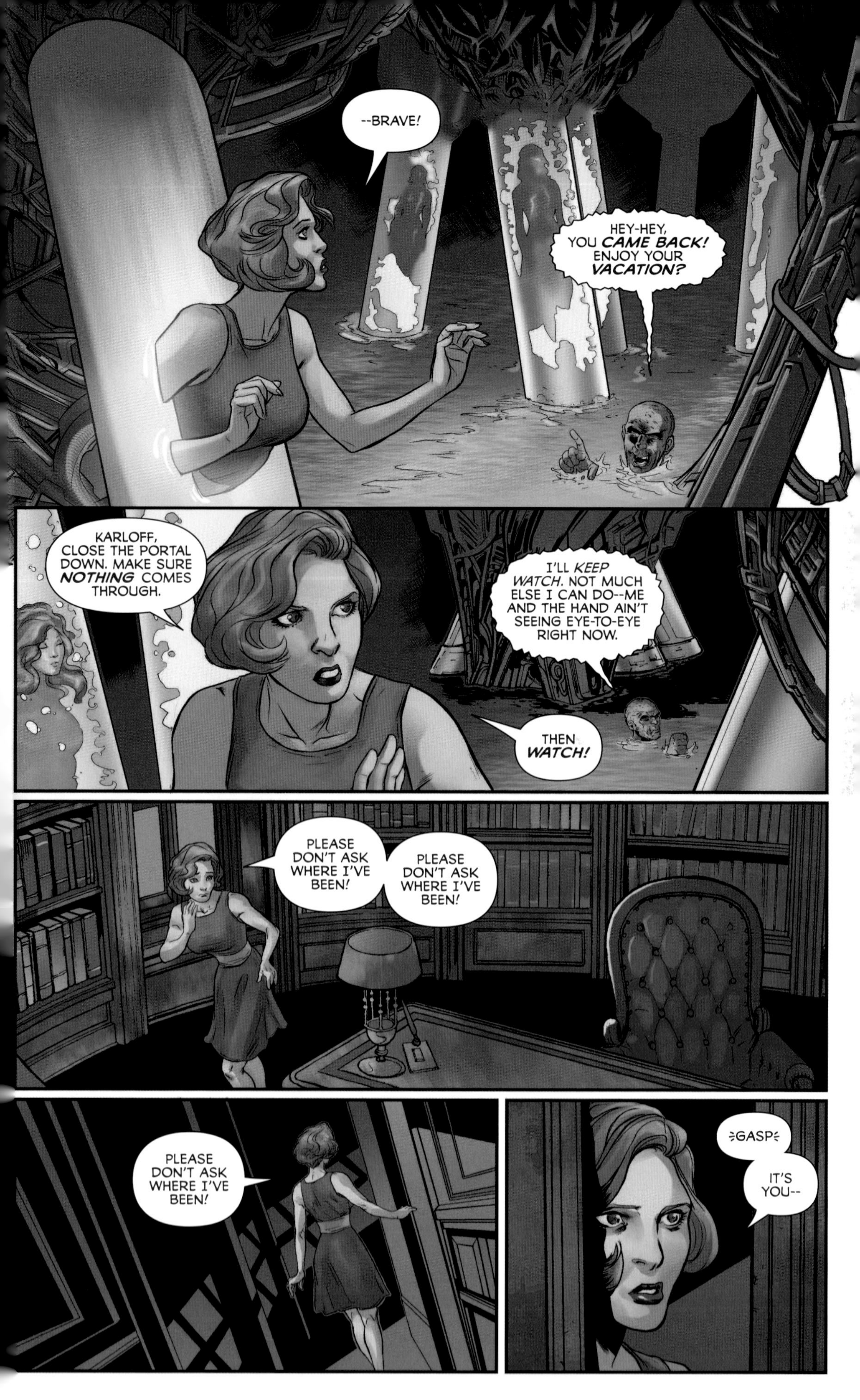
--BRAVE!
HEY-HEY, YOU CAME BACK! ENJOY YOUR VACATION?
KARLOFF, CLOSE THE PORTAL DOWN. MAKE SURE NOTHING COMES THROUGH.
I'LL KEEP WATCH. NOT MUCH ELSE I CAN DO--ME AND THE HAND AIN'T SEEING EYE-TO-EYE RIGHT NOW.
THEN WATCH!
PLEASE DON'T ASK WHERE I'VE BEEN!
PLEASE DON'T ASK WHERE I'VE BEEN!
PLEASE DON'T ASK WHERE I'VE BEEN!
GASP
IT'S YOU--

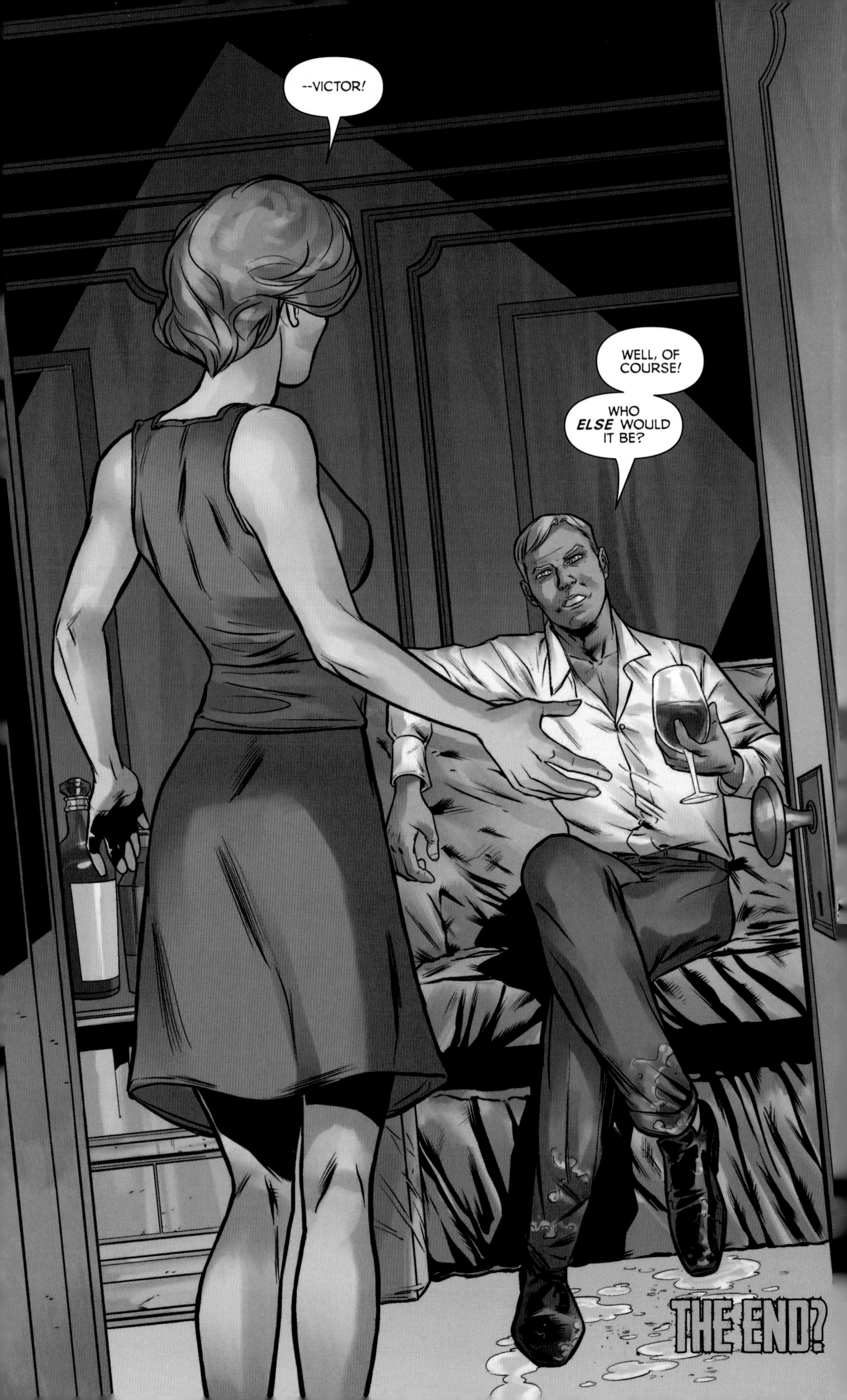
--VICTOR!
WELL, OF COURSE!
WHO ELSE WOULD IT BE?
THE END?

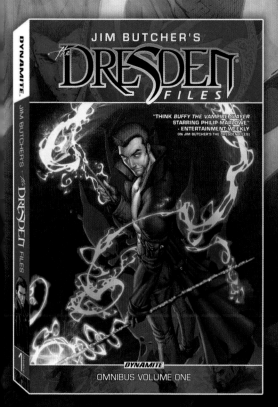